running away to home

jennifer wilson

St. Martin's Press ▨ New York

running away

to home

our family's journey

to croatia

in search of

who we are,

where we came from,

and what really matters

www.stmartins.com

LIBRARY OF CONGRESS CATALOGING-IN-PUBLICATION DATA

Wilson, Jennifer.
    Running away to home : our family's journey to Croatia in search of who we are, where we came from, and what really matters / Jennifer Wilson.—1st ed.
        p.   cm.
    ISBN 978-0-312-59895-2
1. Wilson, Jennifer. 2. Wilson, Jennifer—Family. 3. Croatia—Social life and customs. 4. Croatia—Description and travel. 5. Mrkopalj (Croatia)—Social life and customs. 6. Americans—Croatia—Mrkopalj—Biography. 7. Mrkopalj (Croatia)—Biography. 8. Des Moines (Iowa)—Biography. 9. Group identity—Case studies. 10. Social values—Case studies.   I. Title.
    DR1522.W55   2011
    305.89183'0730922—dc23

                                                                            2011024841

First Edition: October 2011

10   9   8   7   6   5   4   3   2   1

For my sweetheart, Jim.
Without all your steady love,
support, and warm plates of food slid
quietly onto my desk, none of this
would be happening.

acknowledgments

Thanks to Sam, for putting up with the trip and reminding us (often) why we had to go back. Thank you to Zadie, for teaching us by example how to be open-minded, flexible, and joyful travelers. I love you both more than the sun and the moon.

The list of people who helped create the perfect conditions of the petri dish that grew this book is quite long and includes the Jolly Fisherman in Waubon, Minnesota; David Granger; Ryan D'Agostino; William Elliott Whitmore; Michael Diver; the Croatian Tourism Board; Eddie Latovic; Amy Wilder; Sandra Petree; Sharon and Ron Reese; Tomo Cuculić; my grandmother, Kate Fiori; and Jim's mother, Mary Hoff. My gratitude to all players.

And then to Richard Pine and Kathy Huck, for believing in the whole journey before it even began. I can't thank you both enough, though I hope the bootleg *rakija* will tide you over for a while.

A few trustworthy people added insight to this story, and you can thank them along with me if you like the thing: Jeff Inman, Erich Ernst, Dr. Rob Shumaker, Chris Gosch, Terri Stanley, Nicki Saylor, Holli Hartman, Julie Roosa, and especially my first readers, Bil Hoff and Jill Philby—your input was invaluable.

Thank you to Marcus Tanner, author of *Croatia: A Nation Forged in War*, which I referenced heavily for the historical portions of this book. Thanks also to Jason Vuic, author of *The Yugo: The Rise and Fall of the Worst Car in History*.

To our life-support system of family and friends in America: thanks for the love and humanitarian aid.

To our dear and new family in Mrkopalj: thank you for welcoming us home.

ISKRA
FAMILY TREE

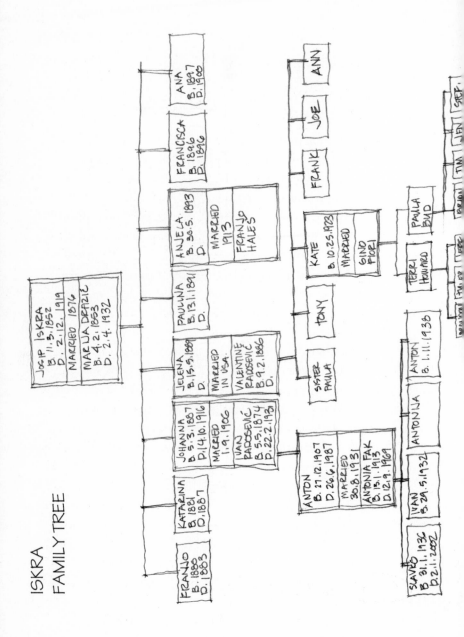

RADOSEVIĆ
FAMILY TREE

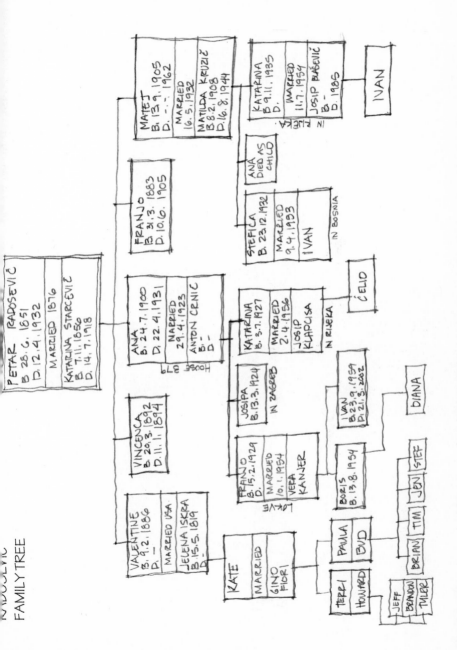

running away to home

chapter one

Dawn had not yet broken as I wrestled my suitcase out of my room above the bar in Mrkopalj, a tiny Croatian village nestled in a low mountain range that looks like the Alps but with fewer people and more wild boars. I sweated my luggage down the creaky back stairway, careful to step quietly for fear that some of the rowdy drinkers whose noise had kept me up all night would now be snoozing somewhere among the empty bottles in the brown-on-brown murk of the bar.

I crept across a quiet courtyard surrounded by weeds, my breath coming in icy puffs, and I threw my stuff into the trunk of my rented Volkswagen Polo. As I hurriedly rubbed the fog off the windshield with my coat sleeve, hungry bears were creeping down those mountains to rob the wilting gardens of the village. They wouldn't find much. Most of the cabbages in Mrkopalj (pronounced MER-koe-pie by the locals) were fermenting in wooden barrels by now; potatoes were stacked in red net bags in root cellars. What the bears did not know (and I didn't know yet, either) is that they would find more action at the local drinking establishment that was now in my rearview mirror, a place operated by a man who was, in spirit, one of them.

The last shreds of night still cloaked Mrkopalj's eight hundred residents and their yard chickens as I skidded past Jesus and the robbers on Calvary, the sheep near the post office, and the dark doorway of a drunken tourism director. This was the land of my maternal ancestors, the village my great-grandparents left behind when they immigrated to America a hundred years ago. From what I'd seen so far, it hadn't changed much since they left. This, in theory, was a good thing, considering that my husband, Jim, and I were planning a back-to-basics family sabbatical abroad with our two little kids as America's economy hit the skids.

In the spirit of scouting possibilities, I planned to explore Mrkopalj for a week.

I fled after thirty-six hours.

The engine of my tiny Euro car whined as I floored it out of last century. One urgent thought pulsed continuously through my mind as the sun began to rise: *Get me the hell out of here*.

I had come to Mrkopalj in search of home. A rustic, simple country home that I hoped to recognize on some deep and spiritual level. Preferably something that smelled like baking bread, or maybe hay. Though I knew so little about Mrkopalj when I set out on this scouting mission, I'd been to enough of my older relatives' funerals to know that I look just like them, with knobby cheekbones and eyes so deep set that I'm pretty sure they'll eventually emerge from the back of my head. In a way, Mrkopalj is an essential part of who I am. Unfortunately, I discovered, this revealed me to be isolated, mildly alcoholic, and dentally challenged.

So that was disappointing. As I mentioned above, Jim and I had been working up the courage to do something we'd always dreamed about: escape to a place where we could live simply with our kids, Sam and Zadie. We'd shared the dream of living overseas ever since we'd met and married ten years before in Des Moines, Iowa. The dream faded as we built our careers—me as a moderately successful travel writer, he as an architect. It disappeared altogether when the kids came along. We dove blindly into the blur of the American family frenzy, with all its soccer practices and frivolous shopping trips to Target. We worked. We drove the kids around. We shopped.

We were chest-deep in the fray when the escape fantasy began to revive in me. I wanted to get back to that essential kernel of connection that had brought Jim and me together in the first place. We'd worked hard and happily to carve out our own version of the American Dream. We renovated a house together in lieu of dating. When we married, we promised that above all, we'd provide each other with an interesting life. We raised two babies in our homemade house, where I planted big gardens under the open sky of the uncrowded state where we both grew up.

Then, somewhere along the line, things got complicated. I worked during naptimes and at night while I stayed home with the kids, writing in my half sleep, parenting in the same manner—I was doing it all but none of it well. I found myself mindlessly rushing to school or to swimming lessons or to ballet or to work or making another trip to the store; anything to distract my mind from the endless needs of the kids and the longest single-syllable word in human history: *Maaaaaaaaaaaaaaaahm*. The manufactured schedule replaced a more tangible life. And really, Sam and Zadie just wanted to hang out at home and wrestle and play beauty shop with Dad, though the 6:00 to 7:30 P.M. window of time that Jim actually spent with his children was filled with the chaos of supper, baths, and bedtime. We ran because we couldn't sit still. Neither of us knew why.

As we were living this life of distraction, we began to accumulate *things*. At final count, Jim had bought three grills—the last one cost us four digits. "You can make naan in it!" he'd announced at the unveiling, stepping aside on the porch to reveal a large oval-shaped ceramic urn mounted on a wooden platform. It looked like an altar. But I wasn't in any position to judge. My shoe collection closely resembled a DSW store in my closet. Restlessness circulated through our house like that one smell that happens when a mouse crawls into the ductwork and dies. Sort of vague. Faint. But pervasive and disturbing. I'm not lodging a complaint here; we were comfortable physically, and that's more than I can say about three-quarters of the world. But for that very reason, it just didn't seem like the right way to live anymore.

Jim and I looked at each other across the shopping cart one Saturday afternoon, both of us holding the Starbucks that accounted for $150 of our monthly household budget, SUV idling in the parking lot, kids grousing that the Lego set they'd chosen was somehow lacking, and asked ourselves: Is this the American Dream? Because if it is, it sort of sucks.

It was into this void that Mrkopalj came calling. In July 2008, my great-aunt died. Sister Mary Paula Radosevich was the last of the immigrant family. Because no one else was interested, the nuns gave me her personal papers, which she'd stored in a bronze-colored tin lockbox. To most of my family, the old relatives were old news. But I thought knowing more about them might help guide my own. My olive-skinned mom rarely mentioned that she was descended from thick-accented immigrants, full mustaches upon both the men and the women. I'd once asked her where our family came from, and she would only answer "Iowa." I sensed some shame about these poor ancestors who'd toiled in coal mines, or maybe it was just her natural reticence.

The night after Sister Paula's funeral, when the kids were in bed, I nestled on the family room couch and sifted through that tin box. I dug out her modestly short autobiography. In shaky upright cursive, she had written that her parents, Valentin Radosevich and Jelena Eskra, had come to America from Mrkopalj, Croatia.

Valentin and Jelena's tale had been furtively tucked away as the Radosevich clan rose to middle-class prosperity. With my generation, their story had nearly vanished. I wished I had more to teach Sam and Zadie about our roots. I knew not one old recipe. Few Croatian words. No helpful bedtime stories in which the misbehaving child gets disemboweled by wolves. But this felt like a start.

I read that Valentin and Jelena had had six children. I didn't know the brothers. But the sisters meant the world to me when I was a girl. The elder Radosevich women, those chuckling old hens, short of stature and big of butt, doted on me, each in her own way.

There was Mary, who became Sister Paula, the oldest, and the only one who went to college. She'd become the principal at a Catholic grade school in Des Moines, and at her funeral her former students told me she was strict but fair. I think that's code for mean. But with me, Sister Paula was attentive and inquisitive. How was I doing in school? Was I making classwork my priority? Higher even than soft-ball and boys? I grew up in Colfax, Iowa, where the only black person in town bagged groceries and lived at the dump, and Sister Paula urged me to broaden my understanding of the world, to consider travel a crucial part of my education. She was the one who after hearing that my parents wouldn't let me see *Grease*, placed a call to my mother to tell her it was a defining movie of a generation and I must see it. And so I did.

Annie was the middle sister, called Auntie by all the cousins. Auntie wore a girdle, a fascinating device of physics with levers and fulcrums, underneath her cotton housedress. I know about the girdle because Auntie would let me come into the bathroom during her morning constitutional so I could snap and unsnap her stockings from her garters. She died when I was a little girl, but not before she sewed an entire wardrobe for my Barbie dolls and ruined my palate by stirring butter and salt into my baby food.

Katherine was the youngest. My Grandma Kate. My mother's mother. I loved her above all others. Toni perms had burnt her jet-black hair until it was crisp and brittle, and her eyebrows were singed from lighting Misty menthols on the coil of her electric stove. Her oversized sweaters sparkled with sequins. She drove her metallic-blue Volare just a few notches below the speed of sound.

I was lonely in my mother's harsh and nervous universe. We seemed so mismatched as mother and daughter. An unhappy woman stranded in a small town, Mom was prone to days of angry silence. I was an intense and curious kid who seemed born to question. In Wednesday-night church school at Immaculate Conception, my class-mates would pass me wadded-up notes bearing questions that they were too embarrassed to ask.

"So if Jesus is real, will he catch this book if I drop it?" I asked a flustered fourth-grade teacher as I held the catechism above the floor.

"If premarital sex is a sin, then how are you supposed to know if you're going to like being married to someone? It seems like a bad idea not to test-drive the car before leaving the lot." That one I floated

out to our priest in high school, who responded with a stumped silence, but I'll tell you that my parents were not pleased when he had a
Why Premarital Sex Is a Sin pamphlet sent to us from the diocese.

And just as I have always been a seeker, my mother has always
seemed one to hide. I wish I could tell you why she spent so many
days isolated from the children so eager to love her, lashing out in bit-
terness from an imagined slight from one of us, her anger often turning to taunting that she would encourage the others to join in on. Or
she'd simply level a stunning silence that would last for days. I don't
know if this was depression, though later I know she struggled with
alcoholism. I also don't know why my dad never stopped it. When I
worked up the courage or indignance, I demanded to know what we
had done wrong, why she wasn't like the other mothers, why she
couldn't offer the simple closeness and openness that we all craved. It
created a friction among us all, a fear and a void. So many of my questions went unanswered. And so perhaps I was also looking for my
mother in that tin box.

From this odd home life as a kid, I found refuge at Grandma
Kate's house in Des Moines. Though her voice was manly and thick
with a staccato Croatian accent, and she had a complete inability to
cook anything flavorful, her unabashed love of my company built a
foundation for my shaky confidence. She was widowed when I was
young, having lost my Italian grandpa Gino to congestive heart failure, so I had Grandma Kate all to myself when I'd visit. We'd spend
whole weekends chatting at her Formica kitchen table or calling her
other daughter, my vivacious aunt Terri, on the phone, only moving
every few hours to lie foot-to-foot on the couch and read romance
novels.

"Boy, Jenn'fer, I tell ya," she'd rumble, "they sure make doing it
with a man sound a lot better than it is."

I would pluck her chin hairs, or we'd head to her Saturday-night
card party, where I'd give all the ladies bouffant hairdos. Around
Grandma Kate, I was no longer the weepy kid obsessed with horror
comics and the *Little House on the Prairie* box set. She thought I was

smart and funny. With Grandma Kate, I was the best version of myself.

She had a stroke when I was in my twenties. Uncle Howard found her on the bathroom floor, where she'd been lying for two days. She grabbed my hand when I walked into her hospital room and told me she'd just had a vision of my long-dead grandpa Gino.

"I almost went, but Gino told me to come back," she cried. "That big dummy."

She should've gone with him. She moved into a nursing home, where I'd find her with bruises on her arms and legs and, once, a goose egg on her forehead that the chief of staff couldn't explain. I'd find her sitting in front of the blaring common-room television, tears streaming down her face.

When she was in the hospital with some sort of complication, I came into her room to find two nurses cleaning her up for the day, one of them swabbing her mouth because she couldn't swallow well anymore. Grandma Kate began choking on the mouth swab, which the nurse had dropped down her throat. They sent me out as she thrashed around in a panic. When I came back, she was dead. I sat by her side, holding her hand as her body went cold, whispering her childhood nickname over and over again: "*Kata. Kata. Kata.*" I have never stopped missing her.

I dug through these memories on the couch until after midnight, pouring over pictures of Mrkopalj on my laptop, dreaming of the village where Grandma Kate's parents had come from, this ghost-like place that was simply never mentioned. It seemed like something out of a storybook: a smattering of gnome houses among fields of spotted cattle and fat sheep, hemmed in by low wooded mountains, less than an hour from the sea. It appeared to have changed little over the centuries. As if it had been waiting for me all along.

Maybe this simple and wide-open existence was just what my family needed. Travel had always renewed me. But could I run away from home—and bring my family, too? Was it even possible? As my wondering turned to obsession, it seemed as if Grandma Kate and Sister Paula and all the old relatives were answering: *Maybe you can.*

The more I thought about transporting us back a century and across the globe, the more I thought it was a very good idea. Which, frankly, is crazy. So I figured I'd check with my human sanity barometer one night after I put the kids to bed. I had married a steady Midwestern man who spent his free time fine-tuning our Ameritrade accounts. If anyone could spot a dumb idea, it was Jim.

"Let's talk," I began, plopping down in front of him as he was watching an ultimate fighting match.

He turned to me. "We are not watching *Rock of Love with Bret Michaels,*" he said. "No matter what you promise me."

"This is better," I said, grabbing the remote and clicking off the television.

He sighed.

"Remember how we used to dream about living overseas together?" I asked.

"I remember," said Jim.

I smiled, trying very hard to look beguiling. "I've been dreaming about it again."

Surprisingly, Jim did not mock this.

So I unveiled my proposal for a return to the old country, where we'd relearn the forgotten lessons of our ancestors and spend uninterrupted time together. It would be a reverse immigration of sorts—my own family starting over where Valentin and Jelena left off. There was a tidiness to the plan.

"I know it doesn't sound sensible," I said. "But for some reason it sounds right."

Now, in most marriages, there is a contented partner and a restless one. You can probably guess which one I am. But Jim wasn't quite the contented spirit he had been. He'd suspected for a long time that architecture wasn't the best career choice for someone who would rather build a house than draw one. At night, he pored over cooking magazines, dreaming of owning his own lunch truck. To most people, he was the same old Jim, the guy who'd push your car out from the snowdrift. But I recognized restlessness when I saw it.

I sat there waiting for the onslaught of Reasons Why We Can't. *We've got a mortgage. We've got pets. We just hooked up the TiVo.* But Jim sat in silence.

Then I realized that he was breaking into the same look he'd had the first time we met, when he was bellied up to a bar with his buddy Dave, pretending to watch Hawkeye basketball but really watching me drink whiskey near the jukebox, harmonizing poorly to the Eagles' "Take It Easy" with my sister, Stephanie.

I liked that look. I married that look. Jim stayed quiet, rubbing his beard and running his hand over his mouth. Then he got up and poured me a glass of wine.

When he sat down again, he spoke. "You know, I don't see any reason why we *couldn't* do something like that. We've got some money saved up. We could rent out the house."

I chimed in. "We're not getting any younger. And it's the perfect timing for Sam and Zadie—they aren't old enough to put up a fight yet."

"I could take a leave from work," Jim said.

I was stunned he was even considering this. "Really?" I said. Maybe we were both crazy.

"Why not?" he asked. "I just sit at my desk all day and think of the things I'd rather be doing—working on the house, making dinner, just hanging out. Do you know how long it's been since I've had a whole day just to *hang out* with my kids?"

He got up and grabbed the atlas. He flipped through it with an enthusiasm I hadn't seen since, well, since he took me home on "Take It Easy" night. We were clicking on this.

We studied the map of Croatia for a while: the funny tilted wishbone shape, all that seacoast, the proximity to Italy.

"The idea of just leaving. Just *walking away*." Jim shook his head. "Can you imagine?"

I wish I could say that our decision to run away to Croatia was more carefully crafted than the drunken midnight talk of two tired parents. But it wasn't. Jim and I could argue for hours about the frequency and aptitude of his lawn-mowing skills, right on down to how he only used the weed eater biweekly. The smallest minutia imaginable. But in regard to the biggest decision we'd ever make in the trajectory of our family, it really was as simple as two restless souls in a rambling mood setting in motion a ball that hasn't stopped rolling since.

Before we did anything rash, we decided I should probably check out Mrkopalj in person. Occasionally countries host travel journalists on familiarization trips, so I wrote a heartfelt letter to the Croatian Tourism Board, begging to be included on one. I received a tepid e-mail brush-off. I called the office. I got a recording. I called again, and got another recording. I called three times, then four. Nothing but silence.

Now, maybe it was that beautiful surfer boy in high school who never called me back, or maybe it's just standard Iowan tenacity, but for whatever reason, when I'm blown off, I develop this epic stubbornness that borders on compulsion. I called again and again, until I lost count. I heard nothing in response.

I was getting the picture that Croatian Tourism did not want me to visit Croatia. I mentioned in my messages that I wrote for *National Geographic Traveler* and *Frommer's Budget Travel*. (I did not mention that my stories were the teensy ones in the front of the book.) Still, no one responded. I couldn't help but wonder: *What are these people hiding?*

Finally, a woman with a deep, harried voice returned my messages. I'll call her Vesna. Vesna told me that a press trip was indeed coming up. I could go if I could get an assignment from one of my magazines.

"I'll do it," I assured her.

But I didn't. I called every editor I could think of. No dice.

A week later, Vesna called again to chew me out.

"What is happening?" she barked. "What is wrong? I try to help you go to Croatia, and now you do not have press letter."

"I want with all my heart to go on the press trip!" I said. "But I can't get an assignment."

Vesna reminded me quietly: "Jennifer, I try to create special circumstance so that you can come to Croatia."

"I understand that, and I appreciate it," I said. "But it's a little-known country and I think everyone has all the Croatia coverage they need right now."

"Croatia is not little-known country!" she yelled. "Rudy Maxa has come to Croatia!"

I did not mention that few people have heard of *The Savvy Traveler* either. Instead, I said: "I'm sorry. I'm just saying I tried to sell the story. No one is biting."

Vesna lowered her voice. "Can't you just make something up? I want you to go. I do this because your people are from Croatia."

I had not thought of this option. And so I wrote my own assignment letter. Something about sourcing posh lodgings and local booze for an upscale home magazine. I figured, reach for the stars, right? And sure enough, by day's end, Vesna had secured my slot on that fall press trip to Croatia and a rental car to visit Mrkopalj afterward—a two-week trip in total.

"Good luck, Jennifer," Vesna said. "You will be very happy there."

I would leave in ten days. There was much to do before my departure. In addition to clearing my desk of work, I had to prepare the house and the pets and the family for an absence of their mama for the longest period of time we'd ever been apart. At some point during the writing of the twelve-page instructional manual for Jim—"Please remember that we have a cat" and "The children will need to be washed periodically"—I realized that my trip research time would be severely limited. For some reason, I didn't use that time to track down a relative or two, or to learn useful phrases in Croatian. Instead, I figured the easiest way to do the trip planning would be to meet someone who was from the area and ask a few questions. Surprisingly, not a difficult thing to do in Des Moines. During my lifetime, Iowa has been a haven for war refugees, including people from the former Yugoslavia fleeing from the wars of the 1990s. I made a few phone calls and connected with a friend of a friend whose family had moved to Des Moines from Rijeka (pronounced ree-YAY-kuh), a port city about a half hour away from Mrkopalj.

The ridiculously attractive Zlatko met me at a local coffee shop, where he quickly assessed the vast abyss of my Balkan knowledge with gorgeous blue eyes in a tanned face. You could practically hear the Al Green song playing as he slid his wraparound sunglasses over his gold-brown hair. He gave me the once-over, finding before him a mildly frumpy mom whose potential for hotness had faded soon after she started getting spiral perms in college. And so he set to work giving me a no-nonsense schooling in the ways of his homeland.

Zlatko borrowed a piece of paper and sketched Croatia. The region my family is from is called the Gorski Kotar, or Mountain District, and is in the northwest corner of the country, the "handle" of Croatia's odd wishbone shape.

So that was the Gorski Kotar geographically. But, running his hands through his continental hair, Zlatko seemed to be having trouble coming up with the right words to talk about the place culturally.

"Gorski Kotar is one of the places . . . ," he began. Then he closed his eyes, resigning himself to something. "There are a lot of crazy people there. They're not as civilized in a traditional way. It's a little more primitive than you think it is."

I stared at him. I considered touching his face.

In the Gorski Kotar, Zlatko said, one of the most ancient dialects of Croatian is spoken. My Croatian phrasebook wouldn't help me all that much. So bizarre was the Gorski Kotar, in fact, that every region surrounding it had been affected by the Balkan wars from 1992 to 1995, and yet it had remained oddly untouched. He had no explanation for why this was.

"What exactly was that war about?" I asked. "I'm sorry to seem ignorant. It's because I am ignorant."

"The Kingdom of Yugoslavia was formed in 1918," Zlatko said.

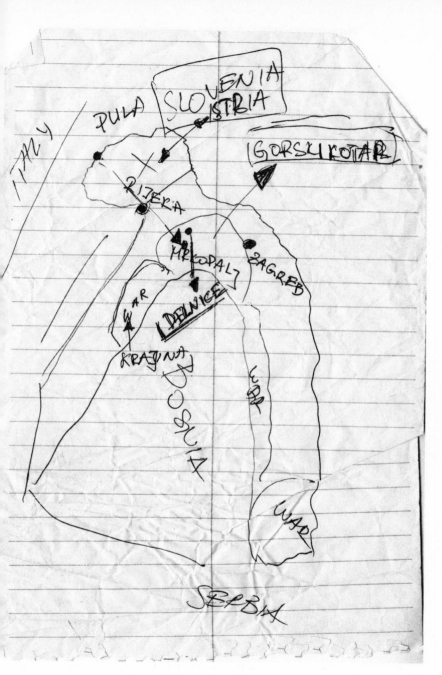

ZLATKO'S MAP

"It was a country with many different nationalities and three different religions—Muslim, Catholic, and Orthodox. During the 1990s, Yugoslavia broke up, and the people had a nationalistic conflict. Everyone wanted more land from the division, and in the end they all went their separate ways."

I'd never heard it explained clearly like this. I'd asked my own brother, Brian, for a *Reader's Digest* version of the war. He served as an Army doctor in Bosnia. "Some guy stole another guy's sheep two thousand years ago," he said. "And they've been fighting ever since." The series of conflicts was so confusing that they didn't even have an official name. I'd done some reading and just referred to them as the Yugoslavian Wars.

"The war is over and has been for a long time," Zlatko said. "It won't be dangerous by any means. Besides, you have the most important thing that you need in Croatia. You have *heritage*."

"So it's not dangerous for us, because we're family?"

"More or less," Zlatko said.

"Well, the wilderness sounds nice," I said. "Maybe my husband will learn to like camping!"

Zlatko leaned forward gravely. "*You need to not go into the woods, Jennifer,*" he said. "There are wolves. There are wild boars. You tell someone in Gorski Kotar that you're going into the woods, and they'll pull out a shotgun from behind the counter and tell you to borrow it for the weekend!"

But it wasn't really *what* was in the woods that got Zlatko worried about my family and me. And on this point, he would not elaborate.

"Jennifer," he said, sighing heavily, "you never know *who* you're going to run into in those woods."

And that was the first indication that perhaps my Motherland wasn't quite the idyllic rustic family vacation destination I'd thought it would be.

chapter **two**

My press trip spanned the Istria and Kvarner regions—roughly that wishbone handle of Croatia jutting into the Adriatic Sea. Another journalist and I were whisked from the airport to the island of Krk by a lovely bald hunk of a guide in dark sunglasses. Siniša (pronounced SEE-nee-shah) herded us through the most beautiful and travel-ready destinations of the Adriatic Coast. Each daily sightseeing itinerary included English-speaking guides expert in Croatian history, sweets shops with effusive proprietors, and the good booze and soft hotel beds I'd requested in my press letter.

The sea was clear as tap water, and the sun warmed terra-cotta rooftops on craggy waterfront cottages. I ate all the food I'd eat in neighboring Italy, at half the price and without as many international males in pointy fashion shoes who, despite a reputation for hitting on any female who isn't their mother, didn't hit on me. In coastal Croatia, the olive oil was so green and fresh that it burned my throat going down. Meals began with hard sheep's-milk cheese and prosciutto cured in a cold sea wind called the *bura*.

In the church of Saint Anthony the Hermit, overlooking the sea-soaked harbor town of Veli Lošinj, a caretaker showed me a hundred sacred relics behind the altar. The leg bone of Saint Clementine. The elbow of Saint Gregor. Below a whale-tendon-covered crucifix, the old stone floor bore the names of ancient sea captains. "It is our history," the caretaker said. "History is everything."

Perched on a rocky cliff over the Adriatic, medieval Vrbnik once produced more priests per capita than anywhere in Croatia because its men wanted to avoid serving on the galleys of the ruling Venetians. There, a woman, upon discovering that I was the returning great-granddaughter of Croatian immigrants, threw her arms open wide and announced: "Welcome home!"

In the harbor city of Pula, in a Roman amphitheater where gladiators once battled lions, a woman with an unearthly shade of burgundy hair told me that being Croatian meant getting used to other countries trying to steal your land—Austria, Serbia, Germany, Italy, Yugoslavia. "We figured they'd take what they wanted and leave," she said. "We were wrong."

In the vegetable market in Rovinj, as artists hung their paintings on the sea walls, a guy with a smile as big as his belly led me to a back-alley stone room, where we drank shots of homemade slivovitz before he sold me truffles.

I drank a goblet of grappa on the island of Mali Lošinj as I walked through gardens of lavender, sage, and rosemary outside a fourteenth-century cottage guarded by a watch-donkey named Dragan.

Old men on mopeds buzzed along cobblestones worn to a fine patina over the centuries. Locals lounged in outdoor cafés on the *riva* as their kids ran in happy packs nearby. Goth teenagers kicked past ancient fortifications built just a few years after Pangaea broke apart. And there was wine. Wine with everything! The Croatians produced all the wines of the world in a country roughly the size of West Virginia; their tart *malvazija* and *graševina* were the first whites I ever truly liked. The olive oil and bread and pasta and fish all came from the ground and sea around them—fresh and natural and wild. Coastal Croatia was the Europe I was looking for when I spent my student loans to go backpacking through skanky youth hostels in college. Lonely and poor, I didn't find it then. I found it as a thirty-eight-year-old mom, hungry for all those connections with land and food and family. Though my ancestral history had faded away, I was drawn to these people who seemed to have it pretty good, despite being mired in war over the years.

Then I waved good-bye to my press-trip compadres, hugging the fantastically large and firm Siniša an extra-long time, and drove away in a rented Volkswagen Polo to Mrkopalj. The land that formed the old family. The land I hoped would mend my new one. Though I missed the hell out of Jim and the kids, I was high on Croatia and its possibilities.

Just east of the country's sunny seacoast is the Gorski Kotar region, where the village of Mrkopalj is located. Called "Little Switzerland" by tourism folks putting a good spin on things, this seldom-explored area might be described by less upbeat souls as Croatia's dark heart. But the English-speaking village tourism director had promised a complete itinerary upon arrival, noting in an e-mail that the tourism bureau was "unusually happy to receive the mentioned journalist." Which made me unusually happy, too. Croatia had been idyllic so far, and I was sure my trip would come full circle with a spiritual connection to Mrkopalj.

But the clouds seemed to drift over that coastal sun as I drove, eventually blotting out the light altogether. I passed very few cars on the highway, and when I exited onto the back roads, none whatsoever. Supernaturally thick evergreen forest and an uneven landscape encroached upon the lonely blacktop. The air took on a wintry chill, and I rolled up the windows of the Polo. Giant spruce trees crowded the narrow, twisting road. Wisps of wood smoke rose from rickety cottage chimneys. Tidy piles of firewood were stacked high against stone walls. The rooftops were Hansel-and-Gretel steep, covered in terracotta tiles or shiny corrugated metal to shed the massive amounts of snow that whomp the Gorski Kotar in winter.

I came over a slight rise and saw a sign for Mrkopalj. Printed underneath the town's name was the word *Kalvarija*, with an arrow pointing up. On a hill above the village were three giant crucifixes staked into the ground. Mrkopalj had re-created the death scene of Jesus and the robbers on Calvary as its welcome sign.

Without fixers like Siniša around to give this foreign land some context, I was intimidated. I guess I thought it would feel more like home right away. We fear what we don't know, and man, I had no idea what to make of a place that appeared to have been suspended in amber since the Radosevich family left. Well, there had been a few changes. The looming hammer and sickle cast in stone on the bridge into town had probably gone up within the last fifty years. Communist rule in Croatia started after World War II and ended with the Yugoslavian Wars. From the looks of things, the Iron Curtain hadn't quite been raised on Mrkopalj.

My mind drifted to Zlatko's warnings about the Gorski Kotar, and there I was, unable to read basic road signs and still slow with the currency. I didn't even have enough words to figure out the tollbooth on the main highway, and a Croatian trucker stormed out of his cab to do it for me. He called me *"shtopite,"* which I added to the very short list of Croatian words I could pronounce. Though calling someone stupid doesn't help a traveler much.

I'm usually pretty good about picking up a few phrases to get by once I'm in a country, but there is no casual picking up of Croatian, which sounds like a normal language that's been bashed by blunt force. The *j* sounds like a *y*, and *c* sounds like *tz*, and regular letters are flagged with little slices and dots and lines that denote that they're about to turn from straightforward sounds into gargling practice.

I wasn't entirely illiterate. I knew a few things from Grandma Kate, such as *prdac, prase,* and *guzica*. I'd always guessed them to be terms of endearment, me being her favorite and all. But when I tried them out on Croatians, I was told that they meant "fart," "pig," and "ass," respectively. Which mostly confused people, and wouldn't go far toward finding a place to stay or a reasonably priced meal.

As I drove into the village for the first time, I resolved to set aside my doubts. I'd come thousands of miles on blind faith. I was the American returning home after a hundred years. Of course this would be awesome! I wondered if I'd see the house of my ancestors. Maybe whoever lived there would even offer to rent it to us. I day-dreamed of a parade. I wasn't counting on the rending of clothes in the streets or anything, but I suspected there might be some weeping or maybe a key to the city.

But Mrkopalj was dead quiet. As far as I could tell, no humans dwelled there, though I did see a few chickens milling around. I drove past the "ski resort" I'd read about on the Mrkopalj website, but in autumn it was empty, its ticket-booth window broken. Nearby, the International School of Peace sat abandoned at the perimeter of town where the houses just sort of died out into the hills, a ramshackle two-story building looking all forgotten and sad.

Along the main road, I spotted a green tourism sign on a squat white building. I pulled over. Inside, I found a series of closed doors and a rickety wooden staircase. Dust motes drifted through the air. I couldn't read any of the signs, but I figured a tourism office would surely have some sort of multilingual welcome on it, so I headed up the steps in search of a friendly face. Or any face, really. The building smelled musty and stale. Where were the people in Mrkopalj?

On the second floor, I spotted a woman furtively walking out of one closed door toward another. "Tourism?" I asked.

She pointed down the steps. "*Hvala*," I told her. "Thank you" was my Croatian specialty. Though the word is produced with the same muscles used when you clear your throat, I had a little in-country cold and could do it pretty well.

As I picked my way down the steps, a wiry old guy in a dirty coat shuffled out a door, locking it behind himself. It was one in the afternoon.

The man stopped when he saw me on the steps. His eyes narrowed, which I mistook for the squint of the aged.

"Are you looking for me?" he asked, his voice echoing in the silence. This was Željko Cuculić, tourism director of Mrkopalj. The name sounds like *TZU-tzu-litch*.

"I am!" I said, relieved. A travel writer doesn't even have to acclimate when she's being led around by guides who explain everything and arrange stuff and grease the way toward the unnaturally happy travel experiences you read about in magazines.

I smiled wide and hurried down the steps. "I'm the American travel writer! My family came to the United States from here three generations ago!"

Cuculić waited until I reached him and leaned in close. "I am here for three hours WAITING!" he yelled. I smelled slivovitz. "And now I leave!"

I took a step backward. "I didn't know I was supposed to be here at any certain time," I stammered.

Sweet Jesus on Calvary, don't leave me alone in this town! I thought. *Please hold my hand and show me the friendly locals and a quaint cafe and explain why a herd of goats just crowded past the front door.*

"You go now to hotel," Cuculić said. He stormed out the door, muttering as he did: "Tomorrow is national holiday. Nobody works. Maybe you call me on the next day."

Dude was no Siniša, I'll say that much. I followed him out of the building, fumbling my keys in my hands, trying not to cry. I had promised Jim a thorough scouting report of Mrkopalj—by the time I left Des Moines, he'd already mentally quit his job and started packing—and I had so many questions of my own. But I wasn't getting a damned thing for at least two days, thanks to this alleged national holiday. And Cuculić smelled like a distillery and looked as if he might be homeless. Except that he had a sweet new cherry-red Chevy.

"I put you in Hotel Jastreb," Cuculić said. "If this is good enough for you. It is only two stars. You follow me."

"Of course," I said. "I'm sorry, I—"

But he was already powering up his saucy ride to lead me to the hotel. I got into the Polo and whipped a U-turn in his wake. I was doing my best not to panic, but I could feel myself breaking into a sweat in weird places. Without assistance from Cuculić, I would have no language here, and that would put a real damper on my fact-finding mission. Now, I'm a mom. It's my job to be competent and efficient and functional. But in Mrkopalj, I felt a tremor in the Force.

Just outside town, Cuculić pulled over. I did the same. We were entirely alone on a backwoods mountain road. He stalked back to my car, short and trim, hands stuffed in his khaki pockets, baseball cap pulled low over his eyes. What was he going to do? Flush me into the woods and hunt me? I didn't roll the window down. I weighed my options. Driving straight to the Zagreb airport for the next flight home seemed like the safest one.

"I make a mistake," Cuculić's voice was muffled through the glass. He put up his hands. "If you want, we have coffee first."

Call it childhood abandonment issues or maybe just the stainless-steel soul of a Midwestern woman, but I avoid vulnerability like the mall on Black Friday. I had a sneaking suspicion that Cuculić wasn't going to be much help in navigating Mrkopalj. Plus, he scared me.

I cracked the window. "No coffee," I answered, though Croatia had a handle on the coffee thing. Every cup I drank—even in scuzzy gas stations—was better than anything back home. "Just get me to the hotel and I'll take it from there."

Cuculić shrugged. "You go up the hill, three miles," he said, pointing along a winding steep path. "Stay on asphalt only."

I drove up the pass to the teeny grain of a village called Begovo Razdolje and lugged my bags across the empty parking lot of Hotel Jastreb, a black-and-white monolith of post-and-beam construction rising from a mountaintop pasture. I checked in with the clerk at the front desk of a sixties-but-not-in-a-good-way lobby; I was Hotel Jastreb's only guest. Under my breath, I chanted a protective mantra— "What would Rick Steves do? What would Rick Steves do?"—as my room's rollaway mattress and faux brick walls conspired against me. Though stone-cold silent is often how I wish a hotel to be—no sounds of whining kids through thin walls, no neighbors boinking against the headboard—when the quiet comes from being the lone guest, it's really an eerie feeling.

I dropped my bag and sat down to assess the situation. Croatia had been entirely dreamy until I hit the Mrkopalj county line. I felt as if I'd traveled from the First World to the Third World in a three-hour drive. Though I'd imagined Mrkopalj might feel somewhat kindred and familiar, I'd never felt so far from home in my life. Was it me? Was I doing something wrong? I might be a mid-level travel writer, but I've always thought myself a really good traveler.

Travel had been no less than a salvation my whole life. As a scholarship kid at Iowa State University, I'd sleuthed the cheapest study-abroad program in the manual, hungry to know what everyone else knew about the world, and when I got to England and the adviser tried to kiss me in a creepy old uncle way, I bartered an A for my freedom and spent the balance of my semester using my train pass as a textbook for my crash course in European icons. Now the Louvre! Now Big Ben! Now the Alps!

Fresh out of college and working as a high-school English teacher for troubled kids, I stepped between an angry student and his social worker, earning a mouthful of stitches and some serious questions about my career choice. So at the end of the school year, I cashed in my 401(k), gave away everything in my Minneapolis apartment that didn't fit into my '87 Honda Civic, and spent one full year traveling around the United States and Canada, crashing in parks and on the couches of friends, trying to get my head right again. It was cheaper than therapy, and it actually worked.

Then there was my favorite and my best road trip: with Jim to Northern Minnesota, where a justice of the peace and part-time moonshiner married us on a lakeshore in the Boundary Waters Canoe Area Wilderness.

For crying out loud, I'd even built an entire career out of successful travels. I did this stuff for a living! And yet this one-chicken town in Croatia's back forty had me completely unhinged. I had no idea what to do for a whole week in Mrkopalj, where the only signs of life had been barnyard animals and Cuculić. I'd dropped down like Dorothy, with a bump and an *oof!* I'd gone from a coastal Technicolor Oz to this dark enchanted forest that was no place like home.

I checked my watch. Seven hours away, on American time, my long tall husband was waking up with the kids. He'd be reminding Sam for the thirtieth time to brush his teeth, and patting Zadie on the back for staying in bed all night like a big girl. In a few minutes they'd head downstairs for breakfast, Zadie dressed in jarring shades of pink with a mop of blond hair in her eyes and Sam re-creating the

Droid Army battle scene from *Star Wars: Attack of the Clones* where Anakin Skywalker loses an arm. I could see them all. I could smell the coffee. I could hear the cereal being poured and the milk being spilled.

I crossed the hotel room to a sliding glass door, stepping warily past the threshold onto a weather-beaten patio that appeared to be whimsically attached to the side of the hotel. The mountain air was sharp with the primordial rot of fall. I dried my eyes with the palm of my hand. What did the ancestors mean by this clipped, indifferent greeting? Was it a message from Valentin and Jelena that this was my starting point? That we had it all, but appreciated nothing? And that this was what nothing felt like? Was this how they felt when they first arrived in America? Confused, scared, clueless? Something told me these emotions were part of my journey. Besides, if I turned back now, I had a haunting feeling that my family and I would spend the rest of our days stagnating on a couch in middle America.

I had to do the thing that had saved me so many times in my life: I grabbed the keys to the Polo and went for a drive.

Down on the main road, dairy cows with bells on their necks grazed in open pastures. A stout woman leaned from the front window of a small cottage, beating a rug. An old man walked along the street in dark pants and a baggy sweater, hands clasped behind his back. Humanity! At last!

I drove both of Mrkopalj's streets, then continued on the blacktop in the direction of the neighboring city of Delnice, pronounced DELL-neets-uh. Delnice had shops and cafés, a bus station, and a nice-looking hotel that advertised wireless Internet. Hotel Jastreb didn't even have phone service. "We lose in thunderstorm," the desk clerk had told me.

In Croatia, you can make calls from the house phone of a post office, then settle up your bill at the counter. I figured that if I could just hear Jim's steady voice, I might be able to pull out of my panic, so I headed for Delnice's post office. But his cell would only relay the slow chant of his voice mail: "This is Jim Hoff. I'm unavailable at the moment. Please leave a message." I called and called and called. Against my better judgment, I finally left a message, but I was snorting and crying, sputtering into the phone and causing that horrible spitty smell that makes people hate public phones. He later told me that the only words he could make out were *drunk*, *homeless*, and *out of here*.

At the counter, the postal worker spoke little English, but her face was kind like a friendly aunt's. I didn't want to leave her. She was the first nice person I had encountered in the Gorski Kotar. Close to the first person altogether, really. I tried to make a few more calls, just to stall. I paid again, and the lady looked nice again, so I hung around some more and bought postcards. I left another message for Jim. I paid again, and watched a couple in matching tracksuits purchase lottery tickets. I bought a phone card, because the post office would be closed the next day—the only useful information imparted by Cuculić—and the lady behind the counter continued to smile at me. If I could have spoken her language, I would have told her I'd had a tough day. That I wasn't usually this soft, and I had such awful PMS that I felt like a tick about to pop. We'd laugh, and maybe she'd share with me the time she went to visit her nephew Svorlag in America, and it was equally bewildering and off-putting. It would've been enough sustenance for me just to communicate that much information with another human being. But instead we just smiled at each other; she did me the favor of not looking as if she felt sorry for me, and I silently submitted to my role as the freaky foreign lady hanging around the post office. Eventually, I hung my head and left, the short drive back to Mrkopalj dark and heavy through a dense canopy of trees.

Passing through town on the way back to Hotel Jastreb, I noticed a sign I'd missed before. This, painted on a section of a tree trunk and slapped on the side of a building: BISTRO STARI BAĆA, M. ROBERT STARČEVIĆ.

I'd heard of this place. A week before, in Rovinj, my tour guide was an aging rocker with a mullet who led us through the city with a black suede fringed jacket hooked over his shoulder. Renato was the lead singer of Le Monde, a band that sometimes played a Mrkopalj bar called Stari Baća because it was the hometown of their keyboardist, Ratko. The bar seemed like a better place to spend the afternoon than the deserted Hotel Jastreb. Rick Steves would surely agree. I landed the Polo in a patch of grass across the street from Stari Baća, scattering a few sheep in the process.

A low white building with brown shutters, Stari Baća (STAR-ee BOTCH-uh) bumped up against main-street Mrkopalj, its steep red metal roof sheltering a stone exterior, front windows thrown open wide, red gingham curtains flicking in and out in the breeze. I walked over the cracked concrete pad of a side courtyard, stepped into a small foyer, and pushed through a second door to find grizzled men sitting with beers at wooden harvest tables covered by red woven cloth. An ox yoke hung above the fireplace. Antique pictures of the town in more bustling times lined the wall below pairs of handmade snow skis. Though Stari Baća's décor seemed to shoot for a nostalgic vibe, the effect was a gloomy reminder that Mrkopalj's best days were long past.

Behind the bar top that separated the pub from the restaurant side stood Robert Starčević, drying a glass that seemed tiny in his hands.

"*Govorite il ingleski?*" I asked, slaughtering his language.

Robert Starčević (the name sounds like STAR-cheh-vitch) was a sleepy-eyed man with a mess of curly brown hair that made him seem physically larger than he actually was. He looked up at me with what seemed like resignation.

"Renato call me yesterday and say you look for your family."

"I do," I answered, eager. "I'm also looking for beer."

Robert lit a cigarette. Croatians are always lighting cigarettes.

"Sit down," he said, exhaling and indicating a table nearby.

Robert uncapped a bottle of Ožujsko and placed it in front of me. I fumbled through my backpack and produced copies of my great-grandparents' naturalization certificates. Robert took them in his paws.

He held up the certificates, pointing at "Radosevich."

The spelling had been Americanized. "No *h*. We spell with no *h* here in Croatia," Robert said, looking up and exhaling a steady stream of blue smoke, "rad-OH-sheh-vitch."

And with that, Robert Starčević retrieved the first shred of my family history.

Robert told me I should head to the church, where I would find an old book. Through the centuries, the village priests had recorded the baptisms, births, and deaths of every family in Mrkopalj. In that book, I would find my Radošević-no-*h* family names.

I drank my beer as we did the math. Valentin and Jelena were born in 1886 and 1889 respectively—though the year of birth mattered little. Family records were kept by street address, which I didn't have, so it would take a while to find them in the book.

Then Robert and I sat and stared at each other. It was unsettling business, this staring, so occasionally he smoked and studied the documents, the papers rasping against each other as he looked at Valentin's, then Jelena's. I nervously peeled the label off my Ožujsko. When the language barrier hangs like a gaping maw between you and everyone you meet, there's a lot of uncomfortable silence and awkward mangling of meaning and intent. You phrase things and rephrase them, hoping to hit the shaky mark of actual communication every now and then. I tried to tell him what I'd seen so far. I tried to tell him that it didn't seem as if many people lived in Mrkopalj. I tried some small talk, just to fill the quiet.

"So," I said finally. "What's the deal with your tourism guy?"

"Cuculić is okay, but he drink too much *loza*," said Robert.

"I *knew* he was drunk!" I slapped the table. "I come back to this town like *a hundred years* after my great-grandparents leave, and the tourism guy who looks like he probably *partied* with them can't even do me the favor of showing me where the bar is!"

Robert Starčević smoked quietly and watched me.

I dropped my head to the table and uttered one of Grandma Kate's top phrases of exasperation. *"Joj meni,"* I groaned. Yoy manny. Oh my.

"Joj meni," Robert mused. "Is very old saying in Mrkopalj." I cut him a look. A slow smile spread across Robert's face. It may have been amusement. Or perhaps he realized that sitting before him was a helpless, moneyed American. A living, breathing entrepreneurial venture, right in front of his heavy-lidded eyes.

Robert got up, grabbed another beer for me, and dialed the phone behind the bar. He spoke into the receiver for several minutes, then returned to the table.

"I have called my niece, Helena," he said. "She speak good English. She will help you."

I drank and waited for Robert's niece, whose maiden name, it turned out, was Radošević. Just like my great-grandmother. Her father's name? Valentin. A sign from the ancestors if ever I saw one.

A half hour later, the door to the bar opened with a whoosh of cold air, revealing a smallish blonde several months pregnant.

Helena unzipped her winter coat and sunk into a chair while her uncle poured her a glass of water. "I am sorry about Cuculić," she said. She looked tired. "It is only because of politics that he has this job. I hate politics."

Helena and her husband, Paul, a local forest ranger, had just moved back to Mrkopalj from Delnice with their toddler, Klara. "It's a better life here for children. More freedom," she said. "I don't like a place with too many people. I don't like Delnice."

Apparently she hadn't been to the Delnice post office.

Times were tough in Mrkopalj, Helena said in a slow lilt. Her words began in the higher octaves and drifted downward until the end of each sentence, where she lingered on the final syllable. Like a noon whistle, but soothing. Helena said young people were moving away to the cities to find jobs. After her baby was born, she said, she'd return to work as a teacher's assistant. "It's boooooring and depreeeeeessing when you live here and have noooothing to dooooooooo."

Still, the woods and mountains were wild and beautiful, and she and Paul wanted their kids to grow up with the old ways. I confided to Helena that Jim and I were longing to do the very same thing: return to Mrkopalj to live the simple life of my ancestors.

I looked around the dank bar. "It sounded fun when we were back home, anyway."

Things did get more interesting with Helena around. She told me that "*mrko*" meant "dark," as the town was covered in shady forest when settlers arrived five hundred or so years ago. The word "*palj*" meant "field" or "ladle" or "loogie," depending on if you asked some-one old, or a woman, or a young person who had to drive all the way to Rijeka to find work.

We talked about Mrkopalj's ancient dialect, and about how Croatian-Americans who visited left some words behind, such as "*ću-guma*," pronounced "CHEW-goo-mah," for *chewing gum*. Or "*lumbrella*," for *umbrella*.

She told me about Mrkopalj's problem with bears. They descended every morning from the mountains to cherry-pick from people's back-yards. "They ruin a garden, but they don't attack people," she said with a coy smile. "They are only huuuuuuungry."

This would bother Jim, who had grown up across the street from a Kmart in Mason City, leaving him largely uncomfortable with the natural world.

"You have the stress," Helena noted. "We will go for a walk."

Outside, the fall air was bracing. She walked me through the church cemetery that spread out toward the foothills, its graves deco-rated with old photos, flickering candles, and plastic flowers.

We crossed the street to the priest's residence to ask about the big book of names, but a tiny nun in full habit told us the priest was not in.

We headed back to Stari Baća, where Helena suggested I relocate from Hotel Jastreb to the rooms above the bar, so Robert and his wife, Goranka, could look after me. Robert worked the phone, and soon townspeople alerted to my presence started showing up. Men peeled off winter coats and greeted each other through a smoky haze, amid the sounds of clinking glasses and occasional spasms of gruff laugh-ter. There were no women except Helena and me and the kitchen helpers.

Robert called from behind the bar as Helena and I settled onto stools. "How is name 'Jennifer Wilson' if you are Croatian? Where is husband from?"

"Well, actually, I kept my name when I got married," I explained. "My husband's name is Jim Hoff. He's Norwegian, mostly."

Robert stood back and studied me, calculating, smirking.

"Do you like Obama?" he asked, his gaze unfocused as if maybe he had been hitting the *loza* himself. This was a different Robert than the quiet one I'd met earlier.

"Oh," I stalled, recalling that my guidebook advised against discussing politics. "Obama is running for president."

Robert leaned in. "You know that he is nigger."

My jaw dropped. Was this a language barrier thing, a word uttered by a guy who'd listened to a few hip-hop songs and thought this was a standard-issue American noun? I just couldn't tell, as I sat in that bar full of drinking men who didn't speak my language. I was nervous and worried, and Robert had just offered to hook me up with a house to rent, so I didn't want to start a fight with him. I had to gather my scouting report in Mrkopalj, and fast. I didn't know how long I'd be able to fly solo in this place.

"We don't say that word where I come from," I said simply. I tried to change the subject. "Hillary Clinton is also running for president."

"Oh ho *ho*!" Robert said in mock horror. "Hillary Cleen-tone!"

Robert fell back to his huddle of buddies, and they conducted a thorough parsing of the American lady traveling without the husband whose name she had not taken and speaking of the Hillary Cleen-tone.

Then Robert called over, "Ronald Reagan was the best president in America!"

"And now he's dead," I noted.

Helena leaned over and nudged me. "Here, men think they know everything," she said, rolling her eyes.

Stari Baća filled up with people stopping by to ogle the curious stranger. Beer flowed. One or two of the younger guys tried out their English skills on me. Someone offered a tour of the family cheese operation. I saw Cuculić at the bar, his thin face lurking in the dark, glaring at me. Old men set up a table to play cards. I could make out the words *Radošević* and *American* drifting through conversations. A couple of guys with the family name stopped by my table, but we couldn't really understand each other, so I don't know if we were related.

We toasted anyway with my new word: *živjeli*! To life! It wouldn't rent me a room or anything, but it would probably point me in the direction of the nearest bar, which seemed equally practical in Croatia.

A startled-looking old Radošević was paraded before me by several others. Helena translated that he knew my great-grandmother's maiden name had been Iskra, not Eskra, as Sister Paula had spelled it. His wife's maiden name was Iskra, too. Many villagers left for America, but he couldn't summon more than that.

"Everything is mixed up," he said sadly, pointing to his head. The men bought him a drink, which seemed to both bewilder and cheer him.

I stuck it out at Hotel Jastreb for the night, its one lonely inhabitant. It was through sheer force of will that I didn't fixate on the notion that my situation was the perfect premise for a horror movie: Cuculić showing up with an angry mob of drunken bears, screaming "You are three hours late!" as he bludgeons me with both a hammer and a sickle. Okay, maybe I fixated.

The next day, after I moved my stuff to Stari Baća, I walked around in the chill of Mrkopalj, silent but for the echo of someone chopping wood. The town was abandoned on the holiday. I meticulously photographed the place, every towering barn and rickety wooden fence. I wrote down phone numbers posted on houses with rooms to let should Robert prove unreliable, which was highly likely. I popped in to Stari Baća once or twice, and a guy asked me if I was married, or if I wanted to be. He seemed to be checking out my teeth.

Someone tried to sell me cabbage from the back of a truck—at least I think that's what he was selling. Another offered in perfect English to sell me his sister's house for half a million dollars. "We can't keep," he said, shaking his head. "We have no reason to stay. No one wants to live here anymore, and tourism is not so good."

I had a good guess as to why tourism wasn't doing so hot, and his name was Cuculić. But I kept my thoughts to myself.

The whole scene was like something from a grainy foreign movie

I would've pretended to enjoy in college. A black cat crossed my path—I'd counted eight such occurrences during my stay in Croatia. I spit three times to my left, a trick Siniša had taught me to ward off evil. Across a meadow, a woman in a black head scarf rounded up sheep. A family herded milk cows over the main street, the grandmother using a stick to tap their bony behinds. I was so engrossed in their movements that I stepped in a big pile of poop.

I was scraping my shoe when Cuculić pulled up beside me in his Chevy. "Why are you walking?" he asked. "What are you looking for?"

"An interstellar teleporter," I said without looking up.

"How did it go with the priest?" he asked.

I dropped my stick and looked up. "He wasn't there. Maybe I'll leave my documents at the church and have them e-mail me an image of the names when they've found them."

"Oh ho ho!" Cuculić sneered, sounding like a bad guy in a cartoon. "I do not believe it would happen!"

"Well, could you maybe help—" I began, but my voice was lost in the grinding of gravel as Cuculić drove away.

I stood there in the road. Cuculić almost willfully avoided doing his job. This offended me on pretty much every level of my Midwestern being. "From this day forward, you are my nemesis," I declared to his taillights.

A flock of little boys on bikes rustled past me, their unzipped coats flapping like wings. I'd hoped to *feel* something in Mrkopalj—a message from my ancestors, maybe even the spirit of Grandma Kate. But there had been no spiritual connection at all, only a simple and desperate need to see Jim and the kids that had turned into a physical ache in my chest and throat.

I knew Robert now and had taken down his phone numbers. I knew Helena, and she had e-mail. In just a shade over twenty-four hours, I'd filled my notebook with a respectable scouting report. I walked across the street to the post office pay phone and used my calling card to change my flight reservation. I would leave at dawn. My urgent-mom-need-to-be-in-constant-motion would not survive a full week in Mrkopalj. I would go crazy here alone.

When I hung up, I stood on the post office steps and breathed a sigh of relief. The village seemed strangely beautiful now that I knew I'd see Jim and the kids soon. I joined the lines of women wearing heavy dark stockings and babushkas filing through the streets to attend evening mass in the tall yellow church with a spire that rose into the mountain sky. As the priest mumbled prayers I'd heard every Holy Day and weekend of my childhood, I whispered along in English, glad of the familiar cadence.

I resolved during mass that I must make contact with the old relatives before I left. They were the most basic reason I was here in the first place. I couldn't do much without an interpreter, so after the service I stood outside and wordlessly held up Jelena and Valentin's naturalization certificates. This time, the travel gods delivered. Soon I was surrounded by old women. I pointed to the papers and then to myself, saying "America!" over and over.

They spoke to me in Croatian, slowly and loudly, as if I would eventually understand. And in a way, I did. The women wanted to help me. When the squat little priest limped out of the empty church, they gently and collectively grasped my arms and led me to him. He was the keeper of the big and ancient Book of Names. A guy walking by the church, the same one who'd tried to sell me his sister's house, paused and offered translation assistance. He introduced himself as Milivoj, and he had a curious speech habit of adding the words "like this" to the end of most sentences.

"Call me Mile," he said, pronouncing it Mee-lay. "Like this."

The women watched with hands folded across their chests as I walked away with the men, waiting to see if they'd righted my ship and if I would now sail. I cast a few glances behind me as we crossed the street to the three-story priest's residence. Each time I looked back, the old women made shooing gestures or nodded enthusiastically.

The priest's English seemed pretty good at first, but by the fourth time he asked if this was my first visit to Croatia, I had a sneaking suspicion that someone's rosary might be missing a few beads.

The priest rotated his head toward me, his large square face dominated by large square glasses. He looked very much like an owl. Again with the repeating, but this time a question that Mile translated: "He wants to know if you can guess how many bibles in different languages he has."

"Holy, Holy Bible," the priest said, grinning.

"Um, five?" I guessed.

"He has a bible in eight languages!" said Mile. "Like this!"

The priest reiterated: "Holy, Holy Bible!"

We climbed a set of side steps and pushed through a channel-glass door. A short hallway led to a seventies-era study, its only sound a ticking clock. Mile and I sat at a table as the priest pulled out a dusty tome that held the history of Mrkopalj.

The priest introduced himself as Father George, and then he and Mile spent forty-five minutes discussing how hard it would be to find the Radošević and Iskra names in the book because I did not have their street addresses. They did so almost entirely without my input, as if my presence—the reason we were gathered to begin with—was entirely extraneous.

"The priest, he says that your great-grandmother cannot be Iskra," said Mile, patiently nestled in his parka. "He has never heard of name Iskra, like this."

"Jelena, Jelena, Jelena," the priest's finger slowly traced the column of the Radošević entries.

"Actually, Jelena is an Iskra," I said. "I know this for sure. You might start with Iskras. I see on that index page that they do exist, and there are fewer of them than Radoševićs."

This confused Mile. "Why look up Iskra?"

"Because Jelena's maiden name is Iskra," I said. "She married Valentin Radošević."

"Valentin? Who is Valentin?" asked the priest.

"Valentin Radošević," I answered. "My great-grandfather."

"Why you say Jelena?" the priest asked.

"That is my great-grandmother," I explained. "Jelena Iskra."

"This is impossible," said Mile. "Jelena did not marry her father, like this."

Language barrier. Language barrier. Language barrier.

There followed a long discussion about how difficult it would be for the priest to check every single Radošević name to find Valentin among them. There were at least fifty Radošević families! Fifty pages to turn! And turning pages was hard.

I listened to them nattering on for a while, then began to inch over toward the book, trying to be inconspicuous.

"Maybe I can just do it myself?" I asked gently, raising my eyebrows as I slowly reached for it.

The priest recoiled as if he'd been burned, pulling the book away protectively. My participation here was minimal, and there would certainly be no book touching by a woman. And so, in an uncharacteristic show of patience, I waited.

After about an hour, when it appeared that the priest had nodded off to sleep, I roused him, and he suggested I check the Internet for my great-grandparents' names. "Not long ago" he had sent the whole book to Zagreb so the information it held could be entered into the Croatian citizen registry. Maybe everything was online now.

Then he wrote down a website, which was illegible, and I was dismissed.

Mile looked at me and shrugged. We rose, the priest slid the Book of Names back onto the bookshelf, and we left the room. Mile bade me good night, and just like that, I was out on the dark street, returning to the bar.

I looked up at the night sky. "Sorry," I said to the dead relatives. "That's the best I can do for now."

Maybe the welcome I received at Stari Baća was an answer from Valentin and Jelena that indeed I'd done just fine on this first go-around, for it was warm and sweet and comforting. Helena and Robert's wife, Goranka, came out of the kitchen as I walked in the door, clucking over me and removing my coat. Where had I been all day? Was I all right? Everyone had been worried.

"I was just looking around town," I said. "Getting the lay of the land."

As I settled in, Helena asked, "Will you come back here with your family?"

I told her I just wasn't sure yet.

"Helena, what would my family do here all day? I mean, seriously. What happens in Mrkopalj?"

"Well, you wake up and have breakfast. Then you go for coffee. Then you have lunch. Maybe a nap. Then go for coffee. Then maybe go for hike in the woods. Then supper," Helena said. "We will think of things to do."

Goranka hovered nearby, awaiting a translation.

Helena tried the hard sell. "We have a good mountain to climb. We have rivers. We can take the canoe out!"

"Maybe we could start a garden together," I suggested.

"Who?" Helena asked.

"We women," I said. "I garden. Maybe you could teach me some new tricks."

Helena translated for Goranka. They stared at me, dubious, then steered me into a secluded dining room just off the bar where the girls in the kitchen had laid out a fresh batch of deer goulash for me. The women shut me away by myself, a peculiar show of respect that made me lonely and fond of them at the same time.

The wild meat was tart and gamey in a thick stew of tomatoes and onions. Helena told me the deer had been shot not long before it hit the table, which explained the tiny pile of bone shards that grew on the side of my plate as I ate. It wasn't a key to the city, but it was the Mrkopalj equivalent, and I was proud to have it. Alongside my plate was a platter of crisp lettuce, unusually thick and stout, peppered and sprinkled with vinegar and oil. The greens had probably been plucked from a garden just before I walked into Stari Baća that night, most likely by the kids peeking at me through a crack in the door.

There was also deep yellow polenta and a glass of *malvazija*. I chewed slowly, considering my short stay.

I'd come to Mrkopalj in search of family, but family had been drawing my thoughts homeward since I'd first arrived. And all news from the States was grim. The America I'd grown up with was wheeling out of control like Cuculić's Chevy on a Saturday night. Friends were losing jobs. The national debt had passed $10 trillion. The wars in the Middle East were putting us right up with North Korea in the international popularity contest. The world was rapidly reconfiguring, and it didn't feel as if the United States was coming out on top this time. This was not a bad time for a sabbatical.

A college girlfriend who worked at CNN had called me before I boarded the plane to Croatia from my connection in New York. "I can't meet you for lunch. The Dow just dropped six hundred fifty points," she said breathlessly. "Time to start living below our means and teaching the kids to do the same."

Wow, I thought then. *Do we even know how?* In his presidential campaign, Barack Obama was calling on Americans to return to their Nation of Immigrant values. I wasn't even really sure what that meant.

But I thought about Helena raising her kids in Mrkopalj, near the wild mountains and with the old ways. I thought about the $25 I paid for my room in Stari Baća, which included the deer in the deal. I thought about those happy boys on rickety bikes. I thought about working in a big garden, baking bread, getting a couple of chickens. I thought about this place where the people knew who they were, because the priest had a big Book of Names that told them. I tossed and turned in my room above the bar, a giant medieval crucifix above my bed. I knew in my heart that if Jim and I were going to forge a new way for our family, it would be best accomplished in a simpler place. But did it have to be Mrkopalj? I mean, we had other relatives with interesting roots. Grandma Kate had married a full-blooded Italian man. Maybe we'd spend our year abroad in northern Italy, where Grandpa Gino's family came from, a place famous for balsamic vinegar, cheese, and wine. I pictured myself riding a vintage bicycle past the Duomo, a baguette peeking out from my fashionable Italian tote. I imagined Jim in a Brad Pitt tweed cap, bringing me a bouquet of fresh flowers after a morning in the vineyard with the kids, ready to share lunch and afternoon grappa, Maria Callas singing on the Victrola in the kitchen. It would cost a fortune, but we had a decent savings account, and at least we wouldn't have to know how to field-dress a boar to survive.

I flew out the following morning, feet firmly planted on the floor of a Boeing 747 to spare my fellow travelers the aroma of Mrkopalj cow poop emanating from the bottom of my Chuck Taylors. I dozed peacefully for the first time in days.

When my flight landed in Chicago, I checked e-mail during the layover. My in-box was flooded with messages I hadn't been able to retrieve in the Gorski Kotar. Scrolling through, I saw a note from Jim. I opened it.

According to Jim, back when times were booming on Wall Street, he had moved our savings into the stock market. The savings for our Great Family Escape. We'd lost a lot of it in the market freefall of the past few weeks. As in *half*.

"We can look at this in two ways," Jim wrote, always the pragmatist. "We can panic and scrap the whole idea. Or we can take this as a sign. They're saying the economy is going to get worse before it gets better. Maybe this is the kick in the pants we needed to do something completely different. There will always be an excuse not to go.

"I hope you're liking Mrkopalj, because at this point, Mrkopalj is about all we can afford."

And that, friends, is how a typically sane middle-aged mother decided to drag her family back to a forlorn mountain village in the backwoods of Croatia.

chapter **three**

I returned home with a troubled mind and possibly a tapeworm. I'd lost five pounds for no reason, but decided to wait it out for another five before calling the doctor. It was a nice souvenir.

In a stunning role reversal, life in Des Moines felt surreal after Mrkopalj. Just driving the familiar route to the kids' happy Montessori school across town could get me disoriented. The signs for weekly deals in our neighborhood grocery store seemed brazen and overzealous. After spending two weeks in a country where I was rarely understood, I felt harassed when ample speech was required of me. Compared to living out of a carry-on for two weeks, managing the sheer amount of stuff in our lives seemed impossible. Three trips to Goodwill later, people started to wonder if I was suicidal.

The only place I still felt okay was at church, a great big Congregational number that I'd settled on after leaving the Catholics. One Sunday, the pastor gave a sermon about repentance, the Greek translation of the word being the more provocative *metanoia*.

"*Metanoia* means a 'change of mind,' not in the sense of a new decision, but in the sense of *a whole new being*," Reverend Ruhe said, roaming the altar. He was short with thick glasses and a sensible black Congregational robe—a smart, sane version of the owl priest of Mrkopalj. "*Metanoia* is coming to a new life. It's like stepping through a door, out of one existence and into another."

I'd never heard of this *metanoia*. It's a tricky word, difficult to define and hard to understand unless you've felt it. But I knew it after visiting Croatia. Everything seemed different, like that day in September when you know summer is over because the afternoon light has changed. I'd walked through the door of what once was. I was about to lead my family through it, too.

Over a series of late nights in front of the fireplace, Jim and I hammered out a loose plan. We would save every extra penny until the kids were out of school in June. At that time we would leave for Mrkopalj, staying through the summer and into autumn—about four months total. Before the snow came (often so heavy that the mountain roads were impassable), we would relocate to the Croatian seaside village of Rovinj a few hours away, spending the first temperate winter of our lives. We would travel until the money ran out, which we'd calculated as just shy of one very frugal year.

We began Croatian language classes. I ordered stacks of history and travel books. But truthfully, it felt as if everything we learned in those months leading up to the trip went in through our eyes and leaked out of our ears. We met some Bosnian couples through mutual friends and they assuaged our worries: Try as we might, the real learning wouldn't take place until we got there.

When Jim and I told the kids we were leaving the country as we were tucking them in to bed one night, they had vastly different reactions.

"No," Sam said simply, tucking his hands under his armpits. He complained bitterly about leaving our dog, a cute and unsuspecting schnoodle, and about leaving his room filled with Legos and Transformers and everything he liked, all in one happy space painted orange, which he also liked. Sam was a sweet kid, but he was fond of the merch.

"I'm not leaving," concluded our son, his big moon face pulled down in a frown. "Granny said people die in airplanes."

That would be my mother, who for several years had not willingly left the house except for holidays and shopping trips to Walmart.

"I'll buy you a hamster," I said.

"I want a snake," Sam said, knowing this might be a deal breaker. I'd been dragging him to garage sales since he was a fat toddler. The kid knew how to negotiate.

"You can only get a pet that you're willing to hold," I said. "If you can hold a snake for fifteen minutes, we'll get a snake."

"I want a hamster," he said. Then he buried his head in my shoulder and cried.

"I'll go to Croatia," Zadie offered, probably because she had no idea what this meant. "But I do not need a hamster."

Now for the hard part.

"When you're traveling, there isn't much room for toys," Jim began.

"So we're going to have a garage sale to sell them," I said.

Sam sat up in bed in horror, as if I'd punched the schnoodle curled at his feet.

"If you sell all your toys, you'll be able to afford a Nintendo DSI," Jim reasoned. "Which fits in a suitcase."

"And also is awesome," I added.

Sam relaxed. "Well, I do want a DSI."

Zadie watched Sam intently.

"If Sam sells his Legos, he will not be happy anymore," she said. "He will not be Sam."

We agreed that Sam could keep his Legos. Still, he only consented to our Croatian sabbatical because he wasn't old enough to stay home alone yet.

"So he's unhappy about moving to Europe for a year," Jim said as we talked in front of the fire later. "I can think of worse problems. It's okay to be unhappy sometimes. He'll have to deal with new things. It'll be good for him."

The next several months were a blur of work. Throughout the winter and into spring, I scrapped for every story I could get my hands on. I dominated Craigslist and held a name-your-own-price porch sale, selling all extraneous detritus in our home. I cleared enough to cover the cost of our visas, the application process of which transformed trip planning from merely difficult into a soul-sucking nightmare.

Just explaining to the Croatian consulate *why* I wanted a visa was complicated.

"I'm a writer interested in returning with my family to my ancestral homeland. We want to move to Croatia for a year," I said during that first phone call.

The woman at the consulate fell silent. I thought perhaps she was overwhelmed with emotion that this great granddaughter of immigrants was returning after all this time.

Instead, she asked in an incredulous whisper: "*Why?*"

Okay, so that caught me off guard.

Before I could rephrase, she asked again: "*Why* would you want to do *that*?"

I ended the phone call quickly, embarrassed that I'd done something wrong. I checked my information again. Yup, in Croatia, if you're staying longer than three months, you need a visa. What I was asking was not unreasonable. In fact, it was the law.

I called back. Again, the odd silence. Then the consulate official suggested in a hushed voice: "Why don't you just leave the country every three months and sneak back in?"

I envisioned Jim being interrogated in a dirty white room by border cops, a single lightbulb swinging above his head as they slapped him repeatedly while the kids and I watched, horrified and clearly without visas. "Why are you forever coming in and out of Croatia? What is your business here?"

But I thought voicing this concern might offend. So I simply answered: "I want to be in Croatia legally."

It would've been easier to do it her way. The visas cost a fortune, and you could be a MENSA scholar and still not understand the application process.

"It is confusing to only you, Mrs. Wilson," the consulate official once admonished me, all steel and nails. "No one else has these problems."

I began to wonder if no one else had these problems because no one in their right mind would apply for a Croatian visa.

Meanwhile, back at the Croatian Tourism Office, they'd gotten wind of my early-morning defection from Mrkopalj on the press trip. I'd called to ask if I could get a little help with the visa application and Vesna slapped me with a "You are very unprofessional!" Why should she help me again?

She yelled and yelled. I took it at first, trying to be respectful.

Then, sort of as an experiment in the Croatian yelling thing, I yelled back.

"Your tourism guy was drunk!" I yelled. "So who's unprofessional?"

"I did not know this," Vesna said, instantly defused.

"Who are you working with at the consulate?" she asked.

I told her.

Long sigh from Vesna. "She is new. I know her mother. I will call you back."

I hung up and called Niall, a Bosnian hairdresser down the street. Niall and his family had fled Bosnia during the war. He invited me to his house for a visit.

"We had the prettiest refugee tent in the camp," he boasted as he sat me down at his kitchen table. He moved gracefully about the room, assembling coffee.

He'd heard of my visa woes through the grapevine, he said. People had seen me walking around the neighborhood, looking stunned and beaten. "I know this look. I am from Bosnia," he winked.

"Just remember this: You are on Croatian time now. Get used to standing in line. Get used to waiting. Do not hurry. Nothing is easy."

He laughed. He poured me some coffee. I asked if he could translate my visa applications for me, one of the consulate's requirements.

"Oh dear, I have no time to do this," he said. But he did give me great advice. "Just find someone who can stamp your papers as many times as possible. Stamp it all, with any stamp you can find. It doesn't matter what type of stamp it is."

"What?" I asked. "A stamp?"

"Yes. Stamp *everything*," he said. "Croatia is still very hungover from those Communist days. They like everything to *look* official even if it is *not* official. So stamp and stamp and stamp!"

I tracked down a Croatian translator in a local hospital. Eddie had married a notary public—meaning she had a stamp and she knew how to use it. They were endlessly patient and painstakingly thorough, and they stamped the shit out of my papers.

Then I asked the Croatian consulate to give me a break on just one of the visa requirements. They'd asked for a rental certificate from my lodging in Croatia, stamped (of course) by a Croatian notary public. I didn't have lodging yet in Mrkopalj. During my brief stay, Robert had assured me he'd have a place for us, but it was under construction. Also, when he assured me, he was drunk. The worst thing I could imagine was arriving in Mrkopalj, with my family this time, and not having a decent place to land.

"I don't think I can get a rental certificate," I told the woman at the consulate. "And I sure as hell can't get a stamp."

"Can't you just put together *something*?" she said. "Anything? Just make it *look official*."

"I'm going to a tiny mountain village where people might very well do commerce by exchanging chickens," I said. "If it's going to be official, it will have to come from here."

"You can try," she said. "But the final decision is up to the Ministry of the Interior in Croatia."

"Will it help that I'm writing a book about how great Croatia is?" I asked.

"No," she said.

Jim would rub my shoulders when I felt defeated. "Eye on the prize," he'd say. "If it were easy, everyone would be doing exactly what they dreamed of."

I was finding that the escape fantasy and the actual *planning* of the escape were two entirely different beasts. When I needed focus, I recalled a conversation with my sister a few years before, when Croatia had not yet overtaken my psyche, but the restlessness had.

Stephanie and I were at our favorite restaurant, Centro, in Des Moines. I'd excused myself to go to the restroom. In the full-length mirror next to the sinks I caught sight of an older, frowning woman. Her chin melted into her neck. She looked a bit stuffed into her skirt. Until this woman reached for the soap dispenser at the exact moment I did, I hadn't recognized the reflection as my own. I'd begun the downhill tumble into midlife malaise and I hadn't even noticed.

"Don't worry about it," Stephanie said when I returned to the table.

"I just read a magazine article that said forty is the new thirty. And thirty is the new twenty! Which works out pretty good, because I'll be thirty this year."

"Magazine stories aren't true," I said, shaking my head. "Articles like that are written by interns in New York barely old enough to vote who will conduct their entire adulthood sleeping around like Tri Delts."

"What a life," Steph said dreamily.

"We are Midwestern women," I said. "Age comes in real time."

"Who knows? We're not plowing fields and popping out whole football teams of babies anymore," she said. "Maybe aging is different now."

"I don't feel like it is," I said, making a grab for the bread basket.

"Why don't you start by putting down the fistful of carbs," Stephanie said.

"There are so many things I haven't done yet," I said to her. "And let's face it, my life is pretty much halfway over."

Stephanie's face sagged, impatient. "Oh come *on*," she said. "What *haven't* you done? You've traveled all over. You have a great job. You lived in *Minneapolis*, for gosh sakes! The mother of all cities!"

"But I accomplished all that stuff before I was a mom," I said. "Since parenthood, what have I done? I've used my kids as an excuse to become lame! My thirties have been this endless cycle of postponement. I'll wait and write a book *after the kids grow up*. Jim and I can travel more *after we retire*. And what does that leave us?"

"A bitchin' retirement," Steph said. "What's wrong with that?"

"What's wrong is that there are *three decades* in between college and retirement that I would like to be more fulfilling."

"Your kids are fulfilling," she answered. "Once they're old enough to be into their activities, things will get even better. I'm pretty sure Zadie's got the Wilson arm. You should probably get her out there throwing the softball now, while her muscles are still forming. Anyway, you'll stay busy. You won't even notice how time flies."

"I don't want to just preoccupy myself for a third of my life," I argued. "I love my kids, but it's my job to show them the options in life, not live it for them. Or live for them."

"Well, what are you going to do then?" Steph asked.

"I want to stop postponing," I said. "I want to be as engaged and curious in my middle years as I was in my twenties."

"So, you want to party more?" Steph asked.

"No. That's not it at all. I'm not a kid. I want to see what I can do as a grown-up woman. See what I've become," I said. "I have no idea what I can accomplish as an adult because I haven't tried much yet."

"Well, you better get on it," Stephanie said. "You and I are not the kind of people who sit around and feel bad. We solve the problem. It might be our only redeeming quality."

Oh, I would get those Croatian visas. By God, I would. I stood fast and firm, assembling all documentation of my family's humanity, and one afternoon in late spring, I got a phone call from the icy voice at the Croatian consulate.

"Mrs. Wilson, I have good news," she said, emotionless. "Your permits to stay in the country of Croatia have been approved."

The kids were still at school. Jim was at work. So I turned off my computer, quietly gathered my purse and coat, and walked the few blocks to my favorite old Naugahyde supper club for a single sublime vodka martini to celebrate before I told anyone. I sat alone in the quiet of an old bar in the daytime lull and enjoyed my triumph. An ancient waitress in a bouffant hairdo walked by, trailing the scent of Grandma Kate: Chanel No. 5 and cigarettes. I knew then that the mammoth boulder of our lives, grown mossy and solid through inertia, was finally starting to give.

Now we just needed to find a place to live in Mrkopalj.

I'd been e-mailing with Helena back in the village, attempting to negotiate a place to stay. At first, she wrote that we could stay in those same rooms above the bar, and it would cost only $1,000 a month! Considering we'd chosen Mrkopalj on the assumption that it was a bargain—and we'd figured about $500 a month for rent in our budget—this was bad news. Plus, those rooms above the bar were awful.

I wrote back to Helena to tell her we would look elsewhere for lodging.

I quickly received another e-mail that Robert's family and friends would renovate the rooms on the second floor of his family's house, and we could stay there! We could have it for the low, low price of $1,500 a month!

Jim and I couldn't decide if we were offended or impressed. Either Robert was shrewd as hell or he thought we were rich. I asked Helena to thank Robert and tell him we appreciated the extra effort but didn't want him to go through all the trouble. We just couldn't pay that much rent.

Eventually we settled on €600 per month for the renovated second floor of Robert's house. About $800 or $850, depending on the exchange rate. It was a stupid price, twice as much as a nice apartment in Zagreb, but we swallowed it. Jim and I have that guilt that all American tourists are pigs. We did not want to be pigs. So we agreed, relieved to have housing at last.

Then, twelve days before we were scheduled to leave the country, in the middle of June, Helena e-mailed again:

Hallo, sorry I'm late because we have some problems in our familiy, our grandmother is very sick she is dieing. I hope that you can understand this situation. She is Robert mother and my grandmother, she is living below your flat where you and your familiy will be settle down so we stop with all works in your flat. We don't know how situation will be with grandmother because every day is different, some day she is very sick and we think that she will die and next day she is better, she is eating and drinking, Today we are not sure that we will finish your flat so Robert offer if you will be at flat where he has caffe-bar, he offer two badrooms, living room and internet, you will be there for some 10 days and than we will transfer you and your familiy at Robert house and if you wants something else call me on my number, today or tomorrow at your time two p.m., I think then is 8 p.m. at Croatia, greetings from all us, Helena.

I made a last-minute scramble for another apartment in Mrko-palj, but it was too late. We had no choice but to trust Robert. Our tenants would move in July 1. The schnoodle had gone to Jim's sister and brother-in-law in Oklahoma. The cat moved in with our retired schoolteacher neighbor. We'd attended our good-bye parties. We'd gotten properly drunk with everybody. We were hungover from hep-atitis shots. Where were we going? Well, we weren't sure. We *might* have a place to stay in Mrkopalj. We might not! It was all the same now. We were stepping through the door, out of one existence and into another. *Metanoia*.

Finally, on June 24, Jim's final day at the office, I received an e-mail from Mrkopalj: Robert's mother had died. They were working on our rooms again.

They had a week to complete them.

Doable in America. But we weren't moving to America.

We just had to have faith in Mrkopalj.

My sister Stephanie drove us to the airport. With one last, shirt-drenching cry, my soul parted from its earthly bindings. Finally, I was becoming a true traveler again, open in heart and mind and schedule. It seemed for the first time entirely possible that I could rec-oncile the free and seeking spirit I had been as a young woman with the tightly tethered mother and wife I had become—it just took a hell of a lot more work. I glimpsed glory in it, though I was unsure how it would go. For the first time in a very long time, I had no idea what would happen next.

We filed onto the airplane hand in hand, all of us quiet. As Zadie looked out the tiny plane window, her face glowed with an angelic glee I recognized. It was how I felt inside, too. This was the prize I'd been keeping my eye on.

"I never been on a plane when I was a big girl before," Zadie said. "I like to be inside clouds."

The crease left my forehead. My shoulders unknotted. My muscles, much tested over the days of packing and hauling, relaxed. I stole a glance at Jim, who winked at me, then pressed his head against his seat back. Sam was absorbed in his brand-spankin'-new Nintendo DSI. Good enough.

On June 29, the Wilson Hoff family lifted off from Des Moines International Airport, having absolutely no idea what to expect from our next year.

Surprisingly, it was a very good feeling.

chapter **four**

Our entrance into Europe was less impressive: Zadie vomited in the Munich airport.

It was a long overnight flight. The attendants startled everyone out of sand-eyed half sleep by snapping open the curtains and windows and serving orange juice and muffins that didn't sit well with my daughter. As we sprawled in the airport chairs, waiting for our final short hop to Milan, where we'd pick up our leased car and drive to Mrkopalj, Zadie leaned over and wretched one convulsive splatter onto the marble floor. Then she quietly asked for a napkin, wiped her mouth, and walked away.

"Are you okay, honey?" I asked, following her and dabbing at her shirt.

"I don't want everybody looking at me," she said, sounding panicky, keeping her eyes trained straight ahead. She stole a glance at me. I saw determination in her face.

Could she be trying to prove herself to me? That she could be trusted to come along when Mom traveled? Zadie had said good-bye to me many times before work trips. She'd always been such a big girl about it that I hardly knew she'd noticed my absences. Maybe she had noticed. Probably she had.

One of the things I'd hoped for most on our trip was to figure out my girl. The previous year, Zadie, who was three at the time, had barely survived full-time preschool while I got back to my writing career in earnest, an anguished decision I'd made after years hun-

kered down in the Stay-at-Home Mommy Cave. Being away from
home all day just wrecked my little towheaded daughter. Zadie threw
fits from the moment she walked in the door until the Grand Finale
Tantrum of Bedtime. Rather than chalking it up to growing pains, I
blamed myself, assuming she felt rejected, as if I'd subcontracted her
toddler years in favor of my own selfish needs and fears. Which was
kind of true. Jim and I worked part-time when Sam was born, raising
him without child care until he was four. By the time we had Zadie,
we were tired of juggling schedules and watching PBS Kids. In the
end, Jim took a full-time gig in one of those places where you have to
talk to your boss to prove you really need a sick day. I accepted more
magazine assignments because the silence of the office was way easier
than parenting two toddlers. And, to be honest, I was probably a little
intimidated about having a daughter. I had no healthy template to
follow. I just didn't know how that mother-daughter harmony thing
worked and, well, I was terrified of failing.

As Zadie hurried toward a restroom sign, I stepped in front of
her and lifted her into my arms. I held her tight, and her body went
limp. Finally she cried. I stepped into the restroom and cleaned her up
properly.

"You are a very good traveler," I told her. "You were very patient
on the airplane."

"I'm tired, Mommy," she said, rubbing her eyes.

"I know you are," I said, wiping her face gently with a wet paper
towel. "You fell asleep on the plane and then slid right onto the floor
and slept all curled up like a little baby."

She smiled at that. "Tell me about when I was a baby."

"You were a very good girl. You were content," I said. "I would sit
in my office and write stories and rock you in your car seat with my
foot. One time, I did a whole interview while I was nursing you."

"That's when I would get milk from your boobs," she said gravely.
Nursing is fascinating business for a four-year-old.

"Yes, it was," I said. "I think we're all cleaned up now. Do you feel
better?"

"Yes," she said quietly. "I don't want to ride on the plane anymore."

"We have one more short flight," I said. "And then we get to swim in a pool."

"Okay," she said, taking a deep breath.

"We'll be together the whole time," I told her. "Like two fancy girls traveling the world."

She seemed pleased at this, and we headed out to wait for our flight.

In Milan, Jim and the kids swam in the icy Novotel pool while I caught the shuttle to pick up the Peugeot we'd leased for a year. A smart black number decked out with a sunroof that spanned the whole top of the car, it was a few inches short of a station wagon, but big enough to fit all our bags and the kids, and it had a very essential GPS, which we set to a prim British voice and named Charla before charting our course to Mrkopalj, Croatia.

We drove a landscape that turned from Italy's dusty vineyards to wide Slovenian meadows to jagged Croatian seafront. Mountains rolled forward, like great stones hidden under a blanket of deciduous trees and, later, the primeval evergreens of the Gorski Kotar. The first time I'd seen this land, alone and afraid, it seemed so foreboding. Now, with my family, the cool green wilderness was the realm of elves and fairies.

It was early evening under a moody sky when we hit the outskirts of town. Jim pulled over and we took a family photo in front of the Mrkopalj re-creation of Calvary. We drove the final mile into the village, where the trees backed away from the road, replaced by tiny stucco houses. Old stoop-sitting men with hands on knees watched us pass.

We rounded the bend onto Novi Varoš. Giddy and curious, we pulled in to Robert Starčević's driveway. The three-story house was bigger than I remembered, a mishmash of diamond-shaped asbestos tiles and thick wood planks stained dark. On each floor, mullioned windows swung wide open to the world.

Robert emerged from a side door, a great brown bear squinting and blinking in the sun. He saw us in our car waving at him and star-tled in a panic. He stumbled down the steps. Was he weaving?

"Oh! Jennifer! Hello!" he said as we stepped out of the Peugeot. I hugged him and he tried to kiss my cheeks but missed. His lips smacked somewhere behind my ears. He smelled like old beer.

"We do not expect you coming today," Robert said, arms up in an expansive shrug. "E-mail says you come tomorrow."

"I sent that last night from our hotel in Italy before we went to bed," I said. "But now that I think of it, I sent it really late. I'm sorry. I meant we were coming today."

"We do not expect today," Robert repeated.

"This is my husband, Jim," I said, standing back a bit and indicat-ing Jim.

"Oh, hey, Jeem!" Robert stuck out his hand. "Is good to meet you, Jeem!"

"*Drago mi je,*" said Jim, busting out his Croatian up front. "Pleased to meet you."

I introduced Sam and Zadie, who hid behind me. Sam was wringing his hands. Zadie clutched my leg. They were jet-lagged and disoriented, and I couldn't wait to get them into their jammies and a comfortable bed and assure their little worried faces that their mama had brought them to a safe place. Because Mama was seeking similar reassurance.

Which Mama did not get. Robert seemed flustered. Flecks of dust and drywall nested in his curly hair. "Your rooms, they are not finished," he said, fishing in his pocket for his cigarettes. "They are finished tomorrow. Finish, one day."

"I'd like to see the rooms," Jim said.

"Yes, of course," Robert said. He walked us up the steps to the sec-ond floor and led us through a narrow foyer toward a pair of French doors.

The rooms of the second floor were under a heavy layer of rubble. The main space was an empty shell of bare studs and stubs of pipes that indicated it would perhaps someday contain a kitchen. Three rooms broke off the main one. Two would likely be bedrooms. A third was sheathed in red tile, and upon that floor was some enormous mechanism—either a giant shower or a time machine, we couldn't tell.

Construction had barely begun, because demolition had not yet ended.

I stole a panicked look at Jim, who had his hands in his back pockets, thoughtful.

Jim looked at Robert and raised his eyebrows a bit. Robert ran his hands through his hair.

"We do not expect you come today. E-mail say you come tomorrow," said Robert. "We finish rooms in maybe two days."

Cuculić appeared behind us. He was shorter than I remembered, his face thinner.

"Mr. Cuculić," I said, and nodded.

"Mizz Veelson," he said, nodding as well.

"This is my husband, Jim," I said.

They shook hands.

"*Drago mi je,*" Jim said.

"Oh ho ho! Your husband speaks Croatian!" Cuculić exclaimed.

"We studied a little bit before we got here," said Jim, all jovial. "We're not proficient or anything, but we do our best—"

I cut him off. "Don't get comfortable," I said. "We can't stay here. Look at this place."

"Take it easy, Jen," Jim said, putting his arm around me.

Robert, sensing he was losing customers, hustled us back to the driveway, away from the chaotic second floor, speaking in Croatian to Cuculić.

"Robert says the rooms are not finished today," Cuculić began. "You may stay here, on the third floor, or you may stay above Stari Baća, until the workers finish."

Zadie put up her arms to be lifted, and I picked her up and pressed her to me. Sam nudged in at my side. The one thing I'd dreaded most about returning to Mrkopalj—that we would get there with no place to call home—was happening. I'd done everything within my supermom powers to ensure that my family would be as safe and settled as possible on this journey. And yet there were details that even I couldn't control. Details that I would have to relinquish either to fate or to the people of this village. On this latter note, the two beery dudes before me did not inspire confidence.

Robert surveyed our family and seemed to come to a conclusion. "We go to Stari Baća for just one beer," he said. Cuculić shrugged, and he and Robert headed to his bright red Chevy, now sporting a great bandage of duct tape across the front bumper. Jim and I followed, driving one block to the bar in anxious silence.

It started to drizzle. I'd picked up right where I left off in Mrkopalj. Lost. Floating. Itching to get out. But this time, I'd dragged my family along. I looked at my kids in the backseat. They seemed to have grown smaller in the past hour. This was all my fault.

"Mom, I'm tired," said Sam. "Where are we going to sleep?" Zadie had been looking out the window, but now she leveled her gaze at me. I didn't know what to tell them.

"Hang in there, guys," Jim said. "We'll get this figured out."

I had to keep it together and get us through this. I took a cleansing breath as we parked, then I led my family into the murk of Stari Baća. Robert retrieved beers and juices from behind the bar and brought them over on a tray.

"You stay in Stari Baća rooms for two or maybe three night," Robert said. "Then rooms in my house finished, and you come."

Cuculić piped up. "Robert says that you can stay in the rooms above Stari Baća until your rooms in his house are finished."

"We are not living in a bar," I said. "We're just not."

"You stay then, maybe on third floor of my house, or in rooms here in Stari Baća, until your rooms are finished. Three or maybe four nights," Robert said, repeating the exact thing that I'd just said I would not do.

"Robert says you can also stay in the third floor of his house, where his daughters sleep now," said Cuculić. "Then maybe in a few days construction on your rooms is finished."

"I heard him," I snapped.

Yes, I am aware that my foul disposition was not helping matters. I was worried about my kids. Zadie crawled into my lap. Sam laid his head down on the table and closed his eyes. They both looked as if they were fighting tears.

The men around me, on the other hand, were kicking back for cocktail hour. I couldn't tell whom I wanted to throttle more, Cuculić or Robert. How long had these guys known we were coming? Nine months? Give me three stay-at-home moms and a pile of lumber and I could've *built* a house in that time. This all would've been a funny bar story if it were just Jim and me and we were twenty-something back-packers. Instead, we were responsible for two increasingly worried-looking kids, and the thought that perhaps I hadn't led us into the safest situation was throwing me into another Mrkopalj panic.

Jim, noting the apprehension spreading over my face, spoke up. "What were the rooms above the bar like when you stayed here last fall?"

"The abandoned set of a slasher movie," I answered.

"You want see?" Robert asked. The men led my husband through the restaurant area up the back stairway. I remembered my night in one of those rooms last fall. Battered doors lined a long linoleum hall-way. Inside those doors, musty bunk beds made up with army blan-kets were shoved against paneled walls. Someone had assaulted the bathrooms with messy and moldering caulk jobs. The main renters of these rooms were visiting hunters and bar patrons wanting to get laid in a clandestine manner. I had been conscious all night of men drink-ing down below. Drinking a lot. And smoking. A lot.

Jim came back downstairs in less than a minute, shaking his head. Robert went to the phone and barked into it. Cuculić floated to the bar.

"Well, those are out," Jim said. He reached over and rubbed my back. "That's where you stayed last fall? No wonder you ran home so fast."

I turned to him and said quietly: "I know we planned to go to

Rovinj in the winter, but why don't we go there now? We could just hang out on a beach until these guys get our rooms done."

"Be patient, Jen," Jim said, hands bobbing in front of him as if bouncing two basketballs simultaneously. "It'll all work out. And hey, you were right—this place is straight out of last century."

"Jim, those rooms in his house aren't going to be finished in one day—or even one month," I said. "Should we maybe talk about an alternate plan?"

"Everything's behind because Robert's mother died," Jim said quietly. "They couldn't help that. I just wish they would've been straightforward about it so we could've found something else."

"*We have nowhere to stay*," I whispered. "Don't you think that's a problem? I'm pretty sure it's a problem."

"You're panicking. Everything seems worse than it is," he said. "But it's actually really pretty here. Is that the tourism guy you told me about? He's being helpful now."

"Judas!" I pointed to Jim, incredulous. "What's so helpful about translating everything Robert says? Robert speaks English!"

"Listen, we're here to find out about your family," Jim said. "We can't do that in Rovinj."

Of course the guy was right. But being a mom and being a free-spirited traveler were feeling like two entirely different things right then.

Robert returned to the table. He explained that his daughters were clearing out their stuff from the third floor. They would move in with him and Goranka on the first floor, where his mother had lived (and died). The workers would complete the second floor quickly, he promised, and all would be well.

"You want, we go see now," Robert said with another exaggerated shrug, his eyebrows raised and his mouth in a questioning frown.

Cuculić stepped forward. "Robert says he wants to show you his third floor now. You may decide then what you want to do."

"I know what Robert's saying," I said to Cuculić. "Because he said it in English."

"Might as well check it out," Jim said, getting up and pulling me up with him. "It's late. We're not going anywhere tonight."

"It's not like we have any other options." I sighed. "Thanks to these yay-hoos."

A friend had given me a piece of advice before we left: Whatever happens, roll with it. We'd come to Croatia to open our lives to the lessons of the ancestors. That meant relaxing the standards a little. Or a lot.

Roll with it. Yes. I could control the planning for this trip, but I had to make peace with the fact that I couldn't control what happened from here on out. I had to find it within myself to let go and trust this journey. I took another one of those cleansing breaths and gathered my son and daughter. We filed out the door in the boozy wake of Robert and Cuculić, who were chatting with Jim in broken English about the drive, the flight, and the weather.

"Mom, I want to go *home*," Sam moaned.

"It's gonna be okay," I said firmly. "We're together and we're safe. That's all that matters right now."

"You look mad," Zadie noted.

"Because I am going to kill Robert and Cuculić as soon as we have a place to stay," I explained patiently. "But that's more a logistical matter than an anger issue."

"Jen," Jim warned.

"And also!" I added, pointing. "Look at the pretty mountains!"

We looked out the car windows and tried to see Mrkopalj as Jim saw it. The earth rose in peaks above the village, vivid green from the rain. Open meadows peeked from behind the houses, blooming with early summer wildflowers in purple, yellow, and white.

When we arrived at 12 Novi Varoš, Robert's home, his daughters stepped out of the side door, inching shyly down the concrete steps. They looked disheveled. Poor things had been frantically packing, rectifying the mistake of their father and I. We were now moving three very sweet-looking little girls out of their home. This did not improve my conscience.

"This is Ivana. She is fourteen," Robert said. Tall and thin, with a head of thick and wavy blond hair, Ivana smiled at us.

"Hi," Ivana said. "Nice to meet you."

"And Karla. She is twelve," Robert said. Karla made a small wave with her long hand. Lanky, with thick brown hair and wire-framed glasses, Karla could have a future as a women's basketball pro.

A third little girl, almost Karla's miniature, pressed against her dad's leg. "This is Roberta," he said, putting his hand on her head. "Roberta is five years old. She is like Zadie."

Roberta smiled at Zadie.

"We go now upstairs," Robert said.

"Robert says that now you go upstairs with him," said Cuculić.

"Seriously?" I turned up my palms at him as I passed.

Robert slid back a rolling wooden door on the third floor of his house. We stepped into a space that was open and dorm-like, with high slanted ceilings. To the left was a bedroom with an upright piano, a wardrobe, a bare mattress, and a desk. Straight ahead was the bathroom. I poked my head in to see a lime-encrusted shower and slanted ceiling of knotty pine. An ominous smell emanated from the direction of the toilet (duly noted by the primary toilet scrubber in our family—me).

On our right was the main living space. Ivana and Karla pulled out a modern red couch with silver pegged legs into a futon. Ivana shook out three child-sized sheets, and smoothed them over the make-shift bed.

"You sleep here," she indicated to Jim and me.

"Mom! Hi!" Sam called. We looked up. Zadie and Sam had climbed into two tiny lofts opposite each other, straight out of a Laura Ingalls Wilder book.

There was a small wood-burning stove. An old rocking chair in front of a big window. A round table and four chairs. A kitchenette with a dorm fridge.

Though it was small, the place was clean and bright, its wide plank floors stained gold. The heavy wood ceiling beams looked more than a century old. The girls had decorated with stuffed animals and snapshots of themselves and pictures of the Virgin Mary Scotch-taped to the wall. Underneath a Catholic calendar, a tiny dried-up holy-water font was draped with an oversized ceramic rosary.

I walked over to the window with the rocking chair. It swung wide onto a full view of the great green mountain Čelimbaša, less than a mile away. The rain had stopped. Black pavement glistened in the dusk. Behind me, Robert said to Jim: "Two, three days here."

I turned. "Two or three days to finish the second floor?"

"Four. Maybe five days," said Robert. "Then rooms: finished."

He coupled this statement with a shrug that seemed to be his signature. One shoulder raised slightly, one eyebrow inched up in equal proportion.

I was feeling very tired. The kids climbed down from the loft and came over to me. I wanted to snuggle close like chipmunks in that stiff-looking red bed and sleep a long, dreamless sleep.

I looked at Jim and nodded once. "This works," I said.

Jim turned to Robert. "We'll stay here, then," Jim said. "Two or three days."

"Maybe one week," said Robert, shaking out a cigarette and casually hanging it on his lower lip, relaxed now. "Not long."

We all left the house. Cuculić or Robert, I can't remember which, showed us the vast backyard with a huge garden planted entirely with potatoes. Robert's backyard and those of his neighbors were not separated by fences. They all ran together into one glorious field of wildflowers, tall grasses, and garden patches, merging in the distance with a lovely low mountain. The girls walked toward the backyard and Ivana beckoned to Sam and Zadie. Surprisingly, my slow-to-warm kids followed.

"Well, shall we get our bags?" Jim asked, giving me a quick squeeze.

"Yes," I said, watching for a few more seconds as my children receded into the wide meadow in the evening light. They'd never had a yard so big in their lives.

Robert and Cuculić smoked in the driveway. Cuculić called to Jim that we should park our car in front of the abandoned house across the street. Jim did so and we began hauling suitcases.

On the way up the stairs, I peeked again at the second floor. Jim and I have renovated a house. I know the look of near-completion, and the second floor did not have that look.

I dropped a few suitcases in the dorm. Jim stepped in behind me, laden with bags.

"This is going to be good," he said, clamping a big hand firmly on each of my shoulders. "I know you're worried, but we're not going to hang around here and be miserable. We're going to settle in to this place and have some fun."

I looked at my husband and nodded, drawing strength from his calm.

Jim chuckled. "What do we have to worry about, anyway? We're all together. That's the main thing."

We all slept on the foldout futon that first night, spooned together, windows thrown open to the cool mountain air. The mattress felt like a countertop and my pillow a sack of flour. I tried not to think of the sea. In the darkness, the silence of the village shattered when a drunken man sang in the night. Cats fought. A dog bayed intermittently. We all slept but Jim, who sat up all night in the big rocking chair, staring out the window with a smile on his face.

chapter **five**

In the morning, I woke to the sound of the dorm's door rolling open. It was Jim. He'd already been over to the little grocery store across the street, and now he unpacked his shopping bag: a jar of Nescafé, a liter of orange juice, crusty bread, yogurt, sausage, and apples.

"How's everybody doing this morning?" he asked.

"Better," I said.

"Good," Zadie's muffled voice called.

From under our pile of blankets, Sam's long arm emerged. He stuck out his thumb, and then slowly turned it down.

"Well," Jim assessed. "The neighbors are out, walking around or riding tractors. The air smells great. It's a little cold. In July!"

The temperature was significantly lower in Mrkopalj than in Iowa during a typical summer. Gone was the soul-crushing humidity of the Midwest. I sat up in bed to stretch and watch Jim rummage around the kitchenette. He boiled water in a tiny pan and cut bread, sausage, and apples on a small wooden board.

"I can totally do this," Jim said. "No work. No computers. No nothing. Just us."

He stirred Nescafé crystals into cracked coffee cups he found in the cupboards. The place was sparse but solidly outfitted, like a park cabin without the mousey smell. Jim handed me a cup of coffee as I lounged. Grandma Kate drank Nescafé, but it was nothing like this nutty European version, which teetered on the verge of tasty.

The kids stirred under the covers. Sam sat up and looked around.

"Awwww," he groaned. "We're still here."

We crowded around the little kitchen table by the window. The kids were sleepy and suspicious of the food, which Jim had placed on a communal plate in the center. They nibbled the food and liked it, but the orange juice didn't taste right.

"Okay, guys," Jim said. "Yesterday was tough, but today will be better."

Sam's head lolled forward and banged against the table.

Zadie crawled onto my lap. I lowered my nose into her hair and breathed.

We didn't know if we should unpack, in case Robert miraculously finished the second-floor rooms, so we dressed from our suitcases and stowed them in the piano room, which we decided would serve as a giant closet. Though it was only ten paces from the main living area, we had this primal urge to stay within sight distance of each other. So we dragged its mattress to a corner near the wood-burning stove for Sam. I unpacked his Legos and found a few wooden folding trays he could build on. This little protected cove would be his own private Tatooine. He seemed relieved.

Zadie dressed elaborately in a princess costume—something she deemed as crucial as air, and in fact had packed alongside her nebulizer—and asked to go outside to find the girls. Jim and I escorted her downstairs as Sam tinkered with his living space. We found Robert sitting on a bench up against the house next door, smoking, wearing spring-green Capri pants, toes poking through worn leather huaraches. A large golden retriever wiggled on his back at Robert's feet.

Jim walked over and rubbed the dog behind the ears. "Who's this guy?" he asked. The dog's tongue lolled out in joy. Jim threw a stick and he bounded away.

"Oh, hey, Jeem," Robert said, taking one last drag of his smoke, then tossing the butt into his neighbor's yard. "This is Bobi. My dog. Karla's dog."

"Boe-bee?" I asked. "Or Bobby?"

"Boe-bee," Robert answered. "Is typical name for dog in Croatia."

Bobi returned with the stick. Jim petted him some more, admiring the dog. Bobi got so excited about the attention that he jumped on Zadie, knocking her over. She didn't make a peep but scrambled to me, and I hefted her onto my hip.

Robert stood up and rustled Bobi into a wire pen attached to the side of his house. "We go now to coffee at house of my first neighbor."

Robert pointed to another three-story house across the street.

"Should we go get Sam?" Jim asked.

"I don't know," I said, looking up at the yellow window of the third-floor dorm. "He seemed pretty peaceful with his Legos."

"Sam!" yelled Jim. Our boy poked his big, tousled head out the window. "We're going next door!"

"Can I stay up here?" Sam asked.

Jim and I looked at each other, worried.

Robert watched us, arms akimbo. He scratched his great curly head. "We go across street," he said, pointing again. "Is near."

"We'll be right over there!" I yelled, pointing across the street. "You can see us from the window! Yell if you need anything!"

"Okay, Mom," Sam said.

Zadie and I crossed the street together. "Now look both ways twice," I reminded her, pausing as a little Fiat zipped by.

"Is small road," said Robert. "Safe."

"Well, we live in the city, and the kids don't cross the street alone yet," I said, still looking both ways to make my point to Zadie.

"Not many cars on road," Robert said.

"What if a car comes when you want to cross?" I asked Zadie.

Robert interrupted. "Car stops for person in Mrkopalj," he said.

I gave up and we followed him across the quiet street.

A tall, barrel-chested man with buzzed white hair wearing brown Carhartt coveralls greeted us. We'd seen him out in the meadow when we'd arrived in Mrkopalj, cutting his grass with a slingblade.

"This is Mario, my first neighbor," said Robert. Because Mario was not Robert's physically closest neighbor, we understood "first neighbor" to mean the one most trusted. Over time, this theory proved true.

Mario stepped forward, shaking Jim's hand and then mine. Mario had rosy cheeks and bright blue eyes and the first full set of healthy teeth I'd seen.

With a nod, Mario indicated a green picnic table in the nearby grass. The meadow sparkled with dew in the morning sun. Zadie slipped onto my lap. Another golden retriever came hustling down the steps of Mario's house, a cacophony of toenails clicking against wood. The dog rushed to the table, silky gold fur lifting and falling as he half walked, half crawled around us.

"*Sidi*, Thor!" commanded Mario. "*Sidi, doli!*"

Thor sat.

Robert tossed Thor a wafer cookie from a plate on the table.

"*Neh!*" Mario said to Robert. Robert harrumphed a little and tossed Thor another cookie. Mario glared at Robert, just the slightest trace of a grin beneath his grimace. Mario turned and cocked his head at me, as if to say: *Can you believe this guy?*

A set of wooden shutters clattered open on the house. An old woman poked her head out. Sun glinted off her glasses to make her eyes look like blank white orbs. She waved one long slow swipe, then clasped her hands in front of her and watched us.

"Mother of Mario," Robert noted.

I waved back.

Mario, who spoke no English, asked a few questions of Jim through Robert. "Mario say what job is Jim do?"

Jim answered. "I'm an architect."

Mario seemed pleased. "Mario is carpenter," Robert said. "Carpenter of the wood." Mario beckoned to Jim and led him to a side door at the back of his house. He opened it, revealing a full workshop. They disappeared inside, power tools being the international language of men.

I pulled Zadie close and clasped my hands around her belly. We looked out onto the low mountains blooming with wildflowers, rolling beyond the yellow spire of what I recognized as the Mrkopalj Catholic church.

"Are the guwls awake yet?" she asked. Zadie couldn't say her *r*'s yet, a trait I secretly loved.

"Ivana, Karla, Roberta wake soon," said Robert, smiling at Zadie.

Sam showed up, walking across the street to join us. Thor tackled him immediately, licking him first, then humping his knee.

"Thor!" Robert called, tossing him a cookie.

Sam jumped up and squeezed in next to Zadie and me at the picnic table.

"Sammy, did you cross that street by yourself?" I asked.

Sam seemed surprised. "Yes," he said. "It's a small street."

Jim and Mario emerged from the wood shop. "Don't cross the street without us," Jim said sternly.

Everyone looked at the quiet paved road. "It's a really little street," said Sam.

"Oh, hey, Jeem," Robert said, grinning. "Mario last name: Fak. Is like American word that sounds same. But is bad word."

Mario shook his head.

"Fak!" Robert said, for emphasis.

A wiry brunette peeked out over the second-floor stair railing and waved a quick, energetic greeting. She brought down a large tray of coffee fixings.

"This is Jasminka," Robert said. "Wife of Mario."

Jasminka smiled, handing bottles of juice to the kids with a wink. She set down a ceramic cream and sugar set and held up a small metal pot with a long handle.

"Is *džezva*," Robert noted. "For coffee."

Jasminka prepared it Turkish-style. When the Turks ruled the area in the sixteenth century, they left behind words—the ski hill, Čelimbaša (CHELL-eem-basha), was derived from the name of a Turkish pasha—and they left coffee, which was as harsh as the warriors who brought it. A thick muck of grounds heaped at the bottom of the *džezva*.

"I'm trying not to get any of the mud in my cup," Jim said, "but it's impossible."

"*I know*," I whispered, stirring in sugar, which kicked up a mess of grounds.

"Gah!" Jim sipped at the mix of grit and nitroglycerine. "That's got a *kick*."

"If we talk fast, nobody knows what we're saying," I said as Mario, Jasminka, and Robert chatted amiably around us. "It's like we have a secret language."

"Wanna make out?" Jim asked.

"You've got coffee grounds in your teeth," I noted.

Robert's daughters appeared.

"Zadie, Sam, you come play?" Ivana said haltingly. Both kids looked at Jim and me.

"Sure," Jim said.

Sam and Zadie held hands and looked back and forth several

times before crossing the street. I'd never seen them hold hands. Here, they'd have to rely on each other more than they ever had.

"Maybe we're being overzealous about the road," I mused, watching them.

"No one ever died from being too careful," Jim said, working at his coffee.

"No siree," I said.

Cuculić vaporized from nowhere. He rocked back and forth on his heels, hands shoved in the pockets of his khakis. The neighbors mildly acknowledged him because their conversation had grown quite lively.

"They are talking about our politics," Cuculić said, nodding toward Mario, Jasminka, and Robert. "Our prime minister has stepped down. We do not know why this has happened."

My heart jumped. Historically unstable Croatia didn't have a leader?

Cuculić said that the day before we arrived, Ivo Sanader had suddenly resigned. But it appeared that the transition would be smooth and fairly quick. His successor, Jadranka Kosor, would be the first woman prime minister in Croatian history.

Jim leveled a look at me. "Well that's ironic," he said. "Hillary Cleen-tone comes to town and the next thing you know there's a woman prime minister."

"I swear I had nothing to do with it," I said. But still I worried. "Is it bad that there's no prime minister in the meantime?"

"Might be bad," Robert shrugged, raising an eyebrow. "Might be bad because now will be woman."

Robert laughed, baiting me. He threw a cookie to Thor.

"What will you do today?" asked Cuculić. He had the best English in town.

"Well, we thought we'd go to Delnice," I said. "The consulate told us that when we arrived in Croatia, we had to register with the county police department."

Cuculić translated for Robert.

Suddenly, Robert was a frenzy of motion. He stood up and patted himself down for cigarettes. He lit up energetically. He ran his hands through his nest of hair, then locked them behind his head. He spoke urgently to Cuculić and then turned to us.

"You go to police, I must come!" he exclaimed. "I must explain for police you stay with me!"

"What for?" Jim said. "It's no big deal."

"*Neh!*" Robert said passionately. "Is complicated. I *must* come to Delnice."

"We have to get groceries, too," Jim explained. "You don't want to go shopping with us."

But Robert would not be deterred. I looked over at Mario and Jasminka, who seemed like the reasonable half of the first neighbor relationship. They watched Robert with amusement.

"Robert say he come with you to police," Cuculić repeated. "I will come, too."

"We can go to the police station alone," I insisted. "We have *visas*. We're not doing anything wrong. We're doing what we're supposed to do."

But nothing I said seemed to register among the din of negotiating men. It was as if my words didn't materialize in the masculine soundscape. No one looked at me when I spoke. I don't even remember what I said, really. That up there is just a guess.

The men, however, listened to Jim. And Jim didn't want them along.

"I don't want a big production," he said. He was trying to be polite, but an edge had crept into his voice. "Is there some sort of danger involved that we need an escort?"

Cuculić stepped forward, one hand extended. "Robert says you may have problems with the police, and he must explain about staying in his house."

"Why would we have problems?" Jim asked. "We paid a lot of money for visas. There should be no problem."

Cuculić shoved his hand back into his khakis. "And also, Robert must tell police that you are his cousins from America, so he does not pay tourist tax."

Jim and I sat there for a moment in stunned silence. So that's what this was all about. Robert didn't want to pay taxes on our rental price, which would cut into his profit, so he was going to claim us as relatives. An agenda. One that might get us in trouble with the police and that nullified getting the stupid visas in the first place.

I tried to say this, but my words turned to meaningless fog. Cuculić went so far as to put a hand to his ear when I spoke. "I cannot understand what you are saying," he said, squinting. "You must speak more slowly, clearly. Like Jim speaks. I understand Jim."

"Of course you do," I muttered. Having a Y chromosome in Mrkopalj apparently made one deaf to the female voice.

We thanked Mario and Jasminka and followed Robert and Cuculić across the street. Meanwhile, Jim agreed that Robert could come along.

"Are you sure this is a good idea?" I asked under my breath.

"Not at all," Jim said.

Neither of us could come up with a better solution, nor did we have the wherewithal or the language skills to argue further. Though it all seemed a little dodgy, Robert was our only real connection to the village. He was intent on doing this his way. Just as he'd been intent on renting us rooms even though he didn't really have any and so kicked his daughters out of theirs to do so.

I guess when you're new to a strange place, and someone offers to help, you're inclined to let them. At that point, just pouring a cup of coffee was mystifying. Jim and I allowed ourselves to be nannied along, even though our nanny was probably drunk. And in the end, it turned out fine. We registered with the police with little trouble, and even stopped for morning gelato on the way home.

"The rules are different in Croatia," Jim explained as he ordered for our two incredulous children. Eating ice cream before noon was awesome. "It's harder to live here, so let's have some fun to make it easier."

The kids were more pleased with those one-euro cones than they'd ever been with mountains of toys back home. Sam licked his delicately so that it lasted for the better part of an hour. Zadie doused her face in creamy chocolate goo immediately and with gusto. In fact, from that day on, Zadie's face was usually covered in some form of chocolate.

"I like it here," she said.

"Me, too," Jim said.

"It's okay, I guess," Sam said.

I ordered an ice cream for myself, but I wasn't as easy as those guys. I still had a case of the nerves. Letting go and rolling with it takes more effort than you'd think, when you're a mom used to calling the shots.

In the Peugeot, Robert rolled down the window and extended a beefy arm. He slapped the dash with his other hand. "Good car," he said to Jim as we drove away.

And then, randomly, he said: "Bon Jovi is also good."

In a loud and husky voice, Robert sang "Livin' on a Prayer."

I had no idea why we aligned with Robert that day. We'd just met the neighbors: a perfectly nice, sober family with a very large house that surely had a few extra rooms to rent. But we were exhausted and disoriented and more than a little shell-shocked. It was 1846 all over again, and we were headed out for a little California vacation with the Donner Party.

Robert was a mess. But we were just going to have to trust him.

chapter six

When we got back to Mrkopalj, we walked with Ivana, Karla, and Roberta up the mountain in their backyard. It was mostly grassy with a few shrubby trees and jutting boulders. Each of us perched on a stone, overlooking the village. Below, in the meadow, an old woman in a housedress, a calico apron, and a babushka gathered bright yellow flowers.

"This is for tea," explained Ivana. Of the three girls, she had the best English. "They are calling this *gospina trava,* this tea."

In Croatia, the girls said, tea was called *ćaj,* pronounced "chai." Now, there was a word I could remember. Thank you, Starbucks.

I walked down the mountain toward the woman picking *ćaj.* She carried a long stick, moving aside grass for the blossoms she plucked and popped into a bag. She looked up and smiled when I approached and extended a wrinkled hand to show how the yellow buds had stained her fingers purple. I picked a few flowers and dropped them into her sack. I examined my fingers. Yep, the yellow flower produced a purple stain. Wild.

The kids ran down to watch an old man release sheep into the field to munch clover.

Ivana, Karla, and Roberta narrated. Sheep are *ovca.* Mountain is *brdo.* The woman picking tea was Manda. The man with the sheep was Josip. Robert's giant garden was filled with *krompiri,* or potatoes. Most people had a *krompir* patch the size of a supermarket and an additional vegetable garden close to the house.

Jim and I walked to the shops across the street from Robert's place to forage for supper. None of the three groceries was bigger than an American living room. Our favorite was Konzum, a Croatian chain with a butcher shop that sold sausages and mortadella and cheeses. The ladies wore red smocks trimmed in green and little red hats.

We picked up sausage, cheese, and blueberries that grew wild in the mountains. When we checked out, we realized that the gardens of Mrkopalj certainly weren't for show. Groceries were expensive, with the exception of domestic booze, which was cheap. Food cost as much as it did back home, though the village seemed quite poor.

Back at Robert's house, Zadie and Roberta were perched on the backyard picnic table holding hands and talking, each speaking her own language to the other. Sam had borrowed Karla's bike and rode the length of the sidewalk, wobbly and unsure of himself.

Jim and I stowed the groceries in the dorm and returned to the backyard, where Ivana hovered over the kids.

"Should we go for a walk?" I asked her. "Can you show us where things are?"

But Ivana misunderstood me. She headed inside then returned with paper and markers. She drew us a map of Mrkopalj instead.

The two main roads of Mrkopalj joined at a T intersection. Robert's street, Novi Varoš, ran roughly north and south from the T to the ski hill, Čelimbaša. It was Mrkopalj's newest road, thus the name, which meant "New Way." The main road ran west to east. To the west, it was called Muževski Kraj ("Man Street," after the migrant men who once stayed in its boardinghouses during heavy seasonal forestry work). Traveling east, when the road T-boned with Novi Varoš, the name changed to Stari Kraj ("Old Street"), where Stari Baća and the church and the municipal building were located.

Ivana explained the map as the kids roamed the yard and meadow. Every once in a while, they'd cross the field over to the *škola* (pronounced SHKO-la), or school, to climb the apple trees in its small courtyard, or pick wild strawberries.

Sam and Zadie had never moved freely this way. Back home, they weren't often out of our sight. It was, I realized, exhausting for all of us. I was pretty sure that my generation spent more face time with their kids than any other before us. The simple freedom made Sam and Zadie giddy. It left Jim and me standing around, wondering what to do.

Jim and I rarely spent time alone without distraction and without the aid of a television. I actually felt awkward. I suppressed an urge to find something to busy myself. It was like learning to breathe in a different way. Imagine having all the uninterrupted time in the world. On one hand, it feels really liberating. On the other, it eliminates everything you've built around yourself that distracts you from, well, you. We just sat down on the yard swing and rocked in silence, getting used to things.

That evening—the night everyone *thought* we were going to

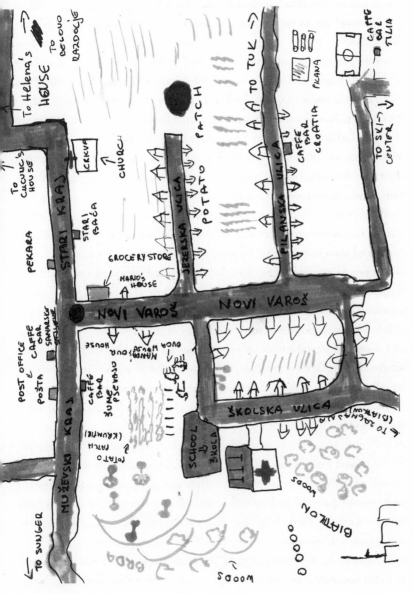

IVANA'S MAP

arrive—Robert's wife, Goranka, made a traditional Mrkopalj picnic dinner as a welcome. Goranka had a gentle face and was built thick and pretty. She commandeered the kitchen on the first floor her family now shared as they, too, waited for Robert to finish our rooms.

Karla and Ivana set the monolithic wooden table in Robert's backyard. Jim and I noticed many of these picnic tables in the village. Giant in size, trestle in design, they still looked a little like the trees they once were, benches just long logs split in half, giant rough-hewn two-by-eights laid side by side for a tabletop. Painted forest green, weathered almost to softness, they blended into grass and trees and meadow and mountain. Simple, magnificent things.

Because winter dominated so much of the year in Mrkopalj, summer was lived almost entirely outdoors. It was the eternal entertainment, reliable even during times of war or poverty or a simple lack of vacation days. The forest and field provided most everything, as it probably had during the time of Valentin and Jelena, and the people of the village simply set up their picnic tables and enjoyed the view. All backyards contained some variation of the basic Mrkopalj combo: giant stone fireplace, fruit trees, gardens, picnic table. Variations came in the details. Viney trellises shading concrete pads. Grape arbors. Chicken coops. Goats. Geraniums in window boxes. The yards of Mrkopalj were like tiny farms, beautiful in their utility, unobtrusive on the earth.

Robert's yard was the least-tended occupied plot on Novi Varoš. It contained a concrete slab, half of which was sloppily stacked with firewood. A clothesline trailed across the yard, irregularly clipped with clothespins drained of color by time and sun. The grass was long and patchy, the *krompir* garden ringed with weeds. A neighbor's plum tree tilted into the yard.

Robert pointed out the tiny concrete outbuilding that had been the family smokehouse when he was a boy and the Starčević family kept a few cattle in their yard.

"Hey, Robert, what are these for?" I asked, standing near Bobi's pen. Next to it was an old wooden door, above which were tacked several small wooden crosses.

"For God to be with animals," he began. The church blessed the farm animals of Mrkopalj every spring. These little talismans were distributed at the conclusion of mass, for people to hang over the barn door. There weren't many families raising animals anymore, but most houses still had those crosses.

Robert pulled the wooden door open to reveal an aboveground dirt-floor cellar.

"Old barn," Robert noted. "In old Mrkopalj, first floor of house: barn."

I'd seen renditions of the house barn in historic villages back home—occupants at one end, animals at the other. It saved work and heat in winter. This was a glimpse into the lives of Valentin and Jelena. Many Mrkopalj houses were built in this manner.

In the backyard, our families gathered around the picnic table. The girls brought out a giant platter of potato halves. Mrkopalj was known for its potatoes, and this recipe was simple: cut them in half, sprinkle with sea salt, and rub the halves together until they foam. When they baked (for forty-five minutes, at 350 degrees), the foam from the rubbing created a smooth, crackly coating. Onto this you could pile the toppings that the girls placed around the table: raw bacon called *spek*, boiled eggs, uncured sausages, squeaky cow's-milk cheese, sliced onions. Fluffy bread torn from the loaf pinched up any extra toppings that fell off when you took a bite.

The potatoes, Robert said, were called *pole*, pronounced POLE-ay. But the whole gathering itself was also called a *pole*.

"Robert, this cheese squeaks when you chew it," said Jim gleefully. "It's squeaky cheese, Jen. Just like in Wisconsin!"

"What is *skeeky cheese*?" Robert asked.

"Cheese that squeaks," I said, mimicking the sound taking place in my mouth.

Everyone around the table lit up.

"Skeeky cheese is Mrkopalj special!" Robert said.

"Skeeky," Roberta said to Zadie, and the girls dissolved into giggles.

My children examined the food and found it benign. Sam grabbed a potato and ate like a monkey working on a banana. Zadie, the dissector, had spent her entire culinary existence picking apart food. In Mrkopalj, there was no need. A boiled egg was a boiled egg, nothing hidden inside. A roasted potato held no mystery. She ate without direction from her parents, who'd issued stern warnings earlier.

"Things will taste different than back home," I'd said, sitting Sam and Zadie down on the hard red futon before dinner. "Try not to think of it as loving or hating anything. It's all just something new to talk about. You're travelers now."

"Also, never say 'yuck' at the table," Jim added.

"What do we say, then?" asked Sam. "Can we say 'gross'?"

"Or poopyhead?" Zadie asked.

I shook my head. "You say thank you and try a bite. That's good manners."

The picnic was eaten communally. Want a potato? Grab one. Curious about the rough sausage? Pop a piece in your mouth. Though forks and knives were present, the food was best eaten by hand, without artifice.

"Everything is domestic," Robert pointed at us with his fork, chewing loosely on a boiled egg. "This is typical *pole.*"

Jim and I brought some wine from the Konzum, and I drank a glass of red, which Robert noted with interest.

"You drink red wine?" Robert cocked an eyebrow.

"Yes," I said.

"Is very interesting," he said with a smirk.

Goranka presented a box of white wine and a bottle of fizzy water. "You mix," Robert said, pouring half wine, half water. "Halp-halp."

"What?" Jim asked.

Robert indicated the wine box. "Halp wine in glass." Then he pointed to the fizzy water. "Halp water. Halp-halp."

Jim loved *gemišt* (gem-EESHT), as the drink was more commonly known. Robert drank like a man filled with a great thirst.

Two young men emerged from the unfinished second-floor rooms covered in construction dust. Robert introduced them as part of his work crew. The electrician also came down, a stocky older guy in gold-rimmed spectacles and blue tradesman's jumpsuit. Robert introduced him as Nikola Tesla, after the Croatia-born ethnic Serb inventor whom you can thank every time you turn on a radio, a light, an electrical appliance, or use a TV remote. Mrkopalj's Nikola Tesla had a little Sean Connery handsome about him. He slid onto the picnic bench, languidly propped his elbow on the table, slapped a hand against the side of his face, and rolled his eyes.

Cuculić appeared from the ether and hovered, pecking at the food, matching Robert and Jim *gemišt* for *gemišt*. He noted that part of Robert's potato garden was actually his, and he tensed as if electrocuted every time the kids accidentally kicked the soccer ball into it.

"*Oprez!*" he'd yell. Careful!

Cousins and friends drifted in and out. The younger ones knew English. Jim and I asked questions about the Gorski Kotar and gathered road-trip recommendations. They asked questions, too. What did Jim do for a living? Why was he not doing it? Jim's position as a stay-at-home dad was the subject of curiosity.

"So, you do not work, but your woman work?" Robert took Jim aside to ask.

"While we're here, yeah," Jim said.

"This is very interesting," Robert mused. "This is a very good situation." Robert took a long swig of halp-halp, lost in thought. As Robert considered his future as a kept man, I could see Goranka's life increasing in difficulty right before my eyes.

We met Robert's niece, a smart blonde named Petra, a law student in Zagreb who'd competed as a biathlete in the 2006 Winter Olympics. She'd been the youngest Olympian in Torino.

"This is something Mrkopalj is known for," Cuculić noted with casual pride, which I believe is the first and last piece of tourism information he ever gave me. "We produce many Olympic athletes. All parents in this village send their children to biathlon training. They do this all year, not only in wintertime."

Everyone ticked off the Mrkopalj Olympians. There was cross-country skier Nada Birko-Kustec in 1952 in Oslo and 1956 in Cortina d'Ampezzo, Italy. Franjo Jakovac competed in biathlon in Sarajevo in 1984. Mario and Jasminka's son, Jakov Fak, would even carry the Croatian national flag in the 2010 Winter Olympics in Vancouver, also competing in biathlon.

It did not surprise me that biathlon, the most confusing sport ever invented, was the Mrkopalj specialty. It involves cross-country skiing a great distance, then lying down to shoot five rounds at a teeny target, then more skiing, more target shooting, and skiing again. Sometimes it snows. Everyone wears a shiny leotard and carries a gun.

"So people in Mrkopalj are athletic?" I asked Petra.

"It is mostly the children who train," Petra said. "Everyone else is losing the vitality of the old ways. They sit too much or watch TV. Not to offend you, but we always hear that Americans are quite fat because of that."

I looked down at my pile of sausage and bacon and potatoes. I wondered how my own figure would fare over the coming months.

Everyone studied us surreptitiously. I blabbered on in English out of nervousness. I hated the me that showed up when I was anxious. I talked and talked, just to fill the quiet. I had not yet learned that once you wade through the language barrier and struggle to the other side of it, silence is a great vantage point. You can learn a lot when you're not gacking up the airwaves with babble. Oh, but there was nothing quiet about me under the darkening sky that night. A sense of isolation was creeping in as the kids and Jim relaxed into the place while I still felt unsettled outside of my well-controlled mommy realm.

Wine flowed. Jim put his arm around me. I looked up at him. When Jim returned my gaze, I prepared for sweet words of comfort. Instead, he said: "I love Mrkopalj. The alcohol is cheap, everybody's really nice, and it looks like I can get away with never wearing a dress shirt."

I blinked.

Jim rubbed my back with one hand. "Good thing I didn't pack a dress shirt!"

Well, it made sense that unfussy Mrkopalj was Jim's latest love. My minimalist husband had packed four shirts, two pairs of jeans, two pairs of shorts, and three pairs of shoes for our entire trip—and he still regretted bringing that third pair of shoes. He'd shaved his head to reduce his grooming needs. He'd already shot a hundred photos, from the spire of the yellow church to the makeshift garden scarecrows made of old clothes and holey straw hats and strung-up wine bottles.

The men at the picnic table pestered Jim to join them at Stari Baća for some serious drinking. I could see that Mrkopalj would quickly become the fraternity Jim had never bothered to join in college. He begged off, opting instead to remain at the table with a slightly higher-maintenance love, also known as his wife.

I could feel the men looking at me, waiting for me to dismiss Jim so he could join them. I would not do it. I needed my husband now. And so we all sat there, staring at each other.

I saw myself through the eyes of this cadre of Mrkopalj men. I bet they wondered if we'd gotten our heritage mixed up. Jim seemed a lot more at home than I did. Next to Jim, I was the uptight, worry-faced lady who drank fancy red wine and talked entirely too much for someone who didn't even know Croatian. I hated being seen as the killjoy, but I suspected that Mrkopalj had an air of male fantasy to it. The women worked. The men drank. I would have to squash that fantasy.

Soon Robert was antsy. He got up from the table and drained his *gemišt.*

"We go now, and look at your rooms on the second floor," Robert said, hitching up his pants and wobbling for balance. "Rooms are finished in one, maybe two weeks."

This was going to be good. We moved toward the house in a pack: Jim and me and Nikola Tesla and Cuculić and the kids. We filed up the steps, through the second-floor door. Proud Robert noted how much progress had been made in just one day.

Robert swung open a second set of French doors off the breezeway. The young workmen had left the picnic table the instant they'd finished eating and were now laying cement board and insulation as the foundation of what would eventually be a floor in the main room. Nikola Tesla and Cuculić eased in carefully, inching along the periphery and stepping only on the heavy beams in between the insulation.

Robert stood directly in front of me in the doorway, extending his arm to reveal the place in a grandiose manner, though it appeared largely unchanged from the night before.

"My American friends!" he said with a flourish. "Your rooms!"

In my peripheral vision, I saw Robert take a step forward. By the time I turned to listen to his speech, he was gone.

I looked all around. Robert Starčević had disappeared.

Then I heard a muffled snorting sound. I looked over to see the young workers trying to keep straight faces. Cuculić and Nikola Tesla broke out in backslapping laughter, clutching their sides, pointing down.

Robert had fallen through the floor.

A mess of brown curls poked out from the sea of insulation. Robert did not move. He'd broken his fall by catching himself with his elbows, and now he hovered above the first floor with his bare arms half-cocked like chicken wings between wooden trusses. He stared straight ahead, stunned.

Then he slowly looked up at Jim, who was holding the camera, unsure if he should snap a photo.

"Just one picture," Robert mumbled miserably. Then he lowered his head to once again stare straight ahead, stone-faced.

The click of a single photograph hung in the air, just like Robert. The entire room burst into laughter.

I started liking him then.

Eventually, Robert swung his lower half back and forth, gaining momentum to pull up. He hefted his body onto a beam. He'd lost a shoe in the fall, and his bare foot dangled into the kitchen below.

When Robert was up and safe, I laughed harder and longer than I had in a long time. Nikola Tesla slapped his knees and wiped his eyes beneath his gold-rimmed glasses. Cuculić sniggered, hands stuffed under his armpits. Jim's laugh exploded like machine-gun fire. The kids ran downstairs to pull off Robert's other shoe. Ivana and Karla began dustpanning the latest of their father's messes.

Robert brushed himself off, shaking loose cement board and insulation, a few pieces of which would stay in his hair for the next several days. He looked up at Jim and me. "Your rooms finished in three, maybe four weeks."

Over the course of the next few days, both Cuculić and Nikola Tesla would also fall through the floor. The job of the workmen would change from installing flooring to patching the ceiling downstairs. Goranka grew tired of the rain of men into her kitchen.

With Robert at our side, everything took on an air of the absurd that afforded me entry into our life in Mrkopalj. I still felt unsteady. Still wondering how we would fill the days and find the old relatives. But I was learning. And I wasn't fleeing.

In his own inadvertent way, Robert was a worthy guide.

chapter **seven**

During those first few days of July, I felt like we'd been dropped, blinking and disoriented, onto a random point on the space-time continuum. I walked Mrkopalj's streets and country roads, peering into crumbling houses and deep-set eyes. I jostled past the herd of goats that twice daily crossed Stari Kraj, driven by a solitary man whose front yard was dominated by a colossal chain-saw sculpture of an attacking bear, and who mercilessly blared from his windows a farflung catalog of music ranging from American cock rock to traditional *tamburitza*. At night, I dropped exhausted onto the stiff futon bed but slept little for its discomfort, our big window thrown open to mountain air that nearly vibrated with energy.

Because we hadn't mastered the grocery store yet, Jim made tasty sausage-and-cheese meals like daily picnics. He never faltered in his immediate and wholehearted embrace of Mrkopalj. As soon as the sun was up, Jim would head outside to study his Croatian language workbook on the front-yard bench. By the second day, a guy named Zoran added Jim to the coffee carpool. Zoran would pull up on Novi Varoš in his battered Renault and honk twice, and Mario and Jim and Robert would pile into the car to be ferried away for morning coffee. They did not choose Robert's café-bar for this outing, or the café-bar at the crossroads of Mrkopalj, which people told us was Serbian, and whose shutters were held back with an iron knob in the image of Leon Trotsky. Instead, they drove to Mrkopalj's oldest café-bar, serving the village for more than a hundred years, Šume Pjevaju, on the outskirts of town on Muževski Kraj. There, they would meet Cuculić and Nikola Tesla and Tomo, Robert's good friend and Cuculić's grim-faced cousin, who had a thick thumb of wrinkle between his eyebrows.

While Jim was busy hanging out with his frat brothers, the kids were absorbed in the playful world of Robert's daughters. Sam scooped endless loops of sidewalk with Karla's bike, breaking only to browbeat her into a round of Money Play, Croatia's version of Monopoly. To Zadie, the Starčević girls were the sisters she would never have. Ivana propped my daughter on her handlebars and drove her around the village like E.T., showing her off to the school friends who roamed the village in a giggly pack.

"It's like I live with playdates," Zadie murmured one night as she went to bed.

The Starčević girls spoiled Zadie to the point that she informed us she would like to live with them, rather than with us. One day I caught her over at the Konzum, having an ice cream without asking permission. It made me mad because dinner was on, and she seemed almost completely interwoven into their family and practically gone from ours. I crossed the street, stalked over to Zadie, and took the ice cream.

The girls stood wide-eyed, horrified. "Why you do that?" Ivana stepped forward tentatively as Zadie cried.

"Because Zadie has to ask her parents if she can have treats," I said. "Zadie, it's easy just to come upstairs and ask."

"But you *always* say no," Zadie sobbed, turning to Ivana for a hug. All three girls stared at me accusingly, standing up for the kid they'd co-opted as their own.

I was probably crabbier than I needed to be. Though I'd made the Herculean effort to get us to Mrkopalj it took *me* the longest to acclimate. The Eastern European lifestyle was a bit of an adjustment for this busy American mama.

I had no understanding of the way time worked here, for starters. People buzzed away to their jobs in little Citroëns in the morning, or they hung around town to move their cattle or weed the garden. I felt too self-conscious to assert myself into any of the situations unfolding around me. How does one walk up to a complete stranger who speaks a different language, and who is herding sheep, and ask to help? One does not.

I began to long for the person who had comforted me most in my life, Grandma Kate. To hear her laugh so hard she spit out her partials, or have her repeat her single bit of sage advice: "You might be poor, but you have no excuse to stink." To hear the jangle of the Virgin Mary medals on her giant bra, or that one bedtime story about the kid whose mother sent him to the store to buy liver but who instead cut it out of the side of a homeless man. My aunt Terri suggested that perhaps this story might be too scary for children.

"It should be scary, Terri," Grandma snapped back. "How else she gon' learn not to be lazy?"

On the afternoon of July 4, Independence Day back in America, Jim and I sat with Robert on his front-yard bench. Robert nursed an Ožujsko and gestured to Novi Varoš.

"I love this . . . everything!" he said, tipping back his head, hands open to the sky. "It's a good situation. This is the Mrkopalj! This is great city!"

Of course Robert loved his village. Here, he could shirk even the most minor responsibilities and someone always had his back. Mario, a nondrinker, walked and fed Bobi regularly because Robert would forget when he was boozing it up. Which was usually.

Robert held up his beer to toast. Jim raised his own Ožujsko. I halfheartedly raised my blueberry juice purchased from the Konzum, where the red-smocked checkers gave me the stink-eye if I paid with anything larger than a 50-kuna bill, roughly $10.

The young workmen turned into the driveway, back from their lunch break in a van decorated with ski stickers. Tomo followed close behind in his own van, an ancient taupe capsule with brown racing stripes. Robert lurched off the bench. He staggered to regain his balance, tugged down his cutoff shorts, and pushed up the sleeves of his denim work shirt.

"Hello! I must work for one week!" Having drunk enough to mess up both his English and his sense of time, Robert saluted Jim and me, turned unsteadily on his wafflestomper boots, and stumbled for the steps to the second-floor construction zone.

Jim looked at me.

"How could you not love this place?" he asked.

"I don't hate it," I said.

"But?" Jim asked, swigging beer.

"All the dudes love you. *You* fit in. I, on the other hand, do not," I said.

He laughed. "You haven't tried to fit in! You're hanging back. You're trying to figure everything out before you actually enjoy this. I don't think the point is to figure anything out. I think your time is better spent getting to know people."

"It's easier to get to know people when they like you," I said. "They recognize a kindred spirit in you."

"What do you mean, 'kindred spirit'? The guys around here either work all the time or they're hammered all the time. I'm neither of those."

"Do you remember before we were married, and I asked you what you would do for a living if you had no social pressures to worry about?"

Jim smiled. "Be a barfly!"

"Exactly. The barfly fantasy is still alive; it's just been dormant," I said. "These guys see it. They're sucking you into their barfly world."

"Jen, that was a joke. And how do you even remember that?" Jim said. He was quiet for a moment, considering me. "We bought a year off from the desk job and the home repairs and the cable bills to live another life. I'm not going to spend the summer standing outside looking in, like Mrkopalj is some weird experiment we'll watch but not dirty our hands with. I have fun. I don't judge."

I set down my glass. "Just be careful. Be a good example for your family."

"What the fuck is that supposed to mean?" he boomed. "I quit my job so I could spend a year doing nothing but be with my family! There's no better example to set! You're just mad because nobody's picking *you* up for coffee in the morning."

He had me there.

"You're right. I know you're right," I said, swallowing hard.

"This is our dream trip, Jen," Jim said, shaking his head. "*C'mon.*"

"It's just not how I pictured it would be," I said quietly. "I don't know what to do with myself. I thought Helena and I would hang out, but she just had her baby, and you know how overwhelming it is when you have your second kid. I just feel like I'm falling into this black hole of nothingness. No one needs me. It's lonely."

"You've got plenty to do, Jen," Jim said. "Get out there and ask questions about your family. That whole process is just another way of meeting people, right?"

I took a big breath. "I'm not sure how to talk to people," I said. "If I speak English, I'm pretty much demanding they do things my way. But what's worse? Speaking asshole English or offending them with my awful Croatian?"

"You're overthinking it," Jim said. "Just march into a situation and be part of it. Stand there and smile. Learn more Croatian words. Like verbs. Maybe a few phrases so that you can say something funny."

I took a sip of juice.

"Okay. It might be hard for you to say something funny," Jim said. "You're not a very funny person."

"People liked me better back home," I said. "Partly because I'm funnier in English."

Jim raised an eyebrow. "You keep thinking that."

"You know," I said, "I study that damned grammar book. But nothing in my language history prepared me for Croatian. It sounds like something Steve Martin would make up for a comedy routine."

"That's an excuse," Jim chuckled. "You're closet shy, aren't you? Never would have guessed that."

"And you're a closet extrovert," I said, pointing at him.

He stood up and offered me a hand. "Let's go upstairs and say hi to the workers," he said. "Betcha they're not any more finished than they were yesterday."

"Or the day before that," I said. I wound my fingers around his, nestling my palm against the warm, calloused dryness I'd loved for twelve years.

We walked up the cement steps on the side of the house. Inside, the second floor exhibited its usual state of chaos. Someone had brought in an old kitchen table and it was littered with Ožujsko and Karlovačko bottles—the Coors vs. Budweiser rivalry of the Gorski Kotar. Most were half-filled with cigarette butts. There was a box of white wine and green bottles of sparkling water for *gemišt*. A little halp-halp to get everyone through the day.

Robert was splayed on the floor. Tomo was setting a countertop and Robert was underneath, helping to level the cabinets. Tomo looked up when we came in and wiggled his eyebrows as if to say *Watch this*, then gave an order to Robert. Robert wormed his body to the left and raised one side of the cabinet slightly. Tomo gave another order and Robert scootched back over to the right and raised the other side. Tomo issued another order, and Robert heaved himself over to dial down the first side. Tomo barked; Robert moved to lower the opposite side. The cabinetry tilted up and down like a funhouse prop until Robert groaned loudly with the effort. Tomo crossed his arms over his polyester sweater and his shoulders shook with silent laughter. Robert pulled his head out to see what was taking so long, and Tomo inadvertently ashed his smoked-to-the-nub cigarette into Robert's hair.

Robert turned away from Tomo and craned his neck toward Jim and me. "My friend, he say he is helping me, but he is not very much helping."

Tomo tried to look innocent.

Jim turned to me. "I seriously can't believe you don't love it here."

I gave my own Robert-like shrug and went upstairs alone to our dorm. I stood in the window, looking out over Novi Varoš. Ivana had lined the kids up for footraces on the sidewalk. Next door, the old man named Viktor, husband of Manda, whom I'd seen harvesting tea on our first day in the village, slingbladed his yard, stopping occasionally to sharpen the tool with a whetstone stored in a ram's horn that was tied around his waist with a piece of leather string. The old people of Mrkopalj worked. Gnarled hands tatted lace on back stoops. An old widow rocked on the porch of the bakery, a single smudge of flour on her black dress.

I heard Jim downstairs, laughing with the older guys, probably drinking a halp-halp. They'd been bragging when I left that they could start drinking at 6:00 A.M. and still remain sober enough to work. All the while, the workmen, sober themselves, were the only ones actually doing something, gently herding the old boys away so they could finish the floors before anyone could find a hole to fall through.

Jim was right. I was *not* the kind of person who just sat around and felt bad. It made me feel unattractive. I made a mental list of things that would lend some mom-like structure to this family sabbatical business.

First, I needed an exercise routine. The endorphins would keep me from going all Sylvia Plath. Plus, we'd had some incarnation of bacon at pretty much every meal in Mrkopalj. I couldn't afford to buy new pants. A little reconnaissance was in order.

Second, I would quit with the random crazy-lady wandering. There would be form and shape to this exploration, starting with afternoon drives a few days a week to get the lay of the land.

Third, I would make a friend or two.

When Jim came back upstairs to start dinner, I told him about the list and he gave me a big, fat hug.

From that day forward, my life in Mrkopalj changed.

chapter eight

In the morning, I took my first jog to the neighboring village of Tuk. I'd driven the smooth blacktop road in the Peugeot, snaking through a flat green cleave between mountains. The odometer read 2.8 kilometers. There and back, just shy of two miles.

Still, I could not make it all the way without stopping. Charla the GPS had told me that Mrkopalj was 880 meters above sea level, about 2,887 feet, roughly comparable to an Adirondack village. The slightly thinner air didn't seem to power my lungs properly, but that probably had more to do with my lungs than the altitude.

I jogged to the sound of the hiss of distance, flanked by the wide-open fields from which Mrkopalj took its name. Long ago, in my great-grandparents' time, every family dreamed of having a plot in this fertile stretch between Mrkopalj and Tuk that they called the *polje* (POLE-yay). Land was everything. Land meant possibility. Houses were crammed into the far corners of properties, to allow maximum space for grazing sheep or extra gardens or another house for a son's family. I learned these things in my fledgling efforts to engage, forcing Robert to translate for me over late-morning coffee in Stari Baća.

I huffed past fields now abandoned to weed and wildflower, a few still planted with *krompiri*. Wooden watchtowers loomed at the edges, lookouts for hunters of brown bear or wild boar or deer. A Renault Twingo whizzed past on the narrow road, so close I could feel the driver's-side mirror shearing the air at my elbow. I braced for death, and the imagined brush with mortality made the exertion even more intoxicating. At the end, I walked home dripping wet down Novi Varoš, feeling watched, seeing no one, exhilarated nonetheless.

At the same time, we commenced afternoon drives in the Gorski Kotar, through tunnels blasted into white rock, under cathedrals of spruce trees so old their needled branches seemed to melt to the earth. The mountains tumbled low and rounded, their thick wig of forest studded with shocking white calcareous rocks. The slopes worked their way up in height to the narrow ridge of Bjelolasica, the highest peak of the Gorski Kotar's Kapela mountain chain at 1,534 meters, or a little over 5,000 feet.

The names of the villages sounded so funny on our tongues: Belo Selo; Zahrt; Čučak; Skrad. We passed river towns plumed with ferns, campgrounds strangely empty but for rows of overturned canoes. We drove mountain roads so cockeyed they felt like amusement park rides, not a guardrail in sight, giving ourselves over to a perpetual state of danger and carsickness. The kids and I got into the habit of tucking extra grocery bags into the pockets of the car doors. "To barf in," explained Sam, when Robert's girls saw us ferreting away plastic sacks. Eventually we figured out that burping eased queasiness, and the Peugeot became a fantastic acoustic stage for great croaks of relief.

We didn't see many people; there hadn't been many to begin with. The five thousand square miles of Gorski Kotar land had barely been populated until the Turks came sniffing around, spurring the Habsburgs that ruled Croatia into protecting their resources by forcing people to actually live here. They had to import settlers: Orthodox refugees from the Ottoman Empire seeking religious freedom, plus large clans of legendary troublemaking coastal pirates called Uskoks. My ancestral land: settled by exiles and criminals. Secretly, I hoped I was a rowdy Uskok from way back.

Because Cuculić remained useless in a tourism capacity, we learned all of this as we would have had we never left home—from Wikipedia. But, like the mosquitoes in Minnesota, the lack of user-friendliness kept the rabble out. We felt like the first visitors to this place. We weren't sure if this was because of the intimidating density of the forest backcountry or the perpetual morning slivovitz buzz of any potential outdoorsmen. Whatever the reason, the upside was a very soft footprint: Nobody had ruined the nature yet. It was the thickest wilderness we'd ever seen.

Plus, the weather was great. Even on warm days, the air exuded a hint of glacial coolness that smelled of bark and rock and moss. The Gorski Kotar seemed both vast and hidden—a curiously tucked-away pocket of backwoods. I've felt this way while paddling through Iowa stretches of the Upper Mississippi River, similarly untouched by people, a lone patch of the original state of things. Traveling in such a place, earning entry to it, is the reward itself for the isolation that goes along with getting there. If you could deal with the narrow roads with the sheer drop-offs, if you could dodge the bears and the wolves and the pine martens, if you averted the GPS mix-up to find the appropriate forest hobbit to whisper the correct password to the wood-sap nymph and snatch the key from the lumberjack troll, you could enter this insanely untamed territory.

We didn't venture far on those first drives, staying within the ten-mile radius. We drove north to the village of Lokve, where we threw rocks into a mirror lake at the foot of a huge mountain and considered walking the lakeside trail. We chickened out when we realized we were the only souls in sight, save for a creepy wooden sculpture of a woman watching over us. So we looped our way south to Fužine, perfectly placed along its own mirror lake, reflecting a pleasing arrangement of quaint houses and a church spire, a scene worthy of its own Franklin Mint plate. Buses discharged hordes of elderly tourists into the streets. We judged them to be German, based on sheer size and paleness of skin.

"What's going on in Fužine?" Jim wondered aloud.

"This must be where all the people live," said Sam. "I think these are the first people I've seen today."

We headed up the street, passing an overcrowded pizza shop before settling on a fancy-looking hotel restaurant. The posted menu declared bear paw as its specialty.

"Don't waste the thirty-five dollars here," Jim said as we sat down. "Edo told me he knows the butcher in Fužine, and he can get us fresh bear much cheaper."

I stared at Jim, incredulous. My husband already knew a guy who knew a guy.

"Who is Edo?" I asked.

"Oh, just a friend," Jim said, looking over the menu. "No big deal."

Jim and I ordered hunter's stew and bacon with a side of sausage and sauerkraut over boiled potatoes. It was an oily mess of goodness that we ate until our faces were slick. We'd switched to Karlovačko because we liked the Croatian checkerboard on the label, and now we ordered two as chasers. The kids picked at their fries, looking disgusted with us.

"They'll eat anything," Sam said to Zadie.

Driving did us all good. It made us feel that we belonged, and gave context to our existence in the Gorski Kotar.

On the first Sunday in July, the Starčević girls mentioned that it was the day of the annual church festival in Sunger, and so we drove a kilometer west to see it. The afternoon rain threatened to electrocute the sound guys amping the string band in matching black suits with peach shirts. All of them looked like Anthony Hopkins. We settled under the awning of a café-bar built right in the church parking lot. The speakers crackled through "Love Me Tender" as the kids browsed the handful of nearby toy vendors. It was kind of a bust, though, as most of the toys were just fake guns. Sam asked for a semi-automatic sniper rifle. Zadie was partial to a fake pistol with a removable chamber called the Warmonger.

"No," Jim and I both stated flatly, in unison.

"I wouldn't mind a plate of those sausages," Jim said, looking out over the rows of picnic tables where churchgoers feasted and smoked and drank and stared at us.

"Same here," I said.

"Well, how do we do it?" Jim wondered aloud. This appeared to be a church picnic. People were even bringing some form of roast beast from a cookfire next door. Was it free? If not, whom did we pay? Small mysteries such as these baffled us most. Our cell phones still languished at the bottom of empty suitcases, because figuring out how to purchase minutes would be a daylong affair.

Jim tipped his beer toward me. "It's your turn to get in there and figure something out."

I looked over at the man frying sausages in the Sunger church parking lot. Stout yet compact, inexplicably tan, he cut the figure of a high school softball coach. Not to be braggy, but I was first-team all-conference my senior year, and The Coach is a breed of man I am familiar with: body of a teddy bear, face like Dick Van Patten. I stood up and straightened my sporty skirt. A captive audience in the steady downpour appeared to collectively wonder what I was going to do next. I took a deep breath, steeled my soul, and made a mad dash across the parking lot, my head down, running as fast as if I'd bunted a dribbler down the first-base line. I slid under the canvas tent top where the Sausage Man of Sunger was lighting a tabletop grill with a rolled-up paper plate set on fire. I felt the eyes of the entire gathering upon me, the interloper at a party that had hosted the same guests for a hundred years. I beat back self-consciousness and pretended I was the kind of person who casually orders meat from a softball coach.

The skinless sausages appeared to be of the Jimmy Dean variety.

The Sausage Man of Sunger basted them in their own grease with a silver spoon before rolling them onto paper plates dabbed with a thick red sauce from a jar labeled *"ajvar."* Next, he piled on sliced white onions and bread and doused each plate with a final blast of oil before handing it to a server. There was more fat involved than at a Wisconsin fish fry.

I stepped forward. The Sausage Man of Sunger looked up from his work and scrutinized me with the full-on Croatian stare. A hush descended on the crowd.

"Slika?" I asked him, holding up my camera.

"Da." He nodded once, his mouth still but his eyes smiling.

I snapped a picture of his shiny hands, fingers thick like sausages themselves.

I held up two fingers. *"Dva, molim?"* I asked. Two, please?

He looked up at me with a radiant smile, his face slick with grease. *"Dobro hrvatski!"* he said loudly. Good Croatian! He pointed to the sausages and named them: *"Ćevapćići!"*

He rolled a few onto a plate for me, pronouncing the word again, something like cheh-VOP-chee-chee, and made another plate for Jim. *"Da!"*

I was so pleased that I actually clapped. I successfully paid for the sausages—another victory!—and returned to the table amid a steady stream of approving words from the Sausage Man of Sunger, who, when I turned to glance back at him, was watching my backside intently as I walked.

The four of us wolfed down the spicy little sausage rolls. There was something familiar about this food, and it made us all happy.

People stared at us. We stared back. Something struck me during all this staring. There wasn't anything menacing about it. We were just getting used to each other. If I was going to meet my goal of becoming a Slavic people person, I would have to submit to the Croatian Stare. It was easier to do with Jim and the kids nearby. Most things were.

With my belly full of sausage in a church parking lot bar, being serenaded by Anthony Hopkinses dressed in formal wear while my kids shopped a toy artillery arsenal, I felt pretty good. I'd accumulated a few tools in my emotional toolbox over the years. It was time to start using them.

chapter **nine**

Closet shy. Huh. Jim had called it.

It's not that I was a loner. It's just that, over time, I'd come to prefer my own quiet company. I used to think this was because I had kids who peppered me with questions all day long and so I craved peace more than anything else. But I guess it was also tied to an emotional laziness I'd developed in my thirties. I'd never been a party girl. Then, somewhere along the line, it got easier to curl up with a book than to go out and be social. Books had beginnings and endings and clear-cut characters I could understand. In real life, my friends morphed into spouses or parents or committed singletons, and suddenly everyone seemed more sensitive and distant than when we were all in college and had the same life, spending full days discussing the intricacies of pizza delivery and the portions of alcohol consumed the night before. As an adult, I went out less and less. Most of my socializing was in the vicinity of my house, talking plants and street gossip with neighbors, or e-mailing with editors I'd never seen in person.

So my friend-making skills were a little rusty. How does one make actual 3-D friends as a grown-up without seeming creepy?

This was on my mind as we began our second week in the village. We'd grabbed our European atlas from the Peugeot on a Monday afternoon, hungry for something to do. We settled on a drive straight north through a splaying mountain valley toward the Slovenian border.

As we drove, a river skimmed alongside the road. It was the sparkly trout-fishing kind, burbling over smooth boulders and pretty as a movie. This was the Kupa, according to the map, and it formed the natural border between northwest Croatia and Slovenia. We'd heard that its source bubbled up from somewhere deep in the woods near Mrkopalj, and we hoped someday to find it.

I unfolded our Gorski Kotar map and scanned the area. I spotted a tiny hamlet to the east called Radoševići and typed it into Charla the GPS. She sent Jim pinwheeling off the main road. The kids groaned from the backseat as we navigated squiggly mountain passes. The nice thing about having our own car was that we could linger in the pretty places, and get the hell out of Dodge when it proved too dodgy, such as the gray smear of a railroad town called Brod Moravice. Later, someone explained that the place was largely Serbian, and it hadn't fared too well after the Yugoslavian Wars. The vibe was pure eeriness, complete with a village idiot rocking back and forth in the town square, his deep-set eyes tracking our slow drive through his haunted realm.

As we continued toward Radoševići, we passed an odd sight: a giant grill set up just a few feet from the road and, next to it, a wheelbarrow of split wood.

"Do you think that's some version of a restaurant?" I asked.

A grill master recognizing his own kind, Jim whipped the car around. "That's gonna be tasty."

We parked the Peug in the gravel lot, where an exhausted-looking blonde smoked in the doorway of a low building. She snuffed out her cigarette and disappeared as we flopped down in plastic chairs under an awning. The waitress reappeared. We pointed to another table, where two men sat, sharing a giant platter of meat.

"And *pommes frites*," I added, for the kids.

Within a few minutes, a burly guy in a jumpsuit walked out of the next-door garage, hauling a dead pig trussed to a metal pipe with its stomach knit shut by a giant nail. When the man passed by the kids, he nodded.

They froze in shock as he walked to the road and staked the pig to the spit.

Minutes later, a platter of unadorned roast pork arrived at our table. Fries on the side, plus a pile of bread slices.

Sam and Zadie turned to me.

I knew I must choose my words carefully now to avoid some hefty therapy bills in their futures. "Remember how I used to tell you guys that meat comes from real animals and not from Styrofoam containers?" I began.

Zadie, who knew where I was going with this, nodded her head. "We're going to eat that pig," she said, poking at the food. "I never eat pig alone. It looks just like meat."

"Meat is just flesh from an animal," said Jim, half a knuckle already in his mouth. "This is pig flesh."

Sam sat down, pale. "No thanks."

"No French fries until you eat some pig," I said. "Actually, it's called pork, and you guys both liked it back home when you didn't know what it was."

Jim slapped a chunk of pork on Sam's plate for emphasis.

Sam took a nibble. The look on his face changed from repulsion to revelation.

"Like this, Zadie!" he chomped. "It's good!"

Zadie hadn't eaten French fries for a long time, so she was willing to gamble.

"I like it, but I feel bad we're eating a pig," she said.

Sam quickly lost his enthusiasm. He'd been seated with an unobstructed view of the roasting spit, which was explicitly illustrating the full circle of this dining experience. I couldn't really blame him. Once, at the Iowa State Fair with the neighbors, we ate next to the lamb barn at a restaurant serving lamb burgers. I couldn't finish mine.

"I don't want to eat meat anymore, if it's just an animal without its fur," said Sam.

Jim and I ate as the kids returned to the spit to watch the pig go around for a few turns. Its eyes had opened in the cooking process. We heard Sam and Zadie mumbling something.

"What are you two doing over there?" I called.

"Counting the pig's teeth," answered Zadie. She came back over and grabbed another piece of pork, examined it, then popped it into her mouth. Jim high-fived her.

"I still feel bad for the pig," she told him.

"Well, since we're eating him anyway, let's not feel sorry. Let's feel thankful," I suggested. "Let's toast the pig."

"Or roast it!" Jim said, chewing.

We raised our beers, and the kids raised their Sprite bottles. "To the pig," I said. "Thank you for lunch."

"The pig," both kids said reverently, a new kind of mealtime prayer.

We returned from the afternoon drive in high spirits, singing along to a Kenny Rogers CD as we pulled the Peugeot onto our patch of grass across the street from 12 Novi Varoš. Robert's girls were hanging around on the cement steps, looking bored.

They rose when we walked up.

"My mother, she say we are having a family meal tonight at Stari Baća," Ivana said. Karla and Roberta nodded solemnly.

At Stari Baća, a checkered cloth covered the long harvest table, in the middle of which sat several pizzas. Goranka hung back in the kitchen, where she'd handmade the whole lot, enough so that each of us could have our own pie. The girls explained that Helena's family once ran a pizza joint out of their house and Goranka had worked there.

"My mother is known for making the best pizza," said Ivana.

Goranka had drizzled a homemade sauce onto thin crust. The chopped-up smoked ham was local. I don't know about the mushrooms, but the Mrkopalj woods held a variety of them, and whatever these were had been diced into tiny bits and topped with cheese. Each pizza had four individual olives dropped on top—the really good green kind with a stone in the middle. The pizza was so spare, and yet so decadent, I felt I needed privacy to eat it.

Sam delicately picked a piece of ham from his pizza and held it up.

"This is pig flesh," Sam said to Roberta, who knew no English except for the English-Croatian blend that we jokingly called Croglish.

Roberta looked over at Zadie and wound a finger around at her temple. "*Ludi* Sam," she said. Crazy Sam.

Zadie plucked the ham from her brother's fingers. "I like pig flesh."

"Attagirl," said Jim.

I looked over at Goranka, who was watching quietly from the doorway. I gave her the thumbs-up. She smiled and nodded once, then receded into the kitchen.

After we ate, the kids played hide-and-seek and Jim and I walked home alone, poured glasses of wine, and headed toward the mountain to watch the sun set.

As we walked, I saw a garden like a furry green blanket laid out on the mountainside, and the hump of a woman's back as she weeded. She'd planted it this way, I guessed, to shed excess water when it rained. I thought of my garden back home, so sopping wet in spring that the earth made sucking sounds. What I needed for my garden, I told Jim, was a mountainside.

"Or you could just go help out with hers," he said, nudging me. "Go on, Jen."

As Jim headed back to the house, I felt the old reticence well up, but I beat it back. There was only so long I could explore the land of my ancestors while avoiding the actual ancestors. I thought of Goranka, who couldn't speak a word of English and so made pizzas as her version of small talk. I picked my way through the flowers and tall grasses and rock—a precarious task when you're carrying a drink.

I reached the woman as she set upon a long row of onions, their green tufts so ridiculously tall and upright that they appeared bionic.

"I have a garden at home," I said in English, hoping for the best.

She straightened and put a hand to her back, jutting out her enormous bosom and squinting to examine me, her sun-browned face thrown back. She wore a hard hat, mud boots, and track pants.

She peeled off one of the plastic surgical gloves she wore and threw it at me, brusque but smiling, speaking rapid-fire Croatian as she did so. I set down my wine and stepped into the light brown clay.

I weeded.

As I worked, she pointed to each of her plants. *Mrkva, luk, kupus, paprika, grašak, grah*—carrots, onions, cabbages, peppers, peas, beans. We didn't talk after that, just weeded. She applauded when I showed her my clean little section of *luk*. Then she slapped me on the back. Hard.

"*Dobro!*" she hollered. Good!

I stuck out my chest in an exaggerated show of pride—I was making a friend!—and we laughed.

The woman gestured toward the waning sun, looked at an imaginary watch, grabbed her hoe and planting dowel, and shooed me out of her garden.

I stuck out my hand. "*Moje ime je* Jennifer," I said.

"Pavice! Pavice Paškvan!" she bellowed, pronouncing it PAH-veets-uh POSH-kvan, indicating herself with a thumb to her chest. Then she pointed to me. "Yenny!"

I shrugged. Sure. I could be Yenny.

We walked down the mountain, and she showed me a hidden patch of wild strawberries on the way. We popped a few in our mouths.

Pavice held up a single berry. "*Jagoda!*" she yelled.

"*Jagoda,*" I repeated.

"*Da!*" she replied. "*Dobro,* Yenny!"

We moved on to a cherry tree in the schoolyard that was stripped bare up to the height of children, but there were plenty of cherries within our reach, so we ate those, too.

"*Trešnja!*" Pavice held up a cherry.

"You bet!" I popped it in my mouth and shot out the pit with a great "Pitooey!"

Pavice smacked my back. I tried not to fly forward with the impact of the blow.

We walked north across the field toward her house, which was just two over from Robert's. Manda and Viktor's place separated us. I stopped to point out the yellow field flowers that I'd seen Manda picking.

"This is *ćaj*, right?" I asked.

"*Da!*" Pavice said. Each successful communication between us was met with her triumphant volume and a great beating of my back. I liked it. I'd had enough of my own mincing worries. Goddammit, we were happy to meet each other! And now there was tea to discuss! Pavice bulldozed right into the tall grass, pulling off yellow *gospina trava* flowers, tossing them at me and calling "*Čaj!*" as they plunked against my shirt.

"Thanks, Pavice," I said. I knew she didn't speak English, but I plowed ahead anyway. "You know, I always have a hell of a period. I wonder if any teas might help."

I traced a finger around my belly, and made a pained face.

"*Da! Da! Čaj!*" She rubbed her hand all around her own generous belly.

We passed a giant mound of manure. "For your garden?" I asked.

"*Aha! Dobro!*" Pavice yelled, plugging her nose. "*Drek!*"

"Oh, my grandma Kate used to say *∂rek*," I said, tearing up a little. "It makes me feel like she's looking down on us right now!"

Pavice kicked manure with her boots. "Yah, *∂rek*," she said, and walked on.

Penned up behind her house were several sheep that I had seen her husband, Josip, and their son—also named Josip—herding through the meadow twice a day. Near them, chickens pecked busily on a slab. At the center of the backyard, a typical stone oven dominated. I ran my hand along the cool rock and flicked my finger over the charred remains of wood. Pavice pointed to the oven, then to me. I wasn't sure what she was saying, but I'm fairly certain it was something like: "If you want to use it, come on over anytime. Just weed my onions first."

"*Drago mi je*," I said to Pavice. Good to meet you. It was getting late, and I could hear that the kids had come home a few doors down.

"*Dobro hrvatski!*" Pavice cried, slugging my arm. "*Dobro,* Yenny!"

I was so jubilant that I had made my very first friend that I nearly skipped home.

Weeding with Pavice had been so successful that I thought I'd reach out again to the neighbor women. I set to work the second weekend of July making the one dish that I could successfully and consistently execute: peach cobbler. We drove to Delnice, where we'd seen a fruit and vegetable market. The friendly Albanian behind the counter, named Aziz, nodded when I busted out yet another Croatian word—*breskva* for peach—and pointed at a giant basket of them. He hand-picked the juiciest ones and threw them into my bag with a wink, and when we got home I baked four of those suckers in pans borrowed from Goranka's kitchen downstairs.

Jim made a pot of chili to share, but it didn't really work out. He walked around Novi Varoš with a giant stainless-steel vat from Stari Baća. Though it was his gold standard recipe, he found no takers. He'd see a neighbor, hold up the pot, and say: "American chili!" But people just reeled away, horrified, clutching their stomachs and fanning their mouths, crying "*Vruće!*" Mrkopalj did not like spicy food.

I delivered the cobblers to all the women who lived near our house, starting with Pavice, sliding them shyly onto porch steps and then scuttling away. The next morning, we climbed in the Peugeot and celebrated our efforts with our first trip to the sea. We'd been anxious to see the Adriatic, which was about an hour away. Robert told us that Mrkopalj families traditionally visited the resort village of Crikvenica, on the north end of Croatia's coast.

The kids were pumped. Beach time was one of the major perks we'd promised on our trip. As we drove the harrowing coastline, both kids retched into plastic bags from carsickness, yet they actually seemed chipper.

"Maybe I can find a pet dolphin," Zadie suggested, her voice muffled in the bag.

"I'm going to look for a shipwreck," Sam said, already wearing his goggles.

We were stunned into silence by our first real view of the Adriatic, a bright blue vista of perfect clarity. Great white boulders edged the water, upon which children sunned themselves like tiny merpeople. Miniature gnarled pine trees grew from the tidy pebble beach, giving the seashore an appearance of a massive bonsai garden. I felt a late-in-the-game surge of gladness that I'd dragged my brood to Croatia.

We spread out under a pine tree as the sun warmed our skin against the cool sea breeze. Like other families around us, we'd brought a picnic. Jim unpacked mortadella, a hunk of cheese, and white fluffy bread. We ate and looked around.

There sure was a lot of skin showing on the Crikvenica beach. We're talking boobies everywhere. Jim and Sam finished their sandwiches and sprinted into the water, barely noticing. From the sound of their screams, that water was quite cold.

Without hesitation, Zadie went native and stripped to the waist. "Let's get in, Mommy," she said. "Like two fancy girls!"

I was less brazen. I'd bought a two-piece swimsuit before coming to Croatia because everyone said I'd look like a moron in a one-piece, unless one-piece meant bottoms only. Jim helped me pick something modest (from a sporting-goods store, no less). Its skirt covered my butt, which had roughly the same layout as those of Sister Paula and Grandma Kate and Auntie. That is to say, it's big and it wanders.

I felt shy compared to my daughter, who left me fretting on the shore as she ran along the shallows with her little belly sticking out like a compass. My own belly more resembled a bagel. I looked great in a wool scarf and sweater. I rocked a suede jacket and boots. But my soft Iowa body hated being unsheathed in public.

Jim, who'd been ducking through the depths with Sam like a walrus, noticed my discomfort and came over, collapsing on his mat as I sat, sweating and fully clothed in the Adriatic sun.

"What's wrong?" he asked, water dripping down his face.

"I'm fat," I said.

"You are *not* fat," he said. "You're beautiful. Knock it off."

I pulled my knees up and put my head down, embarrassed to be experiencing an anxiety attack on one of the most peaceful beaches in the world.

"C'mon, Jenny, look around you," Jim said. "Who here has a perfect body?"

I looked up. Except for the very young people, whose sole job it was to spend entire days in pursuit of looking good, everyone just flopped it all out there. Big white German couples, bobbing like jolly whales on the water. Sleek Italian dudes, wearing swim panties so small I could actually see chicken skin. Naked baby boys, uncut penises floating like little yams on the water. Moms and Dads doing the back float, blissful.

I shaded my eyes and squinted up at Jim. "Just give me a minute."

"Okay," Jim said. "I have to stay with the kids anyway. But come in. Soon."

He sauntered off on long legs, barely-there love handles the only evidence of his weakness for beer and late-night cheese. I loathed the metabolism as I loved the man.

The beach had gotten crowded. I just sat there, roasting, waiting to be thinner. Then I honed in on a tight circle of old ladies. They were bronze and huge and full of rolls that shifted when they resettled themselves on foam beach mats. They passed around a bottle of brandy and gossiped about someone named Hervé and threw their heads back and laughed and pinned and repinned their hair. They were so lovely. Unashamed like Zadie, but slow-moving, with an air of decadence about them. They'd stolen time from husbands and grandchildren and Sunday dinners to be here. There was no time for shame.

My half-naked daughter ran up and knelt beside me, her lips blue with cold, shivering with pleasure as she settled against the warm rocks. With baby hands, she picked up large flat stones and piled them on her thighs.

After a while, she looked up. "Mommy, will you swim with me?"

To Zadie, and to the ladies behind me, the matter of the human body was a very simple thing: Disrobe and it feels good. So easy. I figured, screw it. Who was I kidding anyway? I was a middle-aged woman who'd nursed two children and ate cheese at night with her husband and refused to spend every free moment in the gym. To hell with shyness. It was hot outside. And my daughter was watching my every move.

I pulled off my shirt and shorts. "Let's go, buddy," I said.

"You got a big tummy," said Zadie, pushing her finger into my belly.

"You lived in that tummy for nine months. So did your brother. Respect."

We returned to 12 Novi Varoš that night, our sunburned skin encrusted with a fine coating of sea salt. I flopped down in the rocking chair by the dorm window as the kids headed to the shower in the bathroom that hadn't stopped smelling of sewage.

I closed my eyes, listening to the sounds of my children haggling over who got to go first, when my thoughts were interrupted by a bellowing voice.

"Yenny!"

I hopped up from the rocking chair and looked out the window. Pavice was standing below with Josip next to her, holding what appeared to be a tin pot. Josip was short and stocky with a face like Robin Williams.

"Hi!" I called.

"Yenny!" she bellowed again, beckoning me outside. I skipped down the steps past the second-floor rooms that had recently gone quiet with inaction.

"*Mljeko,*" Pavice announced proudly, nudging Josip roughly with her elbow. He stepped forward to dutifully hand over a pot of foamy milk.

"What's this?" I asked him.

Pavice indicated that I follow them. Josip led me through a little barn door on the first floor of their house, across from the summer kitchen where Pavice, Josip, and the other Josip spent most of their time. It was dark inside, but I could make out three looming shapes. They were cattle. In the house.

I turned to Pavice. "You have cattle in there," I pointed. "Just like old times."

"*Neh* 'cattle.' *Krava!*" She held up the milk again. "*Mljeko!*"

She pointed to the cows, one at a time. "Medo! Kuna! Šarića!"

Teddy Bear, Dollar, and Little Shari.

I took the tin pot from Josip. Pavice slapped me hard on the back. I stumbled forward with the milk, but managed not to spill any. She disappeared into her summer kitchen and came out with a bowl full of powdered-sugar-coated *kolaći*: dough balls fried in oil. "Sam, Zadie," she said to me, handing me the bowl.

Pavice rocked back on her heels, arms crossed proudly over her generous chest. Her chocolate-brown eyes twinkled.

"Thank you!" I said. "This is awesome. I love it. *Hvala. Hvala* so much!"

"*Mljeko, mmmm!*" she laughed, rubbing her belly in a circle.

"Mmmm!" I repeated.

As I crossed the yard to return to the house, Jasminka hollered at me from her window and held up one finger to say: "Wait!"

She hustled down her steps, crossed the street, and added a crystal bowl of mountain blueberries and a decorative bottle of blueberry wine to my armload of gifts.

She smiled and paused, closing her eyes for a second. Then, speaking English to me for the first time, she said, "Thank you for cake. I like for receipt to make for my son Stjepan. He like cake."

She wanted my cobbler recipe! Then Jasminka pointed at the dainty bottle of wine and winked. "Just for women. Only a little."

"*Hvala,*" I said, smiling. I tried out a new phrase. "*Hvala ljepa.*" Thank you very much. Then I bowed. I don't know why.

Jasminka's mother-in-law, Ana Fak, stepped out from her apartment onto her front stoop. Now she, too, crossed the street and added a canister to my growing mountain of plenty.

"Is tea," Jasminka explained slowly. "You say to Pavice you have woman pain. Is tea for pain."

My neighbor ladies may not have liked Jim's chili. They did, however, like dessert. *My* dessert. I rambled toward the house, my arms laden with milk and wine and blueberries and tea and fried dough balls. Then, as if on cue, a preteen girl who seemed to have stepped right out of a Judy Blume novel approached me.

She introduced herself in perfect English as Lucia, the granddaughter of our neighbors to the north, Željko and Anđelka Crnić. Anđelka was pronounced like "Angela," but with a "k" thrown in, just for fun.

A fascinating combination of awkward and confident, Lucia wore blue steel-framed glasses tucked over her long brown hair. Her tippytoes walk with puffed-out chest may or may not have been the result of the brand-new Wheelies with sparkly shoelaces she wore.

"My grandmother Anđelka brought me here from my home in Fužine so that I could translate for her," said the girl.

She seemed so eager to impart the wisdom gained from her twelve years, fired in smarty-pants bursts that left me short of breath: She was Lucia and she had been studying English since she was four, and she could not help but notice that my husband studied his lexicon, but that I did not study my lexicon, and was I not the Croatian one? And why also had I allowed my children to ride their bikes on the sidewalk unescorted? This was not wise, because many people drive crazy in this town.

I stood there for a moment. "Hello," I said.

Lucia toed the gravel of the driveway with her Wheelie. "My grandmother Anđelka would like you to come for coffee tomorrow morning."

I looked up at the Crnić house. Anđelka stood in the window, waving. She had short brown hair and thick round glasses, and was taller than most of the women I'd seen. If I hadn't been carrying so much stuff, I would have waved too.

Lucia produced a small Mason jar from behind her back. "This is jam made from raspberries. We call them *ribizla* in Croatian language," she said. "You should remember this word. You should remember every Croatian word. This jam is from my grandmother. She makes it from the bushes in her backyard."

I could not believe any of this. They liked me! They really liked me!

I showed up Monday morning in Anđelka's kitchen. The old man Viktor sat at the wooden table set for coffee. The two of them were shooting a morning dose of *rakija*, potent country liquor that was clear like water.

"My grandmother says that you must drink *rakija* in the morning," Lucia said.

Anđelka nodded, hands clasped in front of her, her eyes closed with a beatific smile. "*Rakija* is an aid for digestion. My grandmother has heard from the neighbors that you also have lady pain. *Rakija* is also for that."

Anđelka slid a shot glass toward me. I checked my watch. It was ten in the morning. Was it bad to drink before noon? Did it matter?

I'd been telling the kids since we arrived in Europe that the old rules didn't apply anymore. I had to take my own advice.

I picked up the shot glass. "*Živjeli!*" I said.

Wizened nearly to the point of miniature, Viktor raised his glass and smiled slightly, his teeth brown with age. He tipped his head at me.

"*Živjeli,*" Viktor said.

I drained the whole thing.

"Bravo, Jennifer!" Anđelka cheered, rubbing a brisk circle on my back.

With an immediate burn in my belly, I knew I had just been inducted into the village of my ancestors.

chapter **ten**

I blinked awake the next morning, listening as tractors ripped through the streets while the sun colored the sky outside the window. It was the season of making hay, and great clumps of it dropped on the roadside. Chained dogs barked at feral cats, which roamed free, all their parts intact, and multiplied heroically throughout the summer.

Somewhere a chain saw started up. One of the giant produce trucks rumbled through the streets and honked without mercy so that people would come out of their houses and shop for veggies, just to shut up all the honking. There was so much honking in Mrkopalj! Neighborly honks to say hello were short and jaunty. Little Fiat honks. The obnoxious honks—*hooooooooooooooooonk, honk, honk, hooooooooooooonk, honk, honk*—were vendors selling something. If you didn't shop, they'd only honk more. It was a Machiavellian marketing strategy, and I wished that they'd invest in a little bull-horn, like the fishmonger used. He drove from the sea in his white fish truck chanting *"Riba, riba, riba"* like a Little League third base-man taunting a batter. It was a cool sound, as soon as we knew *riba* meant fish, and not, say, "take shelter."

The dorm stirred collectively. Sam gravitated to his Legos. Zadie helped Jim make breakfast. I jogged to Tuk. I came home, showered in the smelly bathroom, and downed some sausage and Nescafé before heading out the door to walk to the priest's residence to see if I might get a look at that Book of Names. We'd spent the first few weeks in Croatia acclimating, and even Mom was getting her bearings. It was time to get down to the work of finding the old family.

The people of Mrkopalj greeted one another on their morning errands, and now they greeted me, too. Everyone including the children said *"Dobro jutro,"* which meant "good morning." In the afternoon it was *"Dobar дan,"* and then *"Dobro večer"* in the evening. The general casual greeting was *"Bog,"* also a Croatian word for God. It felt surprisingly natural to wish everyone a good morning as I did my best to imitate the cadence and the accent of the Mrkopalj dialect. The *r* rolled just the slightest bit, and the final consonant was never dropped. Though language itself wasn't my strong point, I could mimic well, and people seemed generally unruffled at my greetings, so I must have been doing okay.

The villagers were similar to me in a physical way—muscled, but soft around the edges, with funky noses. There was little artifice. Moles stayed intact. The missing digits from war or DUI Friday remained missing. Few women wore makeup. The summer girls Robert hired to cook and bartend at Stari Baća dressed like rock stars, with big sunglasses and enormous studded purses, but for the most part, clothing was simple. Button-down shirts, work pants.

As I made my way down Stari Kraj, I called *Dobro jutro!* to random old women tossing buckets of water on their front stoops. Cuculić leaned in the doorway of the municipal building, apparently on break from drinking at Stari Baća, and we nodded suspiciously at each other. A dirty white Jeep bucked up the road: Helena's husband, Paul, hand raised in greeting, a big smile moving his bald scalp forward an inch.

I was feeling pretty confident on my walk, jaunty even, as I crunched over the empty gravel parking lot at the priest's residence. Alas, no one answered my knock on the channel glass door. This genealogical sleuthing business would be no quick and easy errand for me. From here on out, it was all just part of whatever big, messy journey my ancestors had in mind when they called me here.

I humped it back home, to where the Motherland was providing much easier access to my family. Everyone was across the meadow from Robert's place, playing at the *škola*. I could see Jim sitting on a stone bench, reading a book. Sam, Zadie, and Karla were up in the cherry trees, eating fistfuls of fruit. I headed over.

"Hi, Mom!" Sam called, fingers and mouth stained.

Zadie spit a cherry pit in a graceful arc. "Did you see that, Mommy?"

"I did!" I clapped, settling in next to Jim. "How's the morning going?"

"Good," Jim said. "They browbeat Karla into coming over here to play."

The kids loved the *škola*. God knows why. It was relatively barren, save for the decrepit Communist-era playground, of which they particularly liked the genital-squashing teeter-totter. Being able to climb trees was a revelation, too. They'd hogged most of the cherries, like good little Americans, and were moving on lately to apples, which weren't even close to ripe, but assisted their digestive tracts with all the mortadella and cheese we fed them. It probably seemed like a major adventure, being perched in the crotch of a tree, foraging for food. For my kids' generation, tree climbing was a lost art.

The *škola* also offered Sam and Zadie independence, as it was within view of Robert's house. Sam had always been comfortable with solitude, and Mrkopalj just encouraged it in a prettier setting. Zadie had never been a solo flyer. She wanted to do her own thing, but she wanted someone beside her when she did it. In Mrkopalj, with the Starčević girls at her beck and call, she reveled in exactly this kind of freedom. The stubborn streak that made her seem so obstinate amid the structure of home was entirely relevant in Mrkopalj, where it was safe to wander and we had no particular schedule to follow. In fact, Zadie was physically growing in Mrkopalj, shedding her toddler wardrobe piece by piece. In Mrkopalj, my daughter, who spent much of her second year in time-outs, learned to laugh deep from her belly for the first time. I'd heard her laugh before, but it always sounded odd and tinny to me, as if she'd heard other people laughing and thought she'd better try it every now and then just to keep up appearances. But in Mrkopalj, she howled.

It happened for the first time the night Jim was trying to pass out chili to the neighbors. I was hanging out on the yard swing, watching

Zadie and Roberta kick around a soccer ball. Bobi had been penned up all day, and Karla released him into the yard, where he made a beeline for Zadie, who, as I mentioned before, was often covered with ice-cream residue. Bobi nearly swallowed her whole with licking. Zadie started to laugh, stepping backward carefully until she got to the picnic table and pulled herself up while that great white dog just lick, lick, licked.

Once atop the table, Zadie flopped her hands on her little hips. *"Joj meni!"* she said, exasperated, using that ancient Mrkopaljci exclamation "Oh my!" for the first time. When Roberta had joined Zadie on the table to examine her wet face, the two of them got to laughing. Soon, they were clutching their bellies and rolling. Roberta laughed so hard her wire-rimmed glasses went askew. Every time the girls looked at each other, they'd break out in giggles again. Soon, I found myself laughing too at such a fantastic sound.

The more time we spent with the kids like this, the less they craved our attention. Back home, a sort of desperation lurked beneath all their behavior. In Mrkopalj, they always had the full concentration of at least one of us (and often both of us). They basked in it, relaxing into the place and the circumstances with tree-climbing grace. Even Sam. He still had bouts of teary homesickness, but mostly they came at night when he was tired.

We were adjusting to life in the slow lane. Jim and I wondered how we'd ever gotten by without hour-long coffee breaks. Seriously, how?

Well, I was *pretty much* adjusting. You can take the mom out of Iowa and all. Case in point: After my initial failure in getting to the Book of Names, I began stalking the priest.

Visiting his residence across from the church began as a simple after-dinner stroll. I'd finish washing dishes and shoo the kids out the door to play. When Jim was settled on the lawn with Robert for a man-to-man beer, I'd walk to Mile's house. (Mile was the man who'd helped with the priest in the fall.) I'd knock on his door, and Mile would look out, his sun-sensitive glasses dark though he'd been inside. He'd slip sandals over his dark socks and escort me across the street to see if this might be the night I'd be allowed another peek into the book that held the names of my great-grandparents.

Mile and I would rap on the channel-glass door, and the same tiny nun in a black habit would open it a crack and ask what our mission was. Mile would explain that the *američki* wanted to see the Book of Names. And every night, the nun would deal out an excuse for the priest with a quiet urgency. The priest was sleeping. He was not feeling well. The priest flat-out wouldn't see us. Though she was not five feet tall, I knew I couldn't get past her. She was one of those people who looks delicate and then they lift a tractor to save the trapped farmer.

The priest became the Owl in my mind, both in looks and elusive behavior. I really had no idea why he was avoiding me. Maybe I'd irrevocably offended him when I'd tried to touch the book so long ago. Unfortunately for the Owl, I was a falcon. I would find my great-grandparents in that big ole book if it was my last act on Earth. Besides, I didn't have anything better to do.

One night, the nun answered the door, wringing her hands. "The priest fell down in church. He is sick. Something like this," Mile explained. "He is having a hard time and cannot talk tonight, like this."

I walked to Stari Baća and quizzed the barflies through one of the English-speaking summer girls. Some said the priest was probably drinking. Another said he had Alzheimer's. One guy spoke up and said it was both diabetes *and* drinking.

And then, some useful information: The priest would retire in August. Might I consider laying off the poor man and try again when the new guy got here?

But who knew if the next priest would even let me see the Book of Names. For all I knew, the mere fact that I was a woman might be barring me from my research in this old-fashioned place. I just couldn't take the chance.

The next night, I walked down to Mile's a little early. I figured maybe we had the timing wrong. I knocked for him at 7:45. Mile came to the door, flustered and scolding. "I have told you eight o'clock!" he said. "I am watching now the news of Michael Jackson. Something like this!"

I tried a different tack. "Well, maybe if we try earlier, we'll catch the priest off guard and he'll let us in this time. Then I won't have to bother you anymore."

This seemed like a very good idea to Mile. We walked across the street. To our surprise, the nun beckoned us in.

The Owl sat at a cluttered dining room table, surrounded by religious pamphlets, stacks of loose papers, day planners, and, inexplicably, a PlayStation 2 SingStar Dance Party guide. We sat down. The Owl perched on his chair at the head of the table. I was suddenly struck with a memory: Sister Paula had adored owls. She collected owl figurines and placed them all over her room in the convent. I'd made her an owl latch-hook rug when I was Sam's age. She thought the owl was a sign of good luck.

"How find house number?" the priest asked, face stoic.

"We will have to look through all the Radošević names," I said. "I still don't know the house number."

"And I don't know," he grumbled.

The Owl shook his head, disgusted with me. Had he not told me in the fall that I needed house numbers to find family names? Was I daft? I said nothing but stared back.

"Today is impossible to find," the priest said, looking away from me.

My lack of language skills sharpened the one journalistic trick I knew: I waited him out in silence.

After a full minute of quiet, the priest spoke. "For me, it is best that you come tomorrow in the morning."

"I will still not have the house numbers." I raised an eyebrow and added: "I am happy to look through the book myself."

When Mile translated, the priest shook his head. He'd see me around nine.

Walking out, Mile told me he had an appointment to get his car looked at in the morning. He couldn't join me. The Owl and the Falcon would spar alone.

In the morning, I was allowed entry immediately.

I silently handed over Jelena and Valentin's naturalization certificates.

"Helena, born Iskra. Married to Radošević," the priest said listlessly.

"Married to Valentin Radošević," I said. "Yes."

"Oh! Iskra is *so* many families." He sighed. He stared at the Book of Names lying closed on the table in front of him.

Fortunately for international relations, the doorbell rang. The tiny nun escorted a harried young woman into the room. She talked with the Owl for a few minutes and made some sort of an appointment, I think for a baptism, which the priest recorded in a planner.

The lady then dug into her pocketbook and pulled out a one hundred-kuna bill.

He took it and thanked her. Then he looked purposefully at me.

Joj meni! No wonder I'd been striking out. I hadn't remembered the greatest tenet of the Catholic Church: Pay to play!

I patted my purse on my lap and returned the nod. Understood! He smiled and opened the book at last.

"Iskra, Iskra . . . ," he said, drawing his finger down the columns of all the Iskras who had ever lived in Mrkopalj. Juraj. Matej. Franciska. Ferdinan. Sylvestra. Dragica. Ivana. Školastika. Marija. Karmela. Zlata. Petra. He chanted names of Iskra women, marching through decades of Mrkopalj life, through tens of pages, with a few false starts—Jelena Iskras born much earlier or much later—for about thirty minutes.

Then he hit the jackpot.

"Iskra. Jelena. Born May 15, 1889."

"Yes, yes, yes! That's the right year!" I jumped up from my chair and peeked into the book.

I think I heard a chuckle from deep within his possibly diabetic, possibly Alzheimered, possibly alcoholic chest.

"Parents are Josip and Marija," he said.

I was very happy to see those names. I was allowed to run a finger over them.

The priest read on.

Siblings: Anton, Franjo, Katarina, Johana, Paulina, Anjela, Franciska, Ana.

Her family lived in House No. 40.

I read little scrawled notes in the margins next to the names of Jelena's siblings. *"Udata Mrkopalj "* for Johana. She'd been married in Mrkopalj.

Franjo, Katerina, Franciska, and Ana: all *smrti,* or died, as children.

There were no notes about Jelena after her birth date. It seemed that the Owl could speak English when he wanted to, because he then told me that if it didn't happen in Mrkopalj, it wasn't in the book. I could conclude that Jelena had married my great-grandfather Valentin after she'd arrived in America, because there was no date of marriage entered into the Book of Names.

Next the priest searched for Valentin, chanting the Radošević names one after the other. "Marija, Ivan, Marija, Ivan, Marija, Josip, Marija, Marija."

I laughed. "Everybody's Marija."

The priest remained stone-faced. "Yeah."

In the silence of the room, a fly beat itself against a closed window. The room was hot, and I felt hotter still just looking at the Owl before me, laboring in shirt, tie, and sweater.

After a very long time, the priest read aloud: "Radošević. *Valentin.*"

I took a sharp breath in.

"Son of Petar and Katarina."

"Born in 1886," I said. "That's the one."

"Yeah," said the priest.

"House Number 262."

Siblings Matej, Franjo, Vincenza, and Ana.

As with Jelena, there were no notes about Valentin after his birth date. But we did find another interesting fact on the page: "Mother born Starčević," the priest read. Robert and I could be cousins.

It didn't surprise me. Robert and Cuculić had told me that the Radoševićs were one of the first families in Mrkopalj hundreds of years ago. So were the Starčevićs and the Cuculićs, by the way. Me and Robert and Cuculić: the first pirates and exiles in line to get in. There were now so many people with the same last names that the village had come up with an elaborate nicknaming system. Robert's family, for example, was Baća, which meant "boy." His father had been called Baća before him, and it's where Robert got the name for the café-bar Stari Baća, which translated to "The Old Boy."

As Robert put it: "Every family have nicky-name."

The priest snapped the Book of Names closed. "Enough, huh?" he asked.

"I think for now," I answered.

"Because Radošević has many families," he said, feigning exhaustion.

"Ah!" I said, grabbing my purse. I fell into the pidgin English I used in Croatia when I was nervous. "Right! Thank you so much, your helping of me. Is it good to maybe donate some? Something to the church for the help of finding the names?"

He shrugged and looked down at my tape recorder.

"If you can, if you can," he said.

"I can," I said, rummaging in my wallet. I took out two one hundred-kuna bills. "One for each, Valentin and Jelena."

He made a very big deal out of recording my money in a ledger.

"Jennifer?" he asked, pen poised.

I stood up. "Jennifer," I repeated.

Then I spoke the names as if I'd earned them: "My great-grandmother was Jelena Iskra. My great-grandfather was Valentin Radošević."

I had begun to witness.

After I left I took a quick walk around Mrkopalj, looking for numbers 40 and 262 on the little tin house-number tags. I wanted to see more of my family, now that I'd scratched the surface of their presence. But I could find no houses that corresponded to the numbers written in my notebook. So instead, I turned back toward the church in hopes of beginning my search for the physical remnants of my ancestors in the *groblje*, or cemetery.

My brother, Tim, had sent me photographs of Valentin and Jelena's graves in a Des Moines cemetery—the headstone read "Wally and Helen Radosevich." Easy enough. But finding the graves of Petar and Katarina Radošević, and Josip and Marija Iskra, would be a formidable task. I looked down from the hilltop of the yellow church onto a field below crammed with hundreds of headstones, bounded on either side by tidy rows of tall, oblong cedar trees. I toed gingerly down the concrete steps to follow a paved path canopied at its midpoint by a giant crucifix and trellis. It seemed to lead straight to the foothills beyond, every inch along the way crowded with graves. Each name I'd learned so far in Mrkopalj—Starčević, Cuculić, Fak, Paškvan—had so many representatives among the dead. Of Radošević names, there were hundreds, and several Iskras, none matching the names of Valentin and Jelena's parents. Some head stones had cameo images. In the stiff portraits, I could see Mrkopalj: shadowy eyes, high cheekbones, dark hair.

Many graves had fallen into disrepair over time, untended and forgotten. I suspected my own family was among them. I saw a very old one, open and excavated, the top of a coffin showing inside—families moved relatives when they outgrew a plot or could afford a better one. Lichen covered simple wooden crosses with nail holes where names were once tacked on. Hand-formed concrete stones had worn away to become unreadable. Some could only be identified as graves because they were in a cemetery and they were the appropriate size.

I was beginning to understand why my mother and Aunt Terri scrubbed the family headstones in Des Moines on Memorial Day, the way Grandma Kate, Sister Paula, and Auntie had scrubbed before them. Though it would be tougher to find Valentin and Jelena's parents if their graves were unmarked, my work in Mrkopalj would not be complete until I did. My days of ignorance about my roots were over, and I had to pay my respects accordingly.

After two hours of picking through the weeds and overgrown grass under the full sun, I grew hot and dizzy. I took a bottle of water from my backpack and drank under a tree. I saw two men standing near the headstone of a soldier, kneading knit caps in their hands. Returning to the cemetery over the following months, not once did I find it empty. Old women freshened the flickering candles in red jars. People my age arranged flowers over cousins lost in drunk-driving accidents. Kids dropped by, seeking advice from absent grandparents. Even little-tended graves were decorated with longevity in mind—silk flowers and perpetually blinking electric candles. The Mrkopalj cemetery was a living thing. As I sat there, a tall smooth marble headstone caught my eye. The name upon it was Katarina Radošević. That had been Grandma Kate's maiden name. I took it as a sign not to give up, but I'd had enough for one day.

That night, I told Jim about my fact-finding mission with the Owl and my first round of detective work in town. We were driving home from Delnice, cruising in the Peugeot through the droop of trees in inky darkness, blasting one of the mix discs I'd made at home. We'd discovered a video store where most of the movies were in English, dubbed with Croatian subtitles. This felt like the height of luxury, even if the definition of a "contemporary" movie in Delnice was *K-9*. Even better: We'd discovered "our" place in a joint called Pizza Scorpion. The guy at the wood-fired oven—somebody told me he was the brother of Aziz, the Albanian fruit vendor I liked so much—baked the kids friendly little cheese pizzas, and Jim and I ordered the house special. We couldn't interpret the menu, but it included the ingredient "scurvy," which seemed like a dare from the travel gods. We were not disappointed. Behold the toppings: bacon, mushrooms, cheese, sausage, a poached egg, and a glob of sour cream on top. A real widow-maker. Jim and I were pleased. Total bill: $10.

"I'm proud of you," Jim said. He was hunched over the steering wheel, trying to make out the road. The Delnice drive was deliciously creepy at night; the forest seemed to encroach even more after dark. "It sounds like a productive day."

"It was," I said. "I'm going to see if there's a cemetery map or something. Some of those headstones are so weathered I can't read the names. But I have to find Valentin and Jelena's parents. They're the ones who got this party started. They let their kids go to America. Because of that, there's me."

For some reason, driving the Dramamine Memorial Road in the pitch black canceled out the nausea, and we were all very happy and full that night. Occasionally one of us would wonder aloud what we might do if a zombie walked out of the woods—a legitimate question in this land where *over*forestation was a problem.

When we got home, the kids snuggled into bed and Jim and I lowered our bodies onto that cruel tray of a futon. I looked out the window at the big black bowl of Mrkopalj sky as I drifted off to sleep, Pavice and Josip's dog, Cesar, braying deep into the night, a hunting dog of indiscriminate origin, the only mixed breed in town besides us.

chapter **eleven**

We walked to church together for the first time on the third Sunday in July. We'd been in Mrkopalj for just over two weeks. Our slow-moving herd took a shortcut, ducking past the Konzum and around a shabby bend, where a German shepherd lunged at us the moment we rounded the corner. His snapping teeth barely missed my forearm. Jim and I catapulted the children down the alley as the dog fought viciously against his chain.

So we were particularly thankful to arrive, alive and unscathed, at the stucco church stained a deep shade of goldenrod. Our Lady of Seven Sorrows perched upon the highest elevation of the village, up three sets of stone steps from the road and overlooking the cemetery I'd recently been baking in. The spire reached into the sky, punctuated by a small circular clock face and a bell tower, this simplest of church designs, its only fancywork being marble-framed doors, half-moon stained-glass windows, and scalloped stone edging like the border on a school bulletin board. We dipped our fingers in the stone font of holy water, its contents forever chilling within these walls.

Jim and I huddled in the pews and pulled Sam and Zadie close for heat as much as affection. A spartan wooden kneeler ran the length of our shins. Parishioners shifted in the quiet, waiting for mass to begin. The church was packed, even though this was just one of Mrkopalj's two Sunday masses. With the piercing notes of a mighty pipe organ, the choir rolled out the hymn "O Maria" from high above, in voices triumphant and strong, delineated perfectly between octaves. Loudly, regardless of talent, Mrkopalj joined in with the robust noise of people genuinely glad to be here.

The saint sculptures in Our Lady of Seven Sorrows were painted brightly in metallic colors and flanked by faux marble columns. Crystal teardrop chandeliers twinkled in the light. A strip of red carpeting led up the aisle, past marble statues of the disciples, their names inscribed at the base: Matej, Marko, Luka, Ivan. The shoes of the faithful had worn the crimson and black slate floor tiles to a smooth patina. I held Zadie close, breathing in the warm-bread smell of her. Jim kept his arm tight around Sam. None of us understood a word from the altar, but the heavenly choir of Mrkopalj gave us the general idea. In that cold calm space, I was thankful for my children as they sat, fidgeting but patient, through the long mass.

We stopped at Stari Baća for coffee on the way home. A summer girl, Marija, asked us if we wanted Sunday dinner. Though it was good manners to make a reservation so the women in the kitchen would know how much scratch-cooked food was required of them, we were assured there was enough on this day, so we accepted the offer and she set our table. We liked Marija, who looked like a young version of Dianne Wiest. She made a fabulous cappuccino.

A big redheaded guy and his son, a boy of maybe thirteen, ate dinner, then went outside for a smoke break. Marija's sister, Stefanija, another summer girl sitting at the bar with a coffee, saw my shocked face as I watched them light up outside the window.

"You are surprised?" she asked me, raising her eyebrows. Stefanija looked like a mischievous forest sprite in bubble sunglasses and fashion boots.

"That boy seems a little young to be smoking," I said.

"When we were in grade school, even the kids got smoke breaks," Stefanija said.

Maybe it was considered an act of patriotism in Europe's largest tobacco-producing country.

Marija brought a large bowl of what looked like egg-drop soup. The broth was thick, and we mopped it with country bread. Sam and Zadie held off, hesitant.

"Eat your food, kiddos," I said, mouth full.

"I don't know if I'll like it," Sam said. He hadn't trusted us in matters of food since the roadside pig incident.

"You might not," Jim said. "But chances are it'll be the safest thing for you to eat. It tastes like regular chicken soup. Pretty much."

"Except it's better," I said, my head lowered over the bright yellow broth.

"It is, isn't it?" Jim agreed. In Croatia, Jim and I had begun describing ourselves as feeders, rather than foodies.

"Do I get ice cream if we eat it all?" Zadie asked shrewdly.

"Probably," I said.

"Nothing like some soup!" Sam said, digging in with a big spoon.

They ate cautiously, Sam picking through the broth seeking meat. Finding no definite chunks, he slurped his lunch. Zadie, who hadn't eaten more than a teaspoonful of anything in her life, consumed her standard amount.

Stuffed yellow peppers and potatoes with beef gravy arrived. The kids seemed more grateful for their soup then. Marija served a dessert she called pancakes: crepes with Nutella. I watched the kids finish their soup, uncomplaining, anticipating the chocolatey goo. Sam played Legos at the table. Zadie practiced snapping her fingers. Jim and I had come to Mrkopalj to fix our family, but the kids hadn't needed any fixing. They adjusted to most any situation, as long as their parents were close by.

The bar buzzed with generations of families catching up together. The old neighbor Viktor came in with the church crowd, and sat down to drink *gemišt* with a buddy. Robert's girls rounded up Sam and Zadie and they headed outside in a pack to ride bikes and play in the meadow. Jakov Fak, Mario and Jasminka's Olympian son, streaked by the window on training skates, lean and muscled and tan.

Jim and I finished our meal with two more cappuccinos. Stefanija still perched at the bar, along with a young guy in a stylish sailor's shirt and pressed pants. He introduced himself as Marijan Padavić. Though he was only twenty-eight, he'd already worked as a fashion designer and a graphic artist, and was now studying music and theater in Rijeka.

"I also sing in the Mrkopalj choir," he noted with a slight toss of his head. "I am a tenor." His was the higher male voice that I adored, its soaring sadness the physical embodiment of aspiration, matching the jewel-box beauty of Our Lady of Seven Sorrows.

Marijan was trim and refined in a village of more hulkish men. His father was the mayor. Marijan later told me that he'd been the first kid in Mrkopalj to color his hair. An old woman had leaned out her window as he passed by on his bicycle, screaming "Oh the Satan! Oh the Satan!"

"I'm not that fashionable anymore," he said. "That was in my teenage days."

"So you're the tenor. Who's the amazing bass?" I asked. Matching Marijan at the lower end of the tonal spectrum was a voice as heavy as a tuba.

"Željko Crnić, husband of Anđelka," Marijan said. "Your neighbor to the north."

It pleased me to make those connections to the voices of the church. Plugging in like this felt a lot better than standing on the outside, looking in, wondering what the hell we were doing here.

Jim and I walked home together, at which time he embarked on a favorite pastime of his: staring at Robert's house.

Activity in the construction zone of the second-floor apartment was high during the weeks following our arrival, but nothing ever really got done. The young workmen could only make progress when no one else was around. The whole too-many-cooks thing applied in Mrkopalj. Especially when the other cooks were drunk.

Therein lie the problem: Robert was always there those first weeks, hiding under the pretense of work but really just turning the whole place into a party zone. He would get Cuculić or any other willing conspirator over under the guise of showing him the apartment's progress, and then he'd proceed to talk him into having "just one *gemišt.*" The idea that there was ever "just one" of any drink in Mrkopalj was laughable.

Nevertheless, it was a phrase of Robert's that we came to love. Or at least Jim did. "Just one *gemišt!*" spoken with gusto and impressive frequency. Then, after four or five rounds of "just one," Robert would head over to Stari Baća, where he'd try to keep track of the bar's business by entering drinks into a ledger with hash marks. As the night progressed, Robert's scratchings would become sporadic and confused, and eventually he'd abandon the ledger altogether. It was widely known that if you got to Stari Baća at the right time, you could drink for free and Robert wouldn't notice. Though Robert complained bitterly about Croatia's short-lived smoking ban (repealed by that woman prime minister he'd been so skeptical about), declining business in Stari Baća had much more to do with the owner's tipsy accounting practices.

At the beginning, when we actually thought the apartment might be completed at some point, Robert's work pace nearly killed us. We didn't unpack our suitcases because we didn't know if we had arrived at our final destination. Slowly, by the late days of July, the second floor developed a real kitchen and a modern bathroom with that crazy shower full of buttons and dials just like a spaceship. It had a bedroom perfect for Sam and Zadie, and a separate one for us with an actual bed, hand-carved by Robert's brother. When the bed was

delivered, the headboard was capped by two carved wooden minia-
tures of Robert's signature wafflestomper boots, complete with red
shoelaces.

Unfortunately, at any point during the construction period, you
could find more beer bottles and wine boxes than actual tools. We
began to suspect that we'd be living in the third-floor dorm for the
duration of our stay in Mrkopalj. Eventually, by the end of July, we
simply unpacked and resolved to love our dorm.

The nature of these local construction practices, coupled with
impressive amounts of alcohol, should have explained the haphazard
arrangement of Robert's house. The structure of the Starčević manse
completely baffled Jim's architectural sensibilities. As I had struggled
to find my place in Mrkopalj, so Jim struggled to understand the in-
sane construction of Robert's house. Once he sat down and drew the
thing in detail but even that didn't help much.

I'd often find Jim outside, arms crossed, head cocked, brow fur-
rowed, just looking at the thing. I could almost see smoke rising from
his ears as he tried to comprehend the three stories of hodgepodge
building material subdivided into so many separate compartments that
it laid out like a rural haunted house. Sections that had served specific
uses in the past were simply abandoned when no longer needed. The
barn in the back end of the first floor, for example, remained much a
barn in spirit, though it held only Bobi and a year's worth of potatoes in
its gloomy chambers. The first floor, where the dead grandmother had
lived with Robert and Goranka, emanated the feeling of sagging, deep
settlement. Worn-out burgundy pleather couches ringed a small television. The kitchen floor had softened so much that I sank an inch with
every step across the linoleum on the way to use the washing machine.
A spiral staircase went from the first floor to the second, with a strange
and hidden bedroom wedged between.

This journey to the second floor was the shift of generations. Here
Robert's fancy had taken over—this was where he'd put his mark upon
his ancestral home. Exterior cement steps ascended the side of the
house, lined with a rusting iron handrail of odd sunburst shapes that

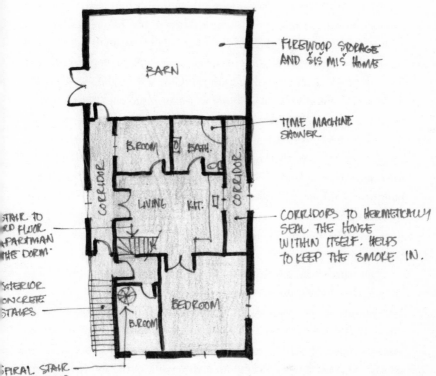

FIREWOOD STORAGE
AND SIS MIS HOME

TIME MACHINE
SHOWER

CORRIDORS TO HERMETICALLY
SEAL THE HOUSE
WITHIN ITSELF. HELPS
TO KEEP THE SMOKE IN.

BARN

B.ROOM

BATH.

CORRIDOR

CORRIDOR

STAIR TO
2ND FLOOR
APARTMAN
'THE DORM'

LIVING

KIT.

EXTERIOR
CONCRETE
STAIRS

BEDROOM

B.ROOM

SPIRAL STAIR
TO FIRST FLOOR

▥ — STAIRS.

▥ — 2ND FLOOR 'NEW' APARTMAN

▥ — BEDROOM FOR 1ST FLOOR.
APARTMAN ACCESSIBLE FROM
1ST FLOOR BY SPIRAL STAIR.

▥ — ODD CORRIDOR SPACES.

ROBERT'S HOUSE (BY JIM)

left one's hand smelling tart and metallic. Once on top of these steps, a visitor might choose the door on the left leading to the construction site. I've mentioned that the second-floor apartment was hermetically sealed within the larger outer shell of the house, as if the smaller box of the renovated apartment fit inside the larger and older version, an odd buffer of dead space all around it. Outside the kitchen window was, a few inches away, another kitchen window, the original one. Before one entered the apartment, there was another, much larger buffer that had been made into a vestibule in which to remove shoes and coats, or place an umbrella. Except that this vestibule was very long, the full length of the house, and packed with firewood at the barn end. From that vestibule one could enter the developing apartment through French doors framed by the original barn wood from the old days. This wood was thick and dark and weathered, and it was one of the best features of the house.

But Robert did not think so. During the last week of July, he recruited Jim to help plaster the entire length of it.

The afternoon was warm. Robert's sister-in-law, a lovely blonde with a darkness about her eyes that could probably be attributed to her job as a cancer-ward nurse, stopped by for a visit as Robert explained the job to Jim. Snijezana introduced herself as the mother of Petra the Olympian, noting that her name was one of the most difficult in Mrkopalj—snee-YAY-zhuh-nuh—so she advised us to call her by its rough English translation of "Snow Girl." Snow Girl stared in horror when she realized that Robert intended to plaster the barn wood.

"I do not like this!" she gasped. "You are covering up the spirit of the old house! You are ruining it!"

But Robert would not be swayed. This would be a plaster wall, decorated with odd antiques he found in the barn, rather than the antique itself. He shrugged at Snow Girl, cigarette dangling from his lips, and smeared the first wipe of thick plaster over the weathered wood. Then he took a deep drink of the halp-halp.

Jim agonized. Should he respect the wood or respect Robert's wishes?

"Jim work," Robert encouraged him. "You are architect for wood."

Jim dug into the bucket and reluctantly applied a thick white coat in a smooth stroke. Robert objected. He reached over and roughed up the plaster with his own trowel.

"Artistic!" Robert roared. He flopped an arm over Jim's shoulders. "Two artistic men!"

Jim would apply his plaster smoothly, and Robert would whip it up like cake frosting, using anything he could to add texture. He ran outside and snapped a pine bough off a tree and mopped it across the plaster. He pressed a pair of old scissors into it and left them there. He applied a metal clothes hanger that wasn't quite flat so it stuck out a little bit. He wrote in the plaster. He pressed his hands into it. Robert, the Brown Bear, did everything but roll his back against the wall to leave his scent on it.

All the while, Jim worked furiously to contribute some sort of smooth continuity to this work that would partially bear his name. In fact, Robert wrote out the date, and the words *Jim Work* into the plaster, which had extended to the ceiling of the kids' bedroom inside the doorway.

Snow Girl, all depressed now, went inside to drink coffee with Goranka. Mario came over to see what was going on. He pointed to Jim's smooth layers. "*Da,*" Mario said. Then he pointed to Robert, who was now pressing a handful of nails into the wall, and shook his head. "*Neh.*"

It seemed that Mario, as Robert's generous and sober first neighbor, had done his best through the years to smooth the rough edges of Robert's life. I noticed that he and Jasminka took the girls on outings, and especially doted on Roberta. Mario helped coach their biathlon team. It was Mario who had built the new pine stairway to the third floor; the old one had included a step so high that I pulled a hamstring on it twice. If it weren't for Mario, I didn't know what would happen to Robert's family.

Soon, Mario was looking out for my family too. The kids in Mrkopalj ran in packs, and when Robert was at Stari Baća and Goranka was working at her part-time job in the Rijeka highway tollbooth, the girls

were relatively unsupervised. A few nights after the plastering incident, a gang of teenagers gathered in front of Robert's house. The
older boys were yelling up to our third-floor dorm, just goofing off,
but I could hear something about Americans, then they were screaming Sam's name.

"What's going on?" I yelled down to Ivana, who was trying to
shush them.

"Never mind!" called Ivana. "They are crazy!"

"They're just being kids," Jim said, looking up from his book.

Then I looked over and saw Mario step out of his house. He
slowly walked down the steps and approached the road, watching the
kids with his arms crossed. He didn't have to say a word: The kids
quieted, then dispersed. He looked up at me and nodded, then went
back inside.

Robert might be our guide. But Mario was the leader. Through
him and Jasminka, Jim and I began to understand the true, and possibly fading, soul of Mrkopalj.

chapter twelve

The week before Robert ruined his foyer, Ivana approached Jim
and me as we sat on the yard swing. She stood on one thin leg, her
wild blond hair captured in a ponytail.

"Mario, he say we go to mountain for wood, and then to eat."

We had no idea what this meant. Ivana struggled with English,
and though we pressed her for details in Croglish, the questions were
like arrows shot into the sky. What exactly would we be doing? When
would we be doing it? And why with wood? Were we going mountain
climbing? Should I get my boots? Should we pack a bag? Soon, Ivana
left us, bored and uncomfortable with being grilled like that, even if
she liked her interrogators fairly well.

We, too, dropped the subject. If Mario was involved we had nothing to worry about. We didn't hear about the matter again until Robert brought it up a week later, as Jim and I were drinking afternoon coffee at Stari Baća.

"Mario, he say we go now on tractor. To cut the grass. Then we eat with the fire. All of the families. All of the children. At four o'clock, or five, or half-past eight."

Jim and I debated this as we walked home. Did Mario need help baling hay? We'd seen farmers hauling bales all week. Or did he just want to show us how he mowed his lawn? I had yet to see a lawn mower. We had just been to Delnice running errands and saw an entire city crew mowing an acre-wide median using only weed-eaters.

And now the kids were invited, too. Which meant what? How far into the mountains were we going? Was it safe? Someone had seen wolves crossing the road near Sunger at eleven in the morning—those were bold wolves. On a recent walk up the mountain, Bobi had pointed out a viper the size of a human arm coiled on a rock. Zadie yelled, "Snake! Mom, snake! It's a snake! Bobi found a snake!" and Sam lunged in for a closer look, but this easygoing Mrkopalj creature remained coiled, its docile gaze flat and uninterested. Still, it was a viper, and technically it could have killed us. So what sort of precautions should we take for this trip?

We decided once again to drop the matter until somebody started a car.

And then, at around 4:30, someone did start a car. We were instructed to follow Robert and Goranka's Renault Kangoo. Bobi was closed into the back, which we figured was adequate protection against wolves and vipers. We drove for fifteen minutes on a mountain road, and then for five more on a cinder trail through deep woods into a breezy clearing of grasses, daisies, wild mint, and mustard plant.

In the middle of the clearing, Mario worked a slingblade back and forth, felling tall swaths with each motion. Jasminka emerged from a little shack at the far end of the field and hurried over to greet us. She swept her arm in a grand manner. "The ranch!"

Back home I'd daydreamed of a country cabin—a retreat from

the world's worries. I was always thwarted by overcomplicating the idea. A cabin must have heated floors! Guest bedrooms! A hot tub! An appliance garage to store the blender for the nightly margaritas we shall enjoy when, at last, we can live the simple life!

But Mario and Jasminka had the right idea with this hand-built shelter just one step above a kid's clubhouse. It was perfect: shaped like a Little League dugout with a corrugated tin roof covered by plywood and tarpaper, sprouting a crooked tin chimney and a mish-mash of shutters. Goranka unloaded grocery bags of chips and meat and beer into the tiny kitchenette/living room with a wood-burning stove and an old couch. A thin wall delineated the bedroom.

"Jennifer!" called Jasminka. She handed me a Dixie cup of *rakija*, and poured one for Goranka. *"Živjeli!"* We shot it quickly and Jasminka discreetly put the bottle away.

She led me to a patch of groundcover. Zadie, Sam, and the girls followed.

"The blueberries!" Jasminka announced. This must have been where she'd picked that first crystal bowlful for us. The kids and I harvested midnight-blue berries. They were tart and juicy and stained our hands. We'd eat them the minute we broke their tiny stems off.

I looked around as the kids foraged. Mario, built like Grizzly Adams, cut grass in wide sweeps. With each rotation of his torso, he cleared four or five feet of ground within a half-inch of the earth.

I walked over and asked to try. Though Mario didn't speak English, and my Croatian remained terrible, he and I always seemed to understand each other. He squinted and muttered something in Croatian. I'm guessing it was: "This is a very bad idea."

Reluctantly, he handed over the slingblade. I placed one hand on the end of the wooden handle, feeling its smoothness, then placed the other on the handle that protruded from the middle of the tool. I swung. The grass, rather than falling as it had under the sure hand of Mario, simply bent to move out of my way. I swung again. Same thing.

Mario stood back and watched, trying not to smile.

"Am I doing this right?" I asked him. *"Dobro?"*

He shook his head. *"Neh."* Then he swept a hand firmly over his upturned palm. He spoke a rare word of English: "Clean."

I tried again, swinging the blade harder and grazing the top of my tennis shoe.

Jasminka hurried over.

"Maybe you rake," she suggested.

Back home, old oak trees line our street, and most of them seem to deposit their leaves into my yard. I've raked. Oh, how I've raked. Mario headed to another section of the field to continue his work while the American clown busted out her lone applicable skill. I raked Mario's shorn grass into giant, neat piles around the cabin.

Within a few minutes, Mario stalked over.

"Neh!" He shook his head. *"Neh! Neh!"*

He said a lot of things to me in Croatian about my performance, none of them good, and gently took my rake. He pointed me toward the campfire that Robert and Jasminka were building. I walked away, feeling bad.

Jasminka directed me to find stones for a fire ring. I reached down to grab one and now Jasminka let loose a steady stream of Croatian. "Not too big!" she admonished.

My confidence was shaken. What size stones? Did it matter if they had moss on them? Was it okay to dig out a stone that was stuck into the ground? Or would that just create a divot for someone to trip over later?

I had to rectify my earlier failure. This was a matter of pride now.

I walked back to Mario.

"Tell me what I did wrong," I said. He looked up at me, confused. I took the rake. I held it up. "Teach me what you want me to do."

Jasminka yelled over to him and Mario nodded. He showed me that this type of raking wasn't piling, it was spreading out. He motioned to the sky. "Sun. Dry."

It was all I needed. I finished the raking, spreading out the grass so that it would dry in the sun, recovering my dignity just in time for dinner.

Goranka set another massive Mrkopalj picnic table. Jasminka

tended the bonfire as the kids gathered around. Mario whittled sticks into skewers, onto which we stuck six-inch slabs of country bacon called *slanina* that fanned out in the fire. The kids roasted hot dogs. When someone's meat finished cooking, they'd carry it to a cutting board laid out on the picnic table next to a giant hunting knife that all but Zadie and Roberta used to slice their own. Sam's chest puffed out a little as Mario handed him the knife with gravity. I glanced over at Jim with the parental "Do you think this is okay?" look. He shrugged. I shrugged too. Sam cut his own meat.

We ate with our hands.

Jasminka brought out thick-sliced zucchini, laid it on a grill grate over the fire, and sprinkled it with coarse sea salt. This we also ate with our hands.

The kids wandered off to pick strawberries for dessert before the sun set. The grown-ups sat around the picnic table. Eventually, Jasminka lit a kerosene lamp. No one said much.

We did as Mrkopalj did, and as we had learned to do in the dorm: We basked in the extravagance of simplicity and the kindness of our first neighbors.

We followed the Kangoo back home, sleepy and content. Sam sniffed a little as I knelt at his mattress to kiss him good night.

"What's the matter, buddy?" I asked, running a hand over his forehead.

"Well, I miss Grandma and Grandpa. I miss my puppy," he began. "And there aren't any boys here to play with."

"Are you lonely?" I said. "You seem to get along with the girls really well."

"I just miss home," he said, eyes heavy and wet.

"Whenever we are together, Sam, that's what home is," I said. "*We* are home."

I pressed my cheek against his.

"Love you, Mom," he murmured. Within minutes, he was asleep.

Sam had always been this way: beset by hard and fast emotions, then, just like that, over it. Boys were easy.

"You know," Jim said when we sat at the kitchen table sharing a beer, "it's okay that the rooms downstairs aren't going to be finished."

"I think you're right," I said. "This is the best spot in the house."

We cataloged the pleasures of our dorm. At all hours, rain or shine, we threw open the windows to the magnificent mountain air. At night, the moon rose over the rooftops of Novi Varoš. There was very little space, but it lived bigger than it was. We all had our own private corner. Zadie snuggled into the children's bed in the room I used as an office. I could see her from the futon, and she slept without moving, exhausted from roving mountain and meadow and running from the drool-soaked jaws of Bobi. Sam commandeered his mattress on the floor near the wood-burning stove, dreaming of home from the largest personal space in the whole joint.

I'd tied up pretty white bunches of yarrow in a window to dry, along with a bowl of yellow *gospina trava* blossoms, which I'd looked up with Jasminka in her herb book and discovered was Saint John's wort. When the flowers dried, I broke them up into small pieces and put them in an empty olive jar that Jim had saved for me, and I drank tea made with them after dinner each night.

I'd pour my tea into a chipped cup and settle in to the wooden rocker beneath the open window to read my Croatian history book and breathe in that perfect air, sometimes with Jim, sometimes alone.

Jim preferred the bench in the front yard at night. He'd stare up at the great black vat of stars, sipping a *gemišt*. Sometimes, he'd head down to Stari Baća to socialize with someone outside his family, just for a change of pace. Both of us were preparing in our own way for a night of sleep in the futon that was as hard as an examining table, with pillows like bags of corn pellets, as the college kids in cars without mufflers raced along Novi Varoš all night.

Sure, we still had complaints. The futon, yeah. The fact that the rank bathroom had a canted roofline that Jim repeatedly smacked his head on. The door on the bathroom also did not latch, and since it was situated directly across from our rolling-door entry, anyone who dared use the toilet did so with the expectation that they'd be in full view of any visitor. The concern about this constipated my husband and me for the entire summer.

Everything about the dorm was spare or makeshift, and learning to live this way was strangely satisfying. The wooden table with four chairs was just big enough. The vintage television was rigged (probably by Karla) for great reception and satellite cable. The Internet was lightning-fast (also Karla). The dorm-sized fridge ensured that we never bought more than we needed. The handle on the stove was broken, so we had to jigger it open with the nubs of plastic that remained, which required a special move like a secret handshake. Jim had to figure out a workaround for its lack of wire racks, and laughed out loud with pleasure the day he discovered that a silver platter in the back of the cupboard doubled perfectly as an oven rack.

At first, Jim was flustered by the minimal kitchenette—odd silverware, a dull kitchen knife so old its wooden handle felt shaggy, one decent bread knife. Three or four pans. A solid stainless-steel boiling pot we'd borrowed from the Stari Baća kitchen. A *džezva*, good for two Nescafés. More saucers than cups. Had we asked Robert and Goranka to outfit us more completely, they would have done so without hesitation. But we didn't. We made one trip to a kitchen store in Rijeka—Jim couldn't bear to be surrounded by so many fresh potatoes without the ability to slice them with a mandoline—but in general we made do.

Yes, we'd gotten pretty cozy in the dorm. Our Victorian house in Des Moines was a needy old girl. No weekend away would go unpunished without days jammed with chores just to keep her moderately clean and functional. Having just a little bit of stuff, and a little bit of space, felt like a luxury in comparison.

"You know," Jim said, passing me the Ožujsko, "you hated cleaning back home. But here, I think you actually like it."

I thought about that for a moment. "Yes, I like cleaning. It clears my head. But I like cleaning when it takes approximately fifteen minutes. Anything more is excessive."

Jim laughed. I passed the beer back to him. We sat in the quiet of the dorm, watching our babies sleep as cool air drifted in from the night, basking once again in the extravagance of simplicity that was uniquely Mrkopalj's.

chapter **thirteen**

Toward the end of July, I began using a more modern method to fill in the blanks that the Book of Names left me with. There's a ton of information on the Internet about genealogy—though most of it could double as a sleep aid. A friend from college was an avid genealogist and sent one particularly useful site that I hadn't heard about back in the States (made even more useful by the fact that is was free, funded by the Ellis Island Foundation). On it, I could look up PDFs of actual ship manifests that listed the 25 million immigrants arriving in New York Harbor at the turn of last century. Its more legible text version was a searchable database, and there I found my people.

Nineteen-year-old Valentin Radošević had declared himself single, "Hungarian," and a resident of "Mrkopat." (I could just imagine a harried-looking scribe set up at some makeshift desk on a harbor dock squinting through tiny round glasses and desperately trying to cipher the answers of the thick-accented immigrants so he might fill out his books properly.) Valentin was delivered on the ship *Graf Waldersee* from Hamburg, Germany. From the look of things, Valentin's ship was delayed: The arrival date had been scratched out from February 17, 1905, to read February 18 instead.

Valentin had sworn by oath that he was not a felon, a polygamist, or an anarchist or deformed in any way, like poor Johann Mave a few lines down, who the "Dr. says conjunctivitis." Valentin had $14.20 in his pocket. He'd never been to prison or an almshouse. He'd traveled with other guys from Mrkopalj, heading to Colfax, Iowa.

This blew my mind. I grew up in Colfax, where my dad's side of the family had lived for as long as anyone could remember. I could recite five generations of Wilson men from Colfax (mainly because their names were Harry, Thomas, Harry, Thomas, and Harold). Valentin Radošević, who'd declared himself a "laborer" on the ship's manifest, started his life in America toiling in the same coal mines as my Wilson grandfathers. Wouldn't it be something if they'd picked at the same sparkling black rock side by side? The thought pleased me to no end, which gives you an idea of how easily entertained one becomes when rummaging through the dusty archives of genealogy.

I searched for Jelena next. I didn't find her quickly. I tried many different spellings, feeling now that I knew that little bespectacled man recording the immigrants' answers at the docks. I imagined he must have grown tired of his work, and was perhaps considering a job in sales, or consulting, as the day-to-day grind of helping shape a nation was really wearing him down.

At long last, I found Jelena Iskra, her name hopelessly and immediately mangled into "Yelena Yskra" from "Mrkopaly, Austria." My great-grandmother was so ungainly at five feet eleven inches tall that the poor woman had been listed as male.

She'd come via Cherbourg, France, on the ship *Philadelphia*, arriving on May 30, 1909, with a boatload of others from Mrkopalj county: Lokve, Sunger, Tuk, Delnice. Jelena traveled with a group heading to Madrid, Iowa, where Valentin had eventually settled as a miner. On the same page as Jelena was an older Starčević man named Anton, perhaps an uncle sent to look out for her.

Jelena listed herself as "farmhand," and her father, Josip Iskra, as her nearest relative. She was twenty, had $100 in her pocket, and was coming to see her "friend," Valentin Radošević. I still couldn't believe they thought she was a man. Maybe she'd told them that herself, out of fear that someone might try to take advantage of her.

I looked out the window onto Novi Varoš as it rolled toward Čelimbaša, a view that never failed to enchant me. What had Valentin and Jelena seen when they looked out their windows before leaving Mrkopalj forever? How had they found the courage to go? The sadness they must have felt as they surveyed their home for the last time made our own emotional dramas seem like surfing on a velvet pillow into a tangerine sunset.

I heard the whirr of a moped and peeked out the window. Outside, the portly Mrkopalj mailman was pulling up the driveway on his government-issued scooter. He'd spoken to Jim and me one day in good English, telling us he couldn't haul the heavy care packages our friends and family had been sending like humanitarian aid drops— peanut butter, ramen noodles, macaroni and cheese, gossip magazines— but we could pick them up at the post office in the afternoons.

No one had been able to tell me why I couldn't find Valentin and Jelena's house numbers. Now I rushed downstairs to ask what the mailman might know about the numbering system.

"Our numbers change three times in past one hundred years," he told me. "What was Number 262 then maybe is not 262 now."

"Book might be wrong, too," he added, turning around and preparing to putt away. "There is more than one Book of Names."

I stopped in my tracks. "More than one Book of Names?"

"*Da*," he said. "There is another."

The duplication of the books had something to do with the Communist government after World War II. I spent the afternoon at Stari Baća reading my history books, seeking clues. As with many things in the village, Mrkopalj's recent history was gnarled with a more ancient one, in which two lines of thought about Croatian identity had caused centuries of bloodshed.

The first kingdom of Croatia was established around the tenth century. Almost immediately, it was occupied by another country. First the Hungarians took over, then the Turks, then the Austrian Habsburgs, then Napoléon, then the Habsburgs again. By the time the 1800s rolled around, smaller Eastern European nations like Croatia (and Serbia and Bosnia) wanted more. Some Slavic people wanted the whole chaotic region to unite under one bigger centralized power.

Others just wanted to strengthen the individual nations they already had, mining rural places like the Gorski Kotar for the Croatian identity, where the same foods and crafts and songs had been passed down for generations. Being Catholic also became a symbol of the Croatian nationality, because it set them apart from their Orthodox and Muslim neighbors. "We are Catholic in Croatia like Israel is Jewish," Helena told me.

At the end of World War I, Serbia was given several Slavic provinces, forming the Kingdom of Serbs, Croats, and Slovenes. Croatia went along with it because it feared Italy and Serbia would soon start snatching up their land. (Italy helped itself to some of the coast and islands anyway.) This was the first *Yugoslavia,* or Land of the South Slavs, and it worked out pretty well for Serbia, as the government was based there, and the Serbian king turned out to be a dictator.

But for Croatia, it was really just more domination. The war had wrecked Croatia's economy, and the people were poor and desperate. The most popular Croatian political party wanted a truly independent Croatia once and for all.

At about the same time, an ultranationalist fringe party called the Ustaše cropped up, led by a guy named Ante Pavelić. Their goal: absolute independence for Croatia, and that meant a racially pure Croatia. Fascist Italy and Nazi Germany knew a needy ally when they saw one and took an interest in the Ustaše, whose leaders had been expelled from Croatia for being bat-shit crazy, among other things.

In 1941, Germany defeated the Royal Yugoslavian Army in about ten days. The Axis Powers first offered the position of Croatian prime minister to the leader of the popular Croatian Peasant Party, but when he declined, Ante Pavelić came out of exile to lead the Independent State of Croatia.

Pavelić's men began forcibly moving or murdering Serbs from the borderlands. Pavelić was Croatia's Hitler equivalent, building concentration camps for Jews, gypsies, Serbs, and political dissenters.

The Ustaše was too roughneck for the vast majority of Croatians. People peeled off to join anti-government rebels, causing a civil war as World War II raged on. A Yugoslavian Communist leader named Josip Broz Tito headed up the movement against the Nazis and Fascists, and by association, the Ustaše. Tito's Partisans fought the bad guys guerilla-style in Croatia, Serbia, Bosnia, Montenegro, and Macedonia, working toward the restoration of a unified Yugoslavia. In the end, the Partisans aligned with Soviet Russia and won. Tito took control of this second attempt at a unified Yugoslavia, and ran it for the next fifty years in a sort of hybrid of communism, socialism, and capitalism—a "middle way" between East and West.

Tito was a big personality, hanging out with famous people like Eleanor Roosevelt and Elizabeth Taylor. He was promiscuous, married several times (first to a fourteen-year-old Russian girl), and carried on juicy affairs. Tito was also a badass. When Stalin repeatedly tried to assassinate him, Tito wrote him a note:

Stop sending people to kill me. We've already captured five of them, one of them with a bomb and another with a rifle . . . If you don't stop sending killers, I'll send one to Moscow, and I won't have to send a second.

Marshal Tito also rebuilt Yugoslavia. He gave people jobs. His young Communist worker crews boosted infrastructure and created fantastic tourist sites that remain today. But in those early years following World War II, Tito's ranks of secret police and informers were also brutal. People who spoke against the government simply disappeared.

You could practice Catholicism, but the government didn't like it. Several prominent priests had sided with the Ustaše. Tito executed some, jailed others. The government confiscated church property. This was the connection to the Book of Names. I called Helena to ask about it.

She told me that indeed Communist secret police had raided Mrkopalj and destroyed village records. In the 1940s, as protection, the clergy from Our Lady of Seven Sorrows made copies of the Book of Names and hid them throughout the village.

That was as far as I got in my research. Stefanija, the summer girl, was pouring me a cup of tea when the Brown Bear rushed in.

Robert spoke hastily, winded from excitement. He grabbed a beer from the cooler and guzzled half of it. Jim had told him about my conversation with the mailman, and Robert knew a retired municipal employee who not only had a hidden copy of the Book of Names, but remembered the old house numbers.

"We go to house of man with another Big Book! Jim drive me!" He paused to catch his breath. "We come, ten minutes!" Then he left.

Stefanija stood behind the bar, looking at me, eyebrows raised.

I just shook my head. "It's a long story," I said.

"And very dramatic," Stefanija agreed.

I packed my computer and notebooks and watched patiently through the red-checked curtains of Stari Baća, waiting for Jim and Robert. And perhaps another man. Who knew? These bewildering Mrkopalj invitations had become the norm. I just went limp in the face of them now, waiting to be acted upon by outside forces. Eventually, Jim and Robert pulled up in the Peugeot and beeped the horn twice, and I joined them.

We drove maybe a block up the street to the house of Zdravko Skender, a Mrkopalj municipal employee for thirty-six years during Communist times who knew the original house-numbering system. As we crossed the street, I could see Skender on a bench in a garden, sitting upright with his hands on his knees, watching traffic go by with his wife. He was old and angular, with bottle-thick glasses. By the time we'd gotten to his front door, he and his wife were up and inside the house, welcoming us in.

There was a faint nervousness in the air. Jim asked if he could take photographs. Skender said no. Skender's wife siphoned me off from the group, and we sat at her kitchen table and watched the men discuss our situation in the living room.

While Robert explained that I was seeking the houses of my ancestors and we would like to see his Book of Names, Skender sat stone-faced and unmoving on his slipcovered couch.

Robert looked over at Jim, filling the silence with nervous rapid-fire words. "This book is *original book*," he said to us with gravity.

Skender had hidden it all these years, safe from the government that employed him, the government that made people disappear if they did things like hide books.

Like the Owl, Skender was intensely protective of the book. I finally understood why.

Skender spoke, indicating my camera and tape recorder. Robert appeared to reassure him that Jim and I were just a couple of American idiots in search of family. We were not in Skender's home for surveillance purposes. I was Mrkopaljci. I could be trusted. To a man who'd spent much of his career protecting public records from destruction, this seemed like a very important point to make.

At least I *hoped* that was the point Robert was making. I longed to hear firsthand Skender's reluctance and Robert's reasoning, but Robert didn't translate. I don't know if this was forgetfulness or a basic lack of language skills. If it was the latter, Robert would never own up to it. He was proud of his role as our village guide.

All this time, Skender leveled a steady Croatian stare at me as I hung back in the kitchen with his wife. So I stared at Skender's wife, because she had a very friendly face, and it made me less nervous. We smiled at each other. Robert fidgeted, hitched up his Capri pants, and cleared his throat a few times. Jim, rattled himself, wandered over toward Robert and hovered behind him, as if seeking protection.

At long last, Skender slapped his hands on his knees. He got up. He crossed the living room to a closet. From deep within, he drew out an oversized rectangular Book of Names, bound in striped green cloth and edged in brown leather. The book didn't look older than the one at the church. Probably Robert had gotten this detail wrong.

Still, I imagined the book when it had first been painstakingly copied out, perhaps by Skender himself. I wondered about its journey to the darkest corner of Skender's house. Perhaps it had been stuffed into a nondescript bag, maybe a potato sack, like the ones I saw beyond open cellar doors in the houses of Mrkopalj, then tossed into the back of an ox cart as if it was just another bit of daily cargo, like hay or bolts of cloth or a mountain of cabbages. Perhaps, upon reaching its destination, the potato sack was hefted into the kitchen of the house, hauled carefully to the cellar by the faithful matriarch of a good Mrkopalj family. Perhaps she stowed the copy of the Book of Names in a hole in the floor, where she also hid extra milk money for the son she prayed would one day go to America to ease the burden on the house and send home a few dollars from the coal mines. There was probably a chain of Mrkopalj people who had risked their lives to keep this book—none of whom I would see or know—until it ended up in the very ordinary surroundings of Zdravko Skender's closet.

Skender hefted this Book of Names onto the couch, then planted himself on an ottoman in front of it. He ran his hands over the cover for a few seconds then opened it. Jim and Robert and I crowded in. The book was tidier and more uniform than the one I'd seen in the church: definitely a copy. Skender licked a finger and paged through. He raised his eyebrows under his glasses and quickly found each of my family's pages, as if he had the thing memorized.

He said that, according to the book, Valentin's House No. 262 was now House No. 48 on Novi Varoš. Did Robert know where this was?

"Yes," Robert assured him. "It is very near to my house."

We'd first see a yellow cottage that was slightly set back from the street, Skender told us. Directly behind it was another house, hidden from casual view, wooden in structure. This hidden structure was the one we were looking for.

Jelena's house, he said, was just a few houses from where we stood.

Jim and I exchanged wide-eyed "No way!" looks.

I was so happy I wanted to hug Zdravko Skender. This, I knew, would not go over well. Instead, I held out my notebook and asked him to write the correct spelling of his name. Robert translated incorrectly, saying instead that I wanted Skender's autograph. It worked out all right, as signing an autograph seemed to please Skender, as if he'd been recognized for being such a discreet keeper of the book, and he had been.

He signed with a flourish. It read, simply, "Skender."

When we'd finished, his wife poured shots of pelinkovac, an herbal Croatian liquor made with wormwood that tasted like earwax.

"*Živjeli!*" we toasted in unison, Skender still looking only mildly amused by our presence. We drank quickly and left, despite urgent pleas from Skender's wife to stick around and do a few more shots. We left them waving on the front steps, a Balkan version of Grant Wood's *American Gothic*, as we piled into the Peugeot like clowns.

Robert, intrigued by how close my great-grandfather had lived to his own great-grandparents, wanted to see Valentin's house first. So Jim executed a tidy three-point turn and raced toward Novi Varoš—a drive that took approximately thirty-seven seconds. As we passed 12 Novi Varoš, Robert, a veteran of ten Croatian rock bands and gifted with a flair for the dramatic, rolled down his window and counted down houses to Valentin's.

"Von! Twoo! Tree! Stop!"

Jim stopped the car.

"No, wait!" Robert said. He waved his hand. "Keep going."

Jim started driving again.

Robert pointed out the houses with dramatic juts of his finger. "Fore! Fie-eev! Seex! Stop!"

Jim stopped.

Robert shook his head. "No, sorry. Go on."

Jim pealed out.

"Okay! Say-van! Now stop!"

Jim slammed on the brakes and we all heaved forward. When Newton's first law of motion had finished with us, we sat in silence.

"Now out!" Robert commanded. Three car doors opened in unison, and we emptied into the street.

We stood before a set-back cottage of faded yellow stucco, just seven houses from where we lived with the Starčević family. Its windows were broken, curtains drawn, lawn overgrown. I'd passed this abandoned place every morning on my walks to Tuk, sometimes stopping to admire its soft shade of paint against worn dove-gray doors closed to the bustle of earthly beings.

"Look here," Robert said, pointing.

We picked through the knee-high grass. Nailed under an eave on a heavy wooden beam was a rusted metal number that read 48. And next to it another number was nailed up, the same one we'd seen in the Book of Names: 262.

As Skender had instructed, we walked behind this first house. Indeed, a second stood almost flush against it, camouflaged by a riot of weedy overgrowth. This, Skender had indicated, was the house of my great-grandfather's family.

"Is born, Valentin Radošević," Robert presented with a flourish.

The old wooden house stood in shadow and sagged against the weight of time. The front appeared to be living quarters, and the back a typical Mrkopalj house barn. A rickety chimney rose from orange terra-cotta shingles, slowly disintegrating against wind and weather. I could almost see Valentin Radošević gazing out the broken six-paned windows, his dream of faraway places eventually leading to me.

I walked toward the place: this physical incarnation of the old family I had crossed an ocean to meet. My steps were tentative in the scrub and brush shrouding it. Carefully I toed closer, as if charging forward might wake the dead. I woke them anyway. When I peeked past the tattered roll-down shades I saw life—many lives—stirring in the shadows.

Though rotted and caved in over time, each room was still strangely intact. Plaster chunks had fallen from the ceiling as if there'd been an explosion inside. An air of hasty abandonment permeated the house, a feeling of action and of flight. No one had bothered to tidy the bed before walking out for the last time, leaving only a slightly rumpled blanket and a faintly dented pillow.

Jim and I barely spoke as we drifted from window to window. Surprisingly, neither did Robert. Undulating walls shed blue toile and hand-painted pink flowered wallpaper. Lace curtains still billowed in

the breeze. Against these feminine touches were sudden stabs of violence: a tall dresser—drawers open and doors askew—run through
with a long, sharp stick like a javelin. Great tufts of gray-brown fi-
brous stuffing erupting from a couch, as if an animal with sharp
claws had been digging inside of it.

Heavy work shirts and jackets hung on a row of hooks, like a line
of ghostly farmhands in rigid formation. On the wall was a picture of
Jesus and the disciples—a smaller version of one I'd seen in the Owl's
residence. A light fixture sagged from the broken ceiling. Tiny white
porcelain doves dangled from its pull string, spinning slow rotations
in the slight cross-draft, turning and twisting in a constant state of
movement, never really going anywhere.

My eyes followed along one wall and met those of a woman staring back at me. In her hands she held a bouquet of peonies and roses.
An elegant eyebrow arched under the wave of dark hair across her
high forehead. Though only a framed portrait in a thick net of cob-
webs, her eyes peered out from beyond, dark and alive.

I stepped away from the window. Without a doubt, I felt a presence in this house. It didn't take much imagination to see women
and men in housedresses and overalls moving through the rooms
as they had a century ago. I glanced at Jim, who was shooting photos through broken windows. I sensed his unease by instinct—
when Jim wasn't sure of something in Mrkopalj, he reached for the
camera.

I walked to the pasture where the barn was collapsing. The doors
to the haymow swayed open like old teeth. A chicken clucked in the
next yard.

Robert came up behind me. "Long ago, is first neighbors of this
house," he said, indicating the tidy property next door, a small home-
stead with well-kept outbuildings and terra-cotta roof tile. The difference between the land of this family and the abandoned property
of House No. 262 was vast. "Name of man is Dražen Horaček."

I'd also noticed this place on my walks to Tuk. The man Robert
called Dražen was among the hardworking contingency of Mrkopalj.

In church, I'd seen him with a big family that included his elderly mother. He was a farmer and a carpenter like Mario. I rarely saw him in a bar.

A noisy bird chattered at me from Dražen's apple trees. Robert and I walked back to where Jim was photographing the kitchen. A beat-up collection of chairs surrounded a simple square table covered by a pink poppy tablecloth. An old-fashioned scale topped the cupboard that shared a wall with a carpenter's bench. I wondered if Valentin's father had built the kitchen table on that workbench. Wondered if his sisters weighed out sheep's-milk cheese to sell on that scale.

Robert walked over to talk with another neighbor, who reported that there were five owners of this property, spread all over Croatia. The family hadn't known how to divide it and so it sat useless in a village where land was the only commodity.

I'd seen similarly abandoned houses around Mrkopalj. Dishes still stacked in collapsing cupboards, rusty razors on sinks, wooden cabinets sinking slowly through softening floors. Houses were passed down through the generations, but the work was in the city. Those who couldn't afford to stay left the houses to decay, and they slowly transformed from homes into archeological digs.

I pressed my hand flat against the side of the wooden house, asking Time to play back the reel of Valentin's departure as he walked down Novi Varoš. Did he look back? Did he understand that he was leaving forever? Perhaps his mother had waved from the doorstep. Maybe Jelena was there, too, tall as a windmill, wondering if she'd ever see her "friend" again. It must have been excruciating for all of them. It had been excruciating for us, and our journey was finite. I couldn't know his path. But I knew where he'd ended up, and I now knew where he'd started from.

chapter **fourteen**

Robert and Jim stood at a distance as I paid my respects to Valentin Radošević.

"Let's find Jelena's house," I said when I finally joined them.

We piled back into the Peugeot and Jim retraced the path we'd driven an hour before, past Stari Baća, past Skender's place. We came to a brand-new house still under construction, a spare square of bricks awaiting a final coat of plaster and paint.

"My friend lives here," Robert realized. He called to ask what the old address had been before the house had been demolished to make way for a new one. The friend said it would remain as it had always been—House No. 40.

Jelena Iskra's home was gone. Leveled.

"Let's have a look around anyway," Jim suggested.

We crossed the mud and dirt of the construction site. The new house promised to be a handsome country cottage. Jelena's home may have been destroyed, but this land was once again a useful thing. Though I mourned the loss of a tangible clue to my great-grandmother's life, it was certainly Mrkopalj's gain not to have another abandoned place.

In the backyard grew a thick and twisted apple tree, so old it had probably stood watch as Jelena packed her bags for America. I moved under it and looked out over the moor at which Jelena had probably gazed a thousand times. It was a relatively plain view in a village that specialized in showstoppers. Just a few bumps in a carpet of grass, breaking into a field, then mountains. But it was *her* view. I took it in for a long time.

How had Valentin and Jelena told their parents they were leaving? How had their parents taken it? Petar and Katarina Radošević. Josip and Marija Iskra. I said the names aloud. Both had made just as great a sacrifice as my great-grandparents. They'd taught their children strength, then sent them on their way. The selflessness of parenthood overwhelmed me.

I imagined the day I would tell Sam and Zadie good-bye. Maybe they'd be packing for college. Maybe they'd be piling into a beater car headed for the big city, just to live the life for a while. I could only hope my kids would leap so energetically into the future. It hadn't been silly to bring them all this way. And it was okay that they were uncomfortable sometimes, or didn't get what they wanted, or lived in conditions that weren't perfect. They were learning, as I was learning, and together we were fine examples for each other. Who knew how long our togetherness would last. Children were born to leave. Parents were born to make sure they were prepared when they did.

Jim kicked through demolition rubble. He reached down and held something up: an old kitchen tile, white with blue daisies painted on. He brought it to me.

"This is crazed," he said, pointing to the minuscule cracks in the glaze. He handed it to me. "This is old. There's concrete on the back. I would bet a lot of money that it's original."

I held up the tile, examined it, then turned to look at my husband. "You're a good man, Jim Hoff," I said.

"Until I stay at Stari Baća too long," Jim said. "Then you'll think I suck again."

"So don't stay at Stari Baća too long," I said. "Problem solved. Do I have to do all the thinking in this family?"

Jim rolled his eyes, and we headed back to the rubble to find more tiles. I looked out at the moor and thought of Jelena Iskra, marveling at the bravery of my great-grandmother.

As we walked off the lot, I noticed something I hadn't seen on my way in. Behind the new house, atop the rubble of Jelena Iskra's family home, a fountain of wildflowers sprouted with abandon.

That night, Jim and I wandered downstairs to ask Robert if we could take the girls for pizza in Delnice. He was well into the halp-

halp, lounging in the rooms on the second floor that, though it was nearing the end of July, were still not even close to finished.

Mario was over. They were parsing our discoveries, and Jim ran upstairs to grab the camera and show them the pictures we'd taken.

"Jennifer is new Mrkopaljci!" Robert toasted me.

I felt proud amid the playful cheer from the room. I hadn't really done much to deserve it, but it felt good anyway.

"I can't believe Valentin's family was living seven houses away from yours," I said to Robert. "That's just nuts."

"I count each house!" Robert said. "Say-van houses! Is very specifical number."

"It's a lucky number," Jim noted.

"You are sad today that house of Jelena is no more," Robert said. He translated this to Mario, who nodded gravely and patted my leg.

Jim sat down and scrolled through the shots on the camera. Mario pointed out an image of the woodworking bench in Valentin's old house. "Is *Hobelbank*," he said. "German word."

We theorized in Croglish about who might have lived there before and how they'd left. How weird that it appeared so hastily abandoned. And were Robert and I really cousins? Whoa.

Cuculić dropped in, listened to the talk for a few minutes, and noted that his mother had twenty-one brothers and sisters. "Maybe *we* are cousins," he told me. "Anything is possible in Mrkopalj."

I told him I was pretty sure this could not be true.

Cuculić pointed his chin toward Mario. "Mario's mother is the cousin of my mother," he said, shoving his hands into his khaki pockets. "Mario and I could be—"

At this, Mario cut him off. "*Neh!*" Mario said firmly and loudly, hands jerking out flat in front of him. "*Ništa!*"

Everybody laughed. Jim volunteered that he very well could be Cuculić's cousin, too. Cuculić slapped the air in front of him, emitting a disgusted "*Eh!*" at all of us.

I was starting to get the picture that Cuculić was universally picked on. I marveled at a realization: I felt for the guy. I was curious about him. He was like the troubled cousin who always hangs back at holidays, looking uncomfortable, trying to act natural.

I surveyed the room of people I hadn't known a month before laughing and speaking in animated tones about the search for my ancestors in their village. I think everyone had wondered if our digging around Mrkopalj was sincere, if the Americans really cared. When both of us were excited nearly to tears about Valentin's and Jelena's houses, it seemed to stir something in our Mrkopalj friends. They were excited with us.

The enthusiasm continued. Mario told Jasminka and his mother, Ana Fak, that I'd been sad about Jelena's house. Jasminka and Ana wanted to give me something that my great-grandmother might have given me, had I known her.

On a Friday night in late July, they taught me about the herbs and *ćaj* of Mrkopalj. The flowers and leaves of the village were often augmented with dried herbs sold in the village *ljekarna*, or pharmacy, a homeopathic version of the drugstores back in the States. I'd gone to the *ljekarna* in Delnice for anxiety constipation brought on by the broken door handle in the dorm bathroom, and they gave me something like a bale of hay in pellet form. It worked pretty well.

Ana Fak and I walked through the meadow flowers. I'd liked Ana since the first morning I choked down mealy Turkish coffee at her family's picnic table. Ana moved slowly, even when approached by something wild and unruly, like Thor, to whom she simply reached a hand downward, calming him instantly. Ana Fak was big-boned but soft, with a low, raspy voice and smooth, tan skin. Like me, she was chilly at all times. I could feel a cool breeze in the desert, and wore a scarf year-round. So did Ana. I'd see her puttering in the yard in a navy-blue quilted vest even as the last days of July ticked off the calendar. I admired such boldfaced declarations of iciness.

Plus, she smelled like my grandma Kate. I took it as a sign from Grandma Kate herself that Ana began, early on, to put her hands on me when we'd greet each other. I'd stop on my morning walk to tell her *dobro jutro,* and she'd squeeze my arm or firmly pat my cheek, laugh her deep chortle, and talk to me slowly and loudly in Croatian.

Ana and I walked through the tall grass, swaddled in sweaters against the seventy-degree weather, the fields flaunting a palette of purple, gold, and green. The forested mounds of Mrkopalj's mountains rose from the plains as Ana guided me to wild thyme or thistle or mint, leading my hand to each plant, showing me how it felt and how to pluck a flower or a leaf. I tried to take notes, but the Croatian plant names were unspellably complicated. I would retain none of it except her touch and her kindness, which were healing in their own right.

Though one plant did require my full attention. I asked about a bristly green monster whose leaves caused terrible itching for hours. I pantomimed the desperate scratching of skin. She leveled her gaze at me, this silly lost American who didn't even know her *bazga* from her *loginja*. A rumbly laugh rose from her chest.

"*Kopriva?*" Ana wondered aloud. She scanned the field, then drifted to a patch of pointy, serrated leaves that just *looked* mean. I nodded and she named it again: "*Kopriva.*"

"Whatever it is, I don't like it," I grumbled. "*Neh kopriva.*"

Ana patted my back and we walked on. She began picking long stalks of yarrow, and we worked until we had a fat bouquet studded with its tiny white flowers. When Ana felt we'd gathered enough, we gravitated back to Jasminka, who waited at the picnic table, surrounded by tins and jars, a Croatian-English dictionary, and a hardbound herbal-medicine book: *Domaće Ljekovito Bilje*. Ana left us because I pulled out my camera, and Ana Fak deserted every situation in which a camera was involved.

Free of housework for the day, Jasminka looked about twenty years younger than the first time I'd seen her. In her hardworking home, Jasminka's idea of downtime was washing the family vehicles.

"You look so pretty sitting there." I smiled, easing down next to her.

She patted her chin-length brown hair. "Is new color," she said.

When we first arrived in Mrkopalj, Jasminka could speak little of the English she'd learned in school decades ago. But the language came back to her as we spent more time together, and we could almost talk in complete sentences now, between my Croatian and her English.

She told me that she and Mario had known each other all their lives, then one day skiing on Čelimbaša with friends, it was as if they were seeing each other for the very first time. "Electricity!" Jasminka winked at me.

Of course this was how love happened in a small village. I smiled at the idea of it. I wondered if it had happened this way for Valentin and Jelena. That magical moment, when someone went from being just another kid at school to someone who inspired a great current through your heart. Jasminka's son Stjepan was experiencing that with Stefanija's sister, Marija. They'd known each other since childhood, and then suddenly, "electricity," and they were cooing in front of the fireplace at Stari Baća.

I pointed at a jar of brown mucky syrup. I hoped I would not be asked to drink it.

"Is *crnogorica*," Jasminka explained. In spring, she cooked tender sprigs of spruce or juniper with honey and lemon, which helped with a cough or the flu. She handed me the jar. "You will need in winter."

Jasminka paged through her book, translating the names of the flowers Ana and I had seen in the meadow. Jasminka patted my bouquet of *stolisnik* or yarrow. It eased period cramps. Ana Fak wanted to make sure I had plenty *stolisnik*.

Jasminka held up a wad of *metvica*, or dried mint. Also good for digestion and cramps, and as an antiseptic. Mint tea would wake me up when I was tired at my desk, she said. Leaves of *borovnica*, or blueberry, would raise immunity. I should take a bath in dried *vrkuta*—lady's mantle—when I suffered pretty much any feminine complaint. *Majčina dušica*, or wild thyme ("Only wild, not in store," said Jasminka), helped a nonproductive cough. She pointed to a picture of *slakovina* and I recognized the invasive binding vine from my gardens back home: morning glory.

"Wraps around," Jasminka described, making the motion with two hands.

"Yes!" I said. "Chokes!"

"Is good for fever," she said.

Jasminka filled a tin with herbs, mixing a blend of the yarrow, Saint John's wort, and mint. "Tea for you," she said, pushing it toward me.

Ana Fak brought out *povitica*, a nut-roll pastry, fresh from the oven. Sister Paula made *povitica* for holidays when I was a kid. But Sister Paula's dry, bland mound of flour tasted nothing like the moist, nutty goodness that Ana Fak placed before me.

"I know this food!" I said excitedly to Jasminka and Ana. "I remember this!"

"Is taking three hours to make," Jasminka said. "Mix, roll, rise. Mix, roll, rise. Even chopping the nuts!"

"Can you teach me?" I asked Ana. "Please?"

Ana Fak looked with sympathy at me, the returning daughter of Mrkopalj who'd been taught nothing useful in her life. She spoke to Jasminka.

"She will teach," Jasminka said. "Ana say you buy butter, milk, flour, walnuts."

Then Ana headed across the street to Pavice's for the news of the day. Pavice was a tremendous gossip. One of the summer girls had broken up with her boyfriend, and within an hour, before her own mother even knew, Pavice called for details. I watched Ana park it on a tree stump outside Pavice's summer kitchen and light up a smoke.

"We finish today with čaj škola," Jasminka announced. "Now you know everything!"

I laughed. "It's about time someone told me that," I said. "Thank you."

"Is no thanking," Jasminka said. "I like."

"Me, too," I said.

"You are liking Mrkopalj," she said as we hugged good-bye. "All Mrkopalj is like family."

Then she leaned forward and chucked me in the stomach with her elbow. "Addams Family!"

I gathered my things and crossed the street to Pavice and Ana Fak. Ana was rolling her eyes and making circular hand gestures as if to indicate something taking a very long time. I guessed she was complaining about having to teach me the epic recipe of *povitica*. This was really busting up Pavice, whose humor was along the lines of the Three Stooges'. She guffawed and slapped me on the leg and Ana just smiled with her eyes, watching me, smoking, as if it was good to be needed all the same.

"Yenny!" Pavice yelled. "Yenny, *dal ti voliš koprivu?*" Pavice started haw-hawing again, slapping her own knees now. Did I like *kopriva*? Sort of like asking someone: Do you like a kick in the pants?

"*Neh, kopriva!*" I shook my head.

Jasminka joined us and looked up the English word for *kopriva*: nettles. Women with circulation problems once beat their legs with *kopriva* to improve the blood flow. Pavice said this was an old Bosnian cure. Jasminka added that *kopriva* was actually good to eat in springtime, when you could pick the young leaves and fry them with potatoes.

"You people have big problems if you think nettles are good for you," I said, rising from my stump, laughing with the ladies. I headed back to the dorm, where Jim was cooking dinner, which would not have anything ridiculous like nettles in it.

As I crossed the yard, my skin prickled with the awareness that I was being watched. I looked around and caught a glimpse of the old woman Manda, wife of Viktor, looking out her window. I'd seen Manda out picking *gospina trava* on my first full day in Mrkopalj; I'd rarely seen her again. As far as I could tell, Manda hardly left the house.

Yet there she was, watching. I raised a hand and waved to her. Manda waved back, then disappeared behind the curtain, joining the ranks of the mysteries of Mrkopalj that now included hidden copies of the Book of Names, the foreboding air of Valentin's house, the use of nettles as a skin bracer, and the fact that a guy like Cuculić could hold one of the most important jobs in town.

chapter **fifteen**

In a dying village where church was everything and few people had babies, Helena and Paul invited us to their new daughter Magda's baptism on the last Saturday of July. It was a great honor.

Robert asked if we'd take his girls. Goranka was working at the tollbooth, and he would be in Stari Baća. All seven of us packed into the Peugeot, breaking every child-safety law on the books, and drove to the church in Sunger.

We pulled into the parking lot, the one with the bar, and parked.

Jim looked over at me. "Remember the first time we were here?"

I did remember. "It wasn't even a month ago," I said as the kids piled out.

"It feels like a year," Jim said.

Our short time in Mrkopalj had been intense. We'd gone from feeling like foreigners to feeling like family in a matter of weeks. We had Robert to thank for that. Without the Brown Bear vouching for us, we never would have had such instant access. After the service, Helena even insisted that we join in the family portrait. To this day, somewhere in Mrkopalj, there are four bewildered Americans peeking out from the pages of the photo album of one little girl's baptism.

The best part came at the end: the after-party at Helena and Paul's house. They'd crammed wooden tables and benches into their living room and the makeshift layout gave the festivities a raucous air. We were greeted by cousins at the door handing out Dixie cups of *rakija*. Sam and Zadie flowed into a river of kids.

The tables were piled with plates of lamb placed every few feet, along with bowls of cucumber-and-tomato salad dressed in oil and vinegar and giant baskets of crusty bread made by Paul's mother, Pavla. Pavla slid a big plate of fresh green onions in front of me, indicating with a proud wink that these were hers, as she was one of the most prolific gardeners in the county. Pavla's onions were so robust they probably could have gotten up and walked to my plate themselves. She showed me how to eat like a real Mrkopaljci: pinching the lamb with bread and following each bite with a chomp of green-onion chaser. Pavla and I cleared a whole platter of this melty, fatty goodness until I was so full I only had room for more *rakija,* a bottle of which sat in the center of the table, the label written out by hand, among so many pitchers of wine and beer.

I introduced myself to Helena's dad a few seats away. *"Moja ime je* Jennifer Wilson," I said.

He shook my hand, his distinct voice like that of the martian in Warner Brothers cartoons. "Valentin Radošević," he answered.

I halted my *rakija* shot in midair. I had forgotten Helena's maiden name. "That is the name of my great-grandfather," I began to explain incredulously, but just then someone handed him a guitar, and Paul took up his *tamburitza.*

Everyone sang and clapped and, after enough booze, danced. We pushed aside the tables and hopped and twirled and hollered. Helena peered into Jim's camera, coquettish as Marilyn Monroe, and gushed: "Hell-o, America!"

Every Croatian village has its own song. That night, Helena's family sang Mrkopalj's. "Malo po Malo," or "Little by Little," had been the village anthem for more than a century. We sang it well into the night, a disheveled bunch celebrating love and family and home.

The next morning, we would rise and attend church, where the Owl would introduce the new priest, all *Thorn Birds* young and dashing in Italian leather shoes. We would drive for our weekly coastal adventure to the seaside town of Čižići (roughly, CHIZH-uh-shee), where we'd spread the black, metallic-smelling muck of its famous therapeutic mud beach all over our bodies before diving into seawater shallow enough that even Zadie could play safely. Afterward, we would drive up the mountain to eat handmade *šurlice* noodles near the church in Dobrinj while feral cats crowded around for handouts. But in the shallows of Čižići, I back-floated while the kids played around me. Fully submerged but for my face, I hummed the tune of "Malo po Malo" as the mud rinsed from my body and bloomed into the clear Adriatic Sea.

Viva! Viva!
Our mountain countryside!
Little by little,
Little by little,
Little by little,
I will come to you.

These were our days of becoming enmeshed in the life of the village. Jim even began walking with me to Tuk.

On a typical morning, we woke when we felt like it, usually at eight, sometimes nine. Jim assembled breakfast—cereal, drinkable yogurt, coffee, juice, and fistfuls of wild mountain blueberries now purchased weekly from Aziz. After we ate breakfast, we'd tidy up the dishes and assign the kids their morning cleaning jobs. Sam swept. Zadie made beds. We allowed Sam to run to the Konzum for milk or other staples, a very grown-up task that he loved, especially when the Konzum ladies, ice-cold to most customers, gave him suckers for his trouble. Once they had completed their work, the kids could watch TV.

Now both Jim and I would put on our exercise clothes and walk to Tuk, leaving Sam and Zadie alone for the first time in their lives. But first Jim would make them recite the order in which they'd go to the neighbors for help, should problems arise.

"Where do you go if you have trouble?" he'd ask, crouching to meet their eyes.

"First Mario, then Pavice," Sam would answer. "If no one else is around, Robert."

Jim would hand Sam one of the cell phones. Sam would make a practice call.

Then we'd leave.

Our forty-five-minute walk was the kids' favorite time of day. They'd literally shoo us out the door. Only once did we have a problem. They'd argued and Sam ended up crying. Robert narced them off the minute we got back from Tuk. Thus, Sam and Zadie learned the valuable lesson that if you're going to fight, be quiet about it so you don't alert the neighbors.

Jim and I talked the entire time we walked, synthesizing the events of our lives in Mrkopalj and making plans for the month of travel in Europe before we settled in to Rovinj for winter. It was the closest thing to intimacy we had in Mrkopalj, not having our own bedroom or even locks on our door, the lack of which was blossoming into our neighbors' favorite joke.

"Oh, hey, Jeem," Robert might begin. "When rooms are finished, you have bed, and door . . . and your wife! Is a very good situation, eh?"

"Maybe you go to Rovinj for to be alone with Jim," Jasminka wiggled her eyebrows.

Then everyone would haw-haw-haw, and our neighbors would dissolve into racy humor, at which time I felt relieved to not know much Croatian and therefore to be considered exempt from the conversation— a state of being I was finding quite peaceful.

Jim loved the walk to Tuk as much as I did, with the jangle of cowbells in the distance and the strong breeze running through the valley to dry our sweat. Jim said the mountains reminded him of the opening credits of *M*A*S*H*, and I think he half expected choppers to crest the ridgeline at any moment. As it was, the only thing he had to fear was being attacked by the animals we passed, none of which had ever bothered me. One house had a guard goose that screamed in outrage when Jim walked by. Its owner looked and dressed like Fidel Castro, but he always waved at us because he was a friend of Josip and Pavice's. Dogs displayed varying stages of viciousness. One wiry salt-and-pepper mutt barked nonstop at Jim, throwing his body against the wrought-iron fence that contained him. We later learned that this dog was from a strain of stringy mutt bred by Stefanija's family, and he was named Bobi, as were most dogs in Mrkopalj.

Tuk looks a lot like Mrkopalj, except that the skyline is dominated by an east-facing Orthodox church spire instead of a Catholic steeple. People told me Tuk was populated by Orthodox Serbs who'd fled from the Turks in the sixteenth century.

We'd turn around at Tuk and jog home to our kids, who were lying inert in front of a television behind a door that did not lock. I'd shower and head to Stari Baća to write. Jim would settle in to a day of hanging out, steeping in the sweet boredom of being entirely absent from the workaday life. His favorite yard buddy, of course, was Robert.

Jim and Robert sat side by side for long stretches of day in red plastic lawn chairs, legs crossed, watching the kids play, sometimes sipping beers, idly chatting like two old geezers in the park. Jim's favorite game was making Robert recite the names of all the bands he'd been in. Jim liked hearing the band names partly because Robert was always verging on tipsy, and recalling twenty-seven years of history put him into a state of great agitation. He also liked it because Robert's band names were awesome.

On the first day of August, I sat with Jim after our morning walk as he asked Robert the band question for probably the tenth time since we'd come to Mrkopalj.

"First band: Emotion," Robert began. Emotion made its debut in 1982, when he switched from *tamburitza* to bass and began riffing with the neighbor boys, Ratko on synthesizer and Butzo on drums. Their first gig was in the Mrkopalj cultural center, across the street from the tourism office.

"Is be good," Robert said.

"What kind of music did you play?" I asked.

"Only rock 'n' roll," Robert said. "Nothing else. Deep Purple 'Smoke on the Water.' Rolling Stones 'Satisfaction.' Eric Clapton 'Layla.'"

Jim threw his head back and busted out some White Snake. "In the still of the night!"

Robert looked at him, nonplussed.

"And domestic rock 'n' roll. We got our own songs, but they never let us to the studio," Robert said.

"Like, what was the best one?" I asked.

"I write 'Bijele Stijene,'" Robert said. "Is about White Rocks, a mountain park near here. And another: 'I Like Mrkopalj.' Text is very provocative because we are teasing every person in the place. But the song about White Rocks is great."

"Can you sing me the lyrics?" I asked.

"No," Robert answered plainly.

After Emotion came Arch, which included Stari Baća regular Frankie, a sweet guy with facial rosacea whose wife had left him long ago. Frankie used to drink *gemišt* with the best of them, but he had switched to red wine, shocking everyone. This is how people came to know that Frankie actually *dated*, unlike other men in Mrkopalj whose wives had left them. The switch to red wine was Frankie's signal that he was seeing someone; the guy knew how to clean things up for the courting ritual. Frankie beat incessantly on the bar at Stari Baća, which is how I knew he'd replaced Butzo on drums.

Arch was a punk trio that played every Saturday in Sunger, perhaps in the bar in the church parking lot.

Robert's next band was simply called White Rocks, like his favorite song of the same title. After that, it was Amadeus, also with Frankie.

Next came M.I.D.I. Band.

"What does that stand for?" I asked. Jim leaned in. This was his favorite part.

"Musical Interface Digital Instruments," Robert fired off. "Very good band. Is very interesting onstage. Is easier to get some girls."

Then Robert got a little serious. "Everything is easier then."

"Okay, so after M.I.D.I. Band, then what?" Jim urged him.

"Next is Cro Voice," Robert lit a cigarette. "Then I have Miloš and the Guys. After this, there is Winch."

"Miloš and the Guys!" Jim clapped. "It's awesome because there was no Miloš!"

Robert rolled his eyes over to Jim, then back to me.

"We play in Istria, mostly," he said. "Tourist towns. We put our hair long. Like Rolling Stones. Sometimes we take off all our clothes or maybe just some part. We thought it was very stupid and funny to piss on the stage."

Jim's head lolled back and he sat that way for a long time, smiling.

Robert said that once, when he and his bandmates were living in an apartment in Istria, they grew pot plants on their balcony. The old neighbors, not recognizing the stuff, watered the marijuana for the boys when they were out on tour. When the band finally harvested the crop, the neighbors mentioned in passing what a pity it was that these pretty plants had been stolen from them.

In 1997, somebody slammed a door on Robert's hand, severing three fingers, only two of which were put back on properly. A surgeon in Rijeka reattached the third one sideways. That 33.3 percent margin of error ended Robert's career as a bass guitar player.

This was Jim's version of playground talk. It beat the heck out of "Which preschool does your kid go to?" or "Do you think this is pink-eye?" and was the high point of Jim's days. He struggled with the typical stay-at-home parent drama—lots of stress, little recognition, the interminable drag of time. But the kids were growing up before our eyes in Mrkopalj. We knew that both our stay-at-home lives would morph into fond memory when Sam and Zadie were grown. I left Robert and Jim to argue about who was better, White Snake or Bon Jovi, and headed out to Stari Baća to write, as both my husband and I continued to live our own versions of our lifelong dreams.

chapter sixteen

On the first Sunday in August, we thought we'd find some relief from the ninety-degree heat with a cool mountain hike. We stopped by Helena's house to get directions to Samarske Stijene, or Summer Rocks, a labyrinth of stone sculptures and sinkholes in the Kapela mountain chain and the geological sister to Bijele Stijene, or White Rocks, the subject of Robert's finest song.

Helena directed us ten miles south of town, where Jim parked the Peugeot at what appeared to be the trailhead, and we started on the path into dark evergreen forest, its floor thick with ferns, a tiny slash of trail cutting through. We never did make it to the signature view—we lost the trail about halfway in and decided to turn back when the forty-five-minute hike Helena described had already taken us two hours. But on the way home we saw a line of twenty-six tall, roughly sculpted rocks like marching soldiers in the waving grass. We pulled into a gravel parking lot that seemed designated for viewing them and got out to stand before a monolithic plaque, inscribed in Croatian, probably explaining the whole thing. Another mystery of Mrkopalj. As always, it was beautiful.

A car rumbled down the road toward us, skidding to a halt where we stood. Helena threw open her door and rushed toward us.

"Where have you been?" she yelled. "You have been gone for almost three hours and I am worried when I go to Goranka and ask if you are home yet!"

"Ah, we're fine," I said. "It just took longer than we thought it would."

"There are downed trees all over the hiking trail," Jim said. "You can't even walk in there."

"I will tell Paul about that," Helena said. "This is the time of the year people are taking trees from the wood for fire in winter."

She paused. "But I am scared you are dead in the woods! The next time you go in there, I must go with you."

"We just followed the trail," I said. "We only saw three bears, a jackal, a wild boar, and a yak. No big deal."

"You are cheesing me," Helena said flatly.

"Hey, what does this say?" Jim pointed to the plaque. "What is this place?"

"This is Matić Poljana," she said. "Soldiers are walking across this field in World War II, and they freeze to death."

She read the plaque:

Empty mountains, nowhere help
Misery and pain sat and stayed
Forever tired, cursed to die,
Left lying without hope.
Living continued with last effort
Travel without end
Speechless
With only a wish
To finally see the saving light of salvation
To finish the sickening battle.

Jim looked at me. Across the gravel road, in the field of stones and wildflowers, the kids chased a grasshopper to put in a Coke bottle.

"Well," he said. "That clarifies everything."

It was Jim's first lesson in the wars of Mrkopalj. We were about to get more.

That night, as I laid on the futon trying to adjust myself into some semblance of flatness so I could read my Croatian history book in relative comfort, Jim returned from his evening nightcap at Stari Baća all aflutter.

"We're going to a party!" he whispered loudly, trying not to wake the kids.

"What for?" I asked, sitting up. "Now?"

"No, on August fifth," he said. "They're killing a sheep and everything!"

"Who is?" I asked.

"Robert and the guys. It's out at the biathlon training field. On Wednesday!"

"What's the party for?" I asked.

"The way everyone explained it to me, it's like Croatian Thanksgiving," he said, pulling on his pajama pants.

Jim had become part of Mrkopalj. He could name every car at Stari Baća when we'd walk down for coffee. My husband, who can drink most people under the table back home, was considered a lightweight in the village, and the men thought it was sweet when he tried to keep up with them. He learned more by gossiping in Stari Baća than I ever did walking around with a notebook. He could tell me who was having marital problems, whose woman was nagging him about the drinking, and why one man refused cigarettes (the old "my dad forced me to smoke a whole pack" story). This "Croatian Thanksgiving" was a yearly event that Robert sponsored through Stari Baća. The guys at the bar assured Jim that August 5 was celebrated nationwide, in honor of the end of the Yugoslavian Wars.

Knowing that few things are that simple in Croatia, I surfed the Internet to learn more. August 5 was the anniversary of the success of Operation Storm, a defeat of Serbian forces in a battle so crushing that it effectively ended the war. President Clinton approved the operation and the Croatian forces were American-trained.

At dawn on August 5, we were awakened by the sound of a buzz saw.

"I swear to God, these people make more noise by six A.M. than most people make all day," Jim grumbled, getting up to make the Nescafé. Later we headed to the south edge of town and a wide patch of cleared forest dominated by a rusty shooting range.

"It's like the Mrkopalj version of Little League fields," Jim noted.

This was Zagmajna, where Jakov Fak and the local Olympians trained to compete in biathlon. Robert welcomed us in a denim jacket and matching jeans, carrying a clipboard and solemnly keeping track of the various field games.

"Go: you get breakfast," he urged us. "You are very late!"

It was only ten, but Robert wanted us up at the campfire with Mrkopalj's war veterans, a great flank of men in sleeveless T-shirts, flannels, and bucket hats roasting gargantuan weenies on sharpened sticks. Sam and Zadie dragged us along.

This burly bunch had been preparing our breakfast from the moment we got out of the car. Our sticks were ready when we walked up, and they stoked the last of the roasting fire that others had abandoned for the field games. Croatian hot dogs were nothing like their dainty

American cousins. Big, hand-stuffed, greasy, and salty—these mirac-
ulous things seemed steroidal in comparison. A man gently handed
Sam and Zadie their sticks, loaded with sausages scored three times
on each side so they wouldn't burst as they cooked. The kids couldn't
believe their good fortune: Sticking stuff in a fire was the best.

One guy unfolded a camp chair and seated me in it, then pro-
ceeded to fuss over my cooking methods. Another hauled out a cutting
board and unsheathed his comically large hunting knife—"Souvenir
from war," he explained—then sliced generous hunks of country bread
and onions as garnishes. In a minor culinary miracle, the kids even ate
the onions. We chewed so enthusiastically that grease dripped down
our chins, pleasing all those present.

We might have eaten more slowly had we known that the sausages were merely appetizers. The war vets moved us along to a picnic
table, where Mrkopaljcis ate bowls of *fazol* soup, an aromatic glop of
army beans and *kobasica* sausage. It was lunchtime at this end of the
field, and nobody would be letting us skip a meal. I'd seen the beans
soaking the day before at Stari Baća, where the summer girls were
chopping tubs of onions and slabs of bacon. I looked around to see
where the soup had come from, and saw the Sausage Man of Sunger
dipping into a giant camouflage-green steel cooler under a makeshift
party awning. He gave me a foxy wink and brought over soup for my
family. Even Zadie wolfed down the thick broth. Sam picked around
the meat. When they finished, full to the point of looking woozy, they
waddled toward the woods to join the other village kids.

"Mind if I have a few drinks with Robert?" Jim asked.

"That's cool," I said. I wandered toward the field games and sat
down on a rock to watch the festivities unfold in celebration of Croatian Thanksgiving. It was such a nice party that I had a hard time connecting it to something as bloody as war, though I suppose American
Thanksgiving is no less bittersweet, when you think about it.

I'd been trying to understand local history better. Croatia's thorny
past was pretty hard to reckon for a newbie like me. But in a way, it was
my own past, and I knew I had to make the effort. This, too, was part

of the journey. Reading Croatian history books, however, was about as exciting as sitting through a PowerPoint presentation. So to get a better handle on the Yugoslavian Wars, I'd visited Mrkopalj's Škola Mira, the International Peace School that had looked so creepy and abandoned when I'd visited Mrkopalj the previous fall. It was there that I met Robert's uncle, Professor Franjo Starčević.

I'd seen him walking around Mrkopalj, slight of frame and milky-eyed old, dressed in a faded flannel shirt, a baseball cap, and black soccer shoes, hip for an old dude. He shambled along, stopping occasionally to gaze at a house or the sky, present but not entirely present.

When I visited the school, I was met at the door by a kid named Danijel, a student in Zagreb with cerebral palsy who introduced himself as the new director. Almost a year after I'd first seen it, Škola Mira was still a mess on the outside and, I soon saw, on the inside as well. Flies buzzed around dishes stacked in the sink. The walls were wavy with water damage. It was a far cry from the jubilant art studios for children of all ethnic backgrounds that Professor Starčević had founded during the Yugoslavian Wars, when Škola Mira had been a beacon of hope.

Danijel led me inside, where Professor Starčević sat at a long table in the empty dining hall. Danijel translated as the old man spoke.

He had been a professor in Zagreb until the "Croatian Spring" in 1971, a thaw in Marshal Tito's Communism when young Croatians agitated for independence from the largely Serbian government of Yugoslavia. When Tito eventually crushed the movement, the students and their leaders were frightened into silence or arrested. Professor Starčević was fired and returned to Mrkopalj to write a book called *The Quest for the Gorski Kotar Soul*. Future Croatian president Franjo Tuđjman, who was also involved, served jail time.

Tito had a way of keeping ethnic tensions and general unruliness in check. Dictators are good at that sort of thing. And then they die, which Tito did in 1980, and Serbia's president Slobodan Milošević tried to assert control over the Yugoslav federation—Croatia, Slovenia, Bosnia and Herzegovina, Montenegro, Macedonia, and the autonomous provinces of Vojvodina and Kosovo. The other republics generally resisted, but rather than keeping the Yugoslavian federation together, Croatia and Slovenia used Milošević's power grab, and the fall of the Berlin Wall, as an excuse for their own aspirations of independence. Whole states were imploding.

In the Gorski Kotar, Croatians and Serbs who had lived as peaceful neighbors for generations were suddenly suspicious of each other. The Serbs felt disconnected from the Yugoslavian government in Belgrade. They worried that the Croatian nationalist furor would end in another Ustaše-style government like the one that killed thousands of Serbs in concentration camps. Croatian-born residents were suspicious that the Serbs would turn on them if Croatia declared independence, trying to claim Croatian territory as their own.

Slovenia peeled off from Yugoslavia in June 1991 in a short ten-day war. Slovenia is immediately north of the Gorski Kotar, and as the Yugoslavian army—it's officers mainly Serbian—pulled out of Slovenia, its soldiers passed through Croatia. Some of the Gorski Kotar villages built barricades with trees felled from the forests that had always sustained them.

Professor Starčević said Croatia had waited for a long time to be a free nation, that his country had been dominated by its neighbors for a thousand years. And it was now prosperous, too. Less prosperous Serbia wasn't about to let Croatia go without a fight, and in July 1991, that fight began between Croatian and Serbian forces. Only the smallest republic, Montenegro, sided with Serbia as war spread through the former Yugoslavia. This time, it was Serbia whose brutality bathed the Balkans in shame. Though violent acts were committed by all sides, the Serbian military was infamously ruthless, laying siege to Sarajevo, Bosnia, destroying the city and starving its people for years, holding women in "rape camps," and slaughtering eight thousand Muslim boys and men in Srebrenica, Bosnia, among other macabre atrocities.

"In each of us, there is good and bad," Professor Starčević said, as if that explained things. "The dualism inside each of us demands a fight between those two components."

Professor Starčević knew that the Gorski Kotar, an ethnic mix of people since anyone could remember, was in trouble. A Serb living in Croatia was once as benign as a Nebraskan living in Iowa. With the breakup of Yugoslavia, that Serb was suddenly a suspicious foreigner who might steal your land. Croatians only wanted Croatians living in their country. Serbs only wanted Serbs. Nobody wanted Muslims around. Serbia and Croatia wanted to divvy up Bosnia and dissolve it altogether. It was a great big bloody mess. To give you an idea, the term "ethnic cleansing" was coined during the Yugoslavian Wars.

Professor Starčević knew something had to be done to ensure harmony between neighbors in the Gorski Kotar. With the help of other peace-minded leaders, he visited villages with large Serbian populations and asked them to pledge peace. Professor Starčević drove from village to village, imploring friends and families to get along as they always had in order to protect their mountain home. Sometimes his car was blocked by barricades and so he walked.

His most famous walk was in 1992, to the village of Jasenak. He'd arranged a meeting with local Serbian leaders, which lasted until after dark. The walk home traversed a stretch of woods along a ridge of Mount Bjelolasica, where Serbian snipers hid in the trees, waiting.

"Don't be afraid; our people won't shoot at you," the Serbian leaders of Jasenak assured the unarmed Professor Starčević as he left their village.

"Were you afraid?" I asked him.

"I was afraid," he said, nodding. His gray hair curled around his ears, framing a narrow face with a thin nose, high cheekbones, and a long upper lip. "I was afraid, but then I thought that if those soldiers shoot, I will die for an idea that is higher than myself. That didn't happen, they didn't shoot, and I am here now with you, boring you with my story."

In the end, war never touched the Gorski Kotar, just as Zlatko had told me back in Des Moines. One by one, its villages agreed to peace, and Professor Starčević started the International Peace School. The village of Mrkopalj gave him the old ski hostel, and there Croatian and Serbian and Bosnian children ran the halls together, painting and making clay models and building their creations in art classes, even as their fathers faced each other on the battlefield. In the strangest story of that morning, Professor Starčević told me that soldiers in the Croatian army even drove out to the peace school to cook lunch and dinner for the children there.

But after peace was negotiated throughout the former Yugoslavia, the school went quiet. People didn't see the point any longer. The director who took over after Professor Starčević retired merely squatted in the place, living there for free and letting it go downhill. Though Danijel had taken over, during the summer we lived in Mrkopalj, the building was bereft of children. As far as I know, it remains that way, though Robert did set up a satellite version of Stari Baća in its dining room during ski season.

I asked Professor Starčević why he thought his peace efforts worked in the Gorski Kotar when they so obviously hadn't worked anywhere else in the former Yugoslavia.

He thought for a moment before answering me, touching the fingertips of his knobby hands together. He'd made a career out of contemplating the soul of the Gorski Kotar people. Who were my people too, he reminded me.

During the war, the good part of our souls won out over the bad, he said. There was peace here, thanks to "the highness of this hillside country, our closeness to the sky, and the fact that the stars don't shoot at each other."

As I sat on my stump at the August 5 celebration, this seemed as good an explanation as any.

I finished my *fazol* and walked to the field. Jasminka and Mario were among the players of a game that looked like boccie but was played with small discs of wood like hockey pucks.

Jasminka walked over to me. "Hello, Jennifer!" she said, her dark eyes sparkly. "You are playing *ploskanje*?"

"I might," I asked. "What is it?"

She explained that the bored shepherds of Mrkopalj once played this mountain game *ploskanje* (plo-SKAN-yay) with discs sawn from tree trunks. She and Mario had made the wooden disks that morning. (Aha! The 6:00 A.M. buzz saw!) As Jasminka and I talked, another woman sidled up beside me. Her blond hair hinted at gray and flowed down the back of her thin ski jacket. She wore typical Euro eyeglasses—rimless lenses framed by a jumble of complex metalwork, a popular look that had disillusioned Jim and me, who'd thought Europeans were more fashionable than Americans in all matters.

Jasminka introduced us with a hint of mischief. "Jennifer, this is Dragica Cuculić," she said. "Dragica is wife of Cuculić."

I shook Dragica's soft hand, her long fingernails scraping my skin a little as it curled around mine. *"Drago mi je,"* I said.

Cuculić's wife fished into her clasped cigarette case. "You smoke?" she asked.

"No," I said.

"You are smart," she said.

I could get behind the kind of person who acknowledged me as smart at a time in my life when my vocabulary never got much beyond the phrase "Where is the food?"

Jasminka pulled the kids into a *ploskanje* game. Dragica invited me to the beer tent, operated by the summer girls from Stari Baća and a giggly Goranka, who handed me a shot of a murky liquid. I noticed people watching to see what I'd do with it. Dragica sniffed my cup and made a face.

"I never drink," she said.

"Your husband sure does," I said without thinking, nearly kicking myself even as the words came out of my mouth.

"I hate it," Dragica said.

I took a deep breath and drained my cup of the sweet, milky liqueur of dubious pedigree. Goranka clapped for me. Dragica shook her head and made a face. It wasn't even noon yet.

I scanned the crowd. Robert lorded over the grounds with his clipboard, mysteriously sober. This was his gig, his yearly show of Croatian pride. Jim hung back at the picnic tables, drinking beer with Cuculić.

"Your husband makes friends with everyone." Dragica laughed.

I smiled, watching him. "He's like the prom queen of Mrkopalj," I noted. Jim looked over at me and waved.

In the afternoon, everyone gathered under a shady clearing where Robert had set up a microphone to award the field day winners.

During the awards ceremony, Robert called the crowd to attention. "Today we have special guest!" he announced. "Jennifer Wilson visits our village with her family to find her ancestors. She is reporter for *New York Times* and a very famous writer!"

People started shouting and clapping, and though I was neither a *Times* reporter nor a very famous writer, I walked forward. Robert squeezed my shoulders, and the applause continued. I felt like an idiot until I saw Jim and the kids on the sidelines, clapping too, their faces smiling and proud. So I took a small bow. This was a celebration of the homeland, and I was part of the show. People had left Mrkopalj for generations because of war or poverty or general misery. I came back, and not because it was some big tourist destination or anything. We were here because something powerful in Mrkopalj had pulled us. My family's return was a source of pride for all of us on that day.

Someone pulled up in a little Toyota, rolled down the windows, and cranked music that sounded like a combination between rock and *tamburitza*. Everyone started dancing.

In the chaos, Dragica came over with Helena's sister, Cornelia.

"We are going to Stari Baća for coffee," Dragica said. "Would you like to come?"

I looked over at Jim. "Go on," he said. "Have fun."

Dragica took my arm. As we reached Cuculić's red Chevy, the Toyota's speakers began to blast Cher. The hardened soldiers of Mrkopalj gave a mighty cheer, threw their arms over each others' shoulders, and began belting out "Life After Love."

By the time Dragica, Cornelia, and I made it to Stari Baća, we were giggly like high school girls on Senior Skip Day. It seemed to me that the more I drank in Mrkopalj, the more I became part of it.

Dragica ordered tea. I had a coffee and so did Cornelia, a Catholic-school teacher from Rijeka with frosted hair, a slight figure, and a shy manner.

"You should come to Rijeka and I will show you around," Cornelia said.

"No way," I said. "Rijeka is a toilet bowl. You just get lost on this maze of roads that go round and round and round."

Cornelia lifted her eyebrows. "But it can be very nice."

"Croatia has such an amazing sea and countryside," I said. "Give me Mrkopalj over Rijeka any day. Or Zagreb for that matter."

"Hear hear!" said Dragica, throwing her head back.

"I don't get it," I said to Dragica. "Why aren't you around more often? You don't live with Cuculić all the time, right?"

Dragica said she lived in Udine, Italy, where she worked as a home health aid. "This is because there are no jobs in Mrkopalj. And I am not from here anyway."

Nikola Tesla pulled up in front of the bar in his natty silver Renault Mégane. He had Cuculić with him. They joined our table.

"Your wife is fun," I told him. "I wish she lived here."

"That is the problem!" he said. "Because of that thing, no jobs, we are apart. My wife must drive hours away to wipe asses for money."

Dragica nodded. This was just a fact of their life. Money was scarce, so they did what they could. They were hosting relatives in town the next day, and they could barely afford meat for a nice meal. I think I saw Cuculić asking the summer girls if there were any scraps in the kitchen that they could use.

"But you have one of the best jobs here," I said. "Why can't you afford food?"

"Oh ho ho!" he said. "*That* is the problem!"

I didn't get it. Then one of the summer girls came over and Cuculić ordered a *rakija*. Dragica looked away. I think *rakija* was the problem, too.

I'd had a few myself, which emboldened me to probe the Cuculić affair.

"But you love each other, right?" I said.

They both emphatically answered "Yes!" without hesitating.

"That's so sad," I said, actually tearing up. "I wish you two could be together."

"Ho," said Cuculić. "That, too, is the problem."

Dragica, Cornelia, Cuculić, and a silent Nikola Tesla all raised their cups and glasses in commiseration with the failed love of the Cuculićs.

chapter seventeen

Ana Fak taught me to bake *povitica* during that first week of August. After the fourth time calling Jasminka down to translate for us, I knew it was time to hire an interpreter.

"Jennifer, you *must* learn more Croatian," Jasminka said, giving me a playful yet stern look. She handed me her Croatian-English dictionary—I'd brought my own from the States, but it was useless against the Mrkopalj dialect. "Use book. Learn more."

I crossed Novi Varoš balancing my *povitica* pan and the dictionary. Were people sick of translating for me? Jasminka's nudge had been gentle, but a nudge nonetheless. It worried me.

Then Pavice saw me from her yard and let out a big whoop, mimicking me balancing my heavy load. "Woohoo, Yenny! Whoa-oh-oh!"

I smiled and yukked it up a bit for her. It seemed as if every time I was unsettled by Croatia—its politics, its wars, its language—the women of the village were there to soften the edges.

I dropped off the book and the *povitica,* but the dorm was empty in early afternoon. I headed back outside.

"Pavice's son shot a boar," Jim said when I sat with him on the yard swing as he watched the kids play. "What's his name again?"

"Josip," I answered.

"That's her husband's name," Jim said.

"Yes," I said. "But it's also her son's name."

"What's the Croatian word for 'two'?" Jim asked.

"*Dva,*" Sam and Zadie said in unison.

"Okay, so Josip Dva shot a boar," Jim began again. "Then he ripped its face off, and it's hanging on a tree behind their house."

"Gross," I said.

"It's cool!" Sam said. "You should go see it."

"It's like a mask," Zadie said. "But with blood."

"*Joj meni!*" I turned to Jim. "What are we doing to our children?"

I looked around the meadow, trying to find the boar-faced tree, but I couldn't. An old man pushed a wheelbarrow across the field, haying his sheep. Someone was burning a weed pile, smudging the air slightly blue.

Viktor walked out from his side porch and fixed a newsboy cap on his head. He crossed Robert's yard toward Anđelka and Željko Crnić's house, pausing to pat Zadie on the head and tip his hat to us.

"How'd *povitica* go?" Jim asked.

"It was sweet," I said. "We should go up and get some while it's still warm. Jasminka made me take her dictionary. Everyone's sick of our bad Croatian."

"People are tired of us already." Jim shook his head. "We've barely been here a month."

Indeed, the invitations to coffee and backyard barbecues had slowed considerably. I knew people weren't really sick of us; we were just part of the scenery now. Still, I couldn't keep relying on whoever was available to translate for me, usually Robert, whose skills were suspect.

People wanted to know us better, too. There was only so much friendship we could kindle without exchanging the most basic details. I felt close to Ana Fak but I couldn't even name one thing about her beyond the fact that she lived with her family across the street. And where the hell had Pavice come from?

"If we haven't learned the language by now, we probably won't learn it," I said. "To be honest, I can't do much more work here if I don't have better communication skills."

"With all the kids home from college, I bet you could find an interpreter," Jim said. "The young people speak good English."

"I've got my eye on Stefanija," I said. "She speaks the best and people like her. When people talk to me, it'll be like they're talking to her. Plus, she's funny in both languages."

"Hiring everybody's favorite bartender to interpret," Jim mused. "That's good, Wilson."

"I thought so," I said. "Unless Robert doesn't want her to have a side job."

"I don't think Robert pays those girls enough *not* to have a side job," Jim said.

"I'm going to head down there, then," I said. "Go grab some warm *povitica*!"

I glanced around for Josip Dva's bloody boar's face before I left. Instead, I saw Manda at her window, looking out at me. Had she been watching us all along?

In Stari Baća, Stefanija was pulling the day shift, steaming milk for a cappuccino. I backed away, as I always did when the Stari Baća espresso machine was in action. It had blown up in the bar about a year ago, breaking every glass, destroying a section of wall, and nearly exploding a tiny summer girl who'd just ducked down to retrieve something from the floor. Robert had patched the wall, and his job looked as sloppy as the work of the doctor in Rijeka who sewed his finger on sideways. I wasn't taking any chances, so I moved to the opposite end of the bar.

"Hello, Stefanija!" I yelled over the steamer noise.

"Hello, Jennifer!" she yelled back, pushing a chunk of her jet-black hair from her pale face. She wore a miniskirt and tights and an oversized *Flashdance* sweatshirt that bunched up beneath her blue bar apron.

"Are you free tomorrow morning?" I bellowed, plugging one ear as I spoke.

"Yes, I am!" she called. "Why do you ask?"

"I was wondering if you'd be interested in doing a little work for me!" I yelled. "I could use an interpreter!"

"She speaks very good English," said a guy hunched at the bar nearby, directly in front of the cappuccino maker. I recognized him as Pasha, the town soccer hero who worked in Rijeka as a "spider"— slang for traffic cop. My gossipy husband (Pavice's American equivalent) had said that Pasha and Stefanija had once been the "it" couple in Mrkopalj. There was still an on-again, off-again aura of nostalgia between them.

Stefanija switched off the machine and rested her hands wide on the counter, her pixie face crinkling into a wry half smile. "Yes, I would be happy to help you."

"I will pay you for your time," I said.

"Just one moment, please," said Stefanija, hustling out to serve the cappuccino.

I looked over at Pasha, who raised his beer to me. A smallish man with a mullet that actually worked for him, Pasha exuded a strong but quiet electrical current. Jim told me that when he went to Stari Baća at night, Pasha was often there and insisted that people speak English when Jim was around, so he felt included.

"How'd you guys learn to speak so well?" I asked Pasha.

He laughed. Stefanija returned and joined us across the bar. "Stefanija, how do we speak such good English?"

"Easy." She winked. "We watched *Santa Barbara*."

Pasha nodded. "In our school, growing up, we have an hour break at lunch. We would go to Stefanija's grandmother's house and watch *Santa Barbara* over that break."

"It was a very dramatic show," Stefanija said.

"I've got some drama," I said. "People are sick of translating for us."

"Yes, I know," Stefanija drawled.

"Why should you have to learn Croatian?" Pasha asked. "Nobody knows Croatian in the world. People here should speak English. It's an international language."

"Well, we're visitors here," I said. "It's the respectful thing to do. All the travel books say so."

"But you're not learning it. Because Croatian is impossible," Pasha said. "It's not disrespectful. You should not worry about things like that."

"I will translate," Stefanija said. "But I will not take your money."

"I need professional work, so I will pay you a professional wage," I said.

Stefanija just shook her head. "What would you like to drink?" she asked, avoiding the money thing.

"I don't need anything right now, except an interpreter," I said.

"Of course I will do this for you," she said. "But if you want to know Mrkopalj, you must meet the old people of the village. I can help you with this. Viktor and Manda Šepić are some of the oldest people here. They are your neighbors on Novi Varoš. They have many stories."

Stefanija thought for a moment.

"Then you will also want to speak with my grandmother. She is very smart. She is all the time reading books. She remembers *everything*."

I nodded. "I look forward to it," I said.

Someone else ordered a cappuccino, so I left in a hurry. Pasha raised a hand in farewell, then turned to face the cappuccino maker head-on as Stefanija hit the steamer.

We celebrated my hiring of Stefanija with a beach trip to the coastal village of Baška, so far south on the Kvarner Peninsula that it was nearly to the Dalmatian Coast.

"I asked Robert if we could bring the girls," Jim said. "Only Ivana and Roberta can come. Karla has biathlon practice."

Zadie was ecstatic. Ivana had continued her role as big sister over the summer, and Roberta was still Zadie's favorite live-in playdate. Sam was the lonely guy, stranded in a sea of girls, but Legos sustained him, and he carefully stuffed his backpack full of them as the rest of us changed into beach clothes.

Downstairs, Robert had lined up both girls against the Peugeot and was talking intently to them. When we approached, he stood back and stuffed his hands in his pockets. "Ivana and Roberta have cell phone," he said. "You must call if there is problem."

Jim and I had been tentative about taking the girls. If they needed anything, it better not be urgent, because paging through Jasminka's dictionary took forever. The cell phone helped. If we dialed Stari Baća, the summer girls could translate for us.

Robert pointed a fat finger at Jim. "You must learn to speak Croatian!"

Jim gave a Robert-style shrug. "If there are problems, we will call."

Robert examined his daughters. Roberta toed at the dirt with her water shoes. Ivana, reed-thin in her swimsuit, pushed up her Euro glasses and impatiently met her father's stare. She wasn't amused by his worrying. She often hounded him to knock off the sauce and straighten out for the family. It was she who was growing into her sisters' protector. Worrying was *her* job, not that of the brown bear before her.

Still, when Robert spoke, she listened. Then I realized: Robert was praying. He bowed his head and grimly recited a brief blessing, and the three of them crossed themselves.

"Really, Robert, we'll be okay." I punched his arm a little. "Is be good!"

"I know this," Robert said, stepping back.

Robert was shy about the religion thing. Every time we passed a roadside shrine in the car, he'd make some great kerfuffle, coughing up a storm or pretending to brush crumbs from his forehead and shoulders, hiding the fact that he crossed himself every single time. On Sunday mornings, Robert blasted a radio broadcast of Catholic mass in Zagreb. He regularly walked to the cemetery to place flowers on the family graves. But we never saw him inside the walls of Our Lady of Seven Sorrows.

I'd asked him about it. "I going to church, but I don't *go* to church," he said. "When people say I have to go to one building to be a good person, I only want to do the opposite thing." In fact, he and a friend once protested this point by stripping down and riding bicycles through the street naked during mass.

"We have fun with them." He shrugged. "Make them talk about us."

"But," he added, "I pray every night."

"For me?" I'd asked him, teasing.

"For everybody."

Jim started the Peugeot, and I patted Robert's arm. I watched him in the rearview mirror, brooding with a cigarette as we drove away.

The scenery on the coastal drive to Baška was deceivingly beautiful. Houses cascaded down mountain slopes of red dirt and green forest. Roadside vendors camped under umbrellas, selling honey and wheels of sheep's-milk cheese. Wide blue sky canopied a clear sea. The effect was a soaring of the spirit that put the viewer into a state of deepest road meditation. Easy floating, baby. But Jim and I knew the scenery was just a mirage. That wicked coastal road craved our unsheathed internal organs and our shattered windshields. As much as it lulled us, it roiled our stomachs and taunted our mortality.

Ninety-degree cliffside turns weren't the problem. They'd just make you throw up. The real issue was all the cars veering across the white line from the sheer centrifugal force of the relentless zigzag. Loose boulders occasionally tumbled down the sheer rock walls. And based on our knowledge of Croatia so far, Jim and I assumed that most drivers were drunk. There was nothing to do but give in to the danger and trust the steel railing bordering a miles-long vertical drop into a stony sea.

If Jim had a tendency toward meekness when it came to matters of nature, then driving the Croatian seacoast developed at least a minimal callus on his sensitive soul.

We needed this on the road to Baška. We left the mainland via the Krk Island Bridge, passing from green coastal mountains to the red-rock rubble of Krk, one of Croatia's 1,185 islands, an exotic Martian landscape.

We'd seen Baška's beach listed in travel stories as one of the world's prettiest. Eventually, it appeared like an oasis, ringed by that distinct white stone beach line. Waves lapped the Adriatic shore. Swimmers bobbed on its cool sapphire plain, content just to float in a body of water that seemed specially made for dipping weary humans. The Velebit mountain range loomed beyond.

Jim found the public parking area, and we walked as a family through the town center. Baška's Mediterranean white plaster buildings baked in the sun. We slid on sunglasses. The whitewashed cobblestone romance made us feel cool.

"Wish we were here by ourselves," Jim said into my ear.

"It feels like Mexico." I sighed.

Jim and I took a yearly winter trip to the Mexican coast, where we acted like boyfriend and girlfriend for five solid days, drinking beer at noon, flirting over dinner. Every once in a while, we just needed that reminder of what brought us together in the first place. Electricity, they'd call it in Mrkopalj.

But in Croatia, our family traveled in a primal herd. Had we been to Baška on our own, Jim and I would have ducked into the ancient shops, where I might find a pretty sundress without having two kids hiding in the clothing rack waiting to jump out and scare me. We'd have wandered those cobblestone streets in search of a back-alley seafood joint, with no tiny humans clinging to our backs like rhesus monkeys, making a steady stream of merchandise requests.

Yes, this trip had helped our family know each other better, but sometimes it felt as if Jim and I were paying for it with our marriage. We were Mom and Dad all the time. Our experience thus far had been rich and full, but by no means perfect. Things could be rough. We spent nearly all our time together, and sometimes this wore on our nerves. For every sight we'd see, there were three that we couldn't because we were traveling with the kids or the budget didn't allow it.

As I struggled across the sand with our beach bags and inflatable toys, I wistfully watched tanned young couples in tiny Euro swim-suits embracing in the water, forehead to forehead. Theirs was just not my life, and truthfully, it kind of bummed me out. Sometimes, there were just days like this.

So instead of being free and young and continental, Jim and I jockeyed the kids around on blow-up rafts. Ivana alternated between walking in the water, dreamily watching the mountains beyond, and lounging in the sun, serene away from the chaos of her home. Begoggled and water-winged, Roberta stayed just deep enough to get a good eggbeater going with her legs. She bobbed on the waves for most of the day, facing the waterfront where kiosks sold beachwear and cheap jewelry, grinning at the buzz of beach life.

Instead of foofy drinks under a pastel umbrella, Jim ordered us deep-fried minnows that still had their eyeballs, and he ate them whole. In the evening, rather than enjoying a romantic seaside dinner with a bottle of wine, we picked a family-friendly fish joint where Sam immediately melted from his chair when we confiscated his video game, claiming exhaustion and lolling under the table for the rest of the meal. Zadie, in a bizarre accident I still can't figure out, broke her glass by biting into its rim really hard. The Starčević girls ate in horrified silence as I frantically searched Zadie's mouth for shards, thankfully finding none.

It had been a visually gorgeous day, and an entirely exhausting one.

We walked along the beach at dusk, the kids goofing off, expending the last of their sun-sapped energy. I walked alone, away from the group, trying to find some peace. Our breaks from Mrkopalj always seemed to get me emotional and introspective, but I rarely had the breathing room to sort out my feelings.

I looked out on the water and the Velebit mountains, Croatia's largest range, an odd mix of windswept karst and lush forest. Venice was built on pillars made from its trees. Among its incredible caves was the largest hole in the world at almost 1,700 feet deep. (For comparison, the Empire State Building is 1,250 feet tall.)

I'd dreamed of this trip as an escape when we were back home. But life follows us everywhere. I could be as restless in Croatia as I was in Iowa. Jim was still a mother hen. The kids were still four and seven. Parenthood still had a tendency to trump romance. The lesson sank in as the sun set: You can't run from those things that make up the very fabric of your life—even if you change the scenery. You just have to ride the waves. Roll with it.

The sea had smoothed into a mirror, reflecting a pink sky. The entire stretch took on a rose and gold cast. Jim snapped a photo of me as I walked.

"You've been in such a rotten mood all day," he said. Then he flipped to the image and showed me. "But you look really peaceful in this one. And pretty. Then again, I always think you're pretty."

I bumped him with my hip. It was only a glimpse of the boyfriend I married, but it would do. In his photo, I really did appear more calm and free than I'd felt for a long time.

As we drove home, I kept my eyes on the Velebit mountains, where the world's largest hole gaped in the darkness. Both Zadie and Roberta snuggled against Ivana's shoulders. Sam played out the *Star Wars* Battle of Endor under his breath.

When we left the island road and hit the straight-on highway, Jim took my hand. I resolved not to fall into the hole of the darker side of our journey and of myself—the part where I felt lost and adrift— but instead to stay on the surface and see.

chapter eighteen

To thank the August 5 party planners, Robert threw another party three days later. Same place—Zagmajna—different menu.

At dawn, the men had impaled a full-size male sheep on a mechanical spit hooked up to a car battery. We roasted slabs of bacon for breakfast as it cooked. *Gemišt* flowed as a few of the men sliced bread and green onions. Tomo, outwardly grimacing, grumbling like a troll, asked Jim to help heft the sheep onto a great wooden plank when it was done.

While the men worked, I wandered around the forest edge, seeking herbs and tea flowers. When Tomo saw me puzzling over a delicate purple blossom, he slid on a pair of small gold bifocals and walked over to identify it for me. Just for fun, he named every tree, too. If I couldn't understand a botanical term, he'd gently take my notebook and write it down.

As crabby as he looked, Tomo was surprisingly sentimental, and a bit mysterious himself. He'd been some sort of special-ops guy in Tito's private guard. When Jimmy Carter visited Yugoslavia, Tomo was assigned to protect Carter during his morning jogs, hiding in the bushes all along the route because Marshal Tito didn't want the American president to think Yugoslavia was dangerous. But we didn't learn this about Tomo until our last days in Mrkopalj. He didn't talk about himself. These were just the facts of his life; no big deal. And he was a rare moderate in a village of passionate politicos. The guy who identified alpine plants for me, then returned to violently hacking up a sheep with a meat cleaver. I liked him.

Tomo severed the sheep's head from its body, and it sat there, looking at us, next to its own torso, as Tomo sharpened his knives. He pointed to the sheep face as Jim and I stood watching. He raised his eyebrows in question. Did we want to eat some of it?

"Why not?" Jim said. "*Da.*"

Tomo carved off a bit of sheep cheek. Jim flicked it into his mouth. Tomo stood back, apprising Jim's reaction.

Jim smiled and nodded. "*Dobro,*" he said.

Cuculić sidled over. "Do you want this face?" he asked Jim.

"No," Jim answered. "We were just tasting it."

"I will make a soup from it," Cuculić said, grabbing for the head.

Tomo held up his hand. The two men spoke in Croatian.

Cuculić sighed. "My cousin says maybe you want to taste more of this."

Tomo cracked the skull with the meat cleaver to reveal grayish, pulpy matter. His greasy fingers slipped into the cavity to work the bones loose, carefully removing the mass of brain about the size of a fist. Bobi the dog lingered nearby for scraps. The brain turned goopy when Tomo scooped it into a sticky pile on the cutting board. He indicated that we eat with our fingers, his mouth turning up at one corner ever so slightly.

Jim nudged me. "You go first," he said.

"Negative," I said.

"Same time," Jim said.

"Okay," I agreed.

Then he lunged at the stuff, pinched out a piece, and dropped it into his mouth. I did the same, placed it on my tongue, and closed my eyes, not wanting to see Jim's reaction because I thought I would retch.

The brain was soft and fatty, faintly tasting of liver, like a weak and foamy pâté. Though I couldn't get past the texture of it, Jim was goofy with pleasure. "That's really good!" he said, toasting Cuculić with his *gemišt*. The men nodded all around, loving Jim for his enthusiasm. I tried to stay game, but truthfully, the brain was gross.

Tomo, whose forehead wrinkles could be read for mood, changed his expression to one of joking. "This"—he indicated the animal— "man sheep."

He tipped his head toward us and waggled his eyebrows. It was the first English we'd heard him speak. Jim and I caught his drift. Tomo fished inside the sheep to retrieve its *jajas*, or balls. He set down each egg-sized testicle on the cutting board as tenderly as if they were his own, and sliced them with a large knife. At silver-dollar-sized, they were awfully big pieces, considering I'd have to eat one.

This time, I joined Jim in his enthusiasm. The *jajas* were tastier than I'd suspected, like super-rich roasted chicken. Much better than brain.

Tomo finished butchering, using wire cutters to crack the bones. He cut the sheep into manageable chunks and laid them out before calling in the crowd: the kids; Cuculić; Robert and Goranka; Mario and Jasminka; Tomo's wife, Dubravka; Nikola Tesla; and Coffee Carpool Zoran. We gathered around the giant cutting board piled with Man Sheep. Tomo sawed off pieces, taking requests for favorite sections.

"Hey, Jeem!" Robert called. "Tomo is architect for the sheep!"

For a few hours, in this forest clearing of centuries-old *smreka* and *jela* trees, we ate too much, talked a bit, sipped cheap wine, and laughed together. Robert drank so much that he slumped over in his lawn chair with one eye open and one eye closed.

"Dad," Sam leaned over to Jim, "Robert's not looking so hot."

"Quiet," Jim said. "You'll wake him up and he'll start drinking again."

Tomo silently got up, put a callused finger to his lips, and picked up the shovel he'd been using to put out the fire. Then he pretended to bash Robert over the head with it, a jarring movement that propelled Robert out of his chair in a panic. Tomo chuckled like a schoolboy as Robert tried to collect himself.

"Robert, it looked like your friend just tried to kill you," Jim pointed out.

"Is joke," Robert mumbled. "Is Croatian joke."

"When someone pretends to kill you, that's a joke in Croatia?" Jim asked.

"Yes, something like that," Robert said. "Or just to hurt."

Jim shrugged. So did Robert.

Jim scootched up next to me as we sat around the fire, finishing our food, taking bets on whether Robert would fall over or remain upright, as the towering trees bowed in the breeze and scented the air with goodness.

It was that day, buzzed and confident in our new Mrkopalj insider status, that we resolved to find the source of the Kupa River. We'd wanted to do this ever since we'd heard about it. Word on the streets was that the two-hundred-mile-long river that formed the northwest border of Croatia sprung from a petite pool of milky blue-green water a thousand feet deep, beneath vertical cliffs another thousand feet high.

"Let's not just sit around today," I said one afternoon in the middle of August. "Let's go find where that big river starts."

"Do I have to walk a lot?" Sam whined.

"Will I throw up?" Zadie moaned.

But Jim was already out of the yard swing and heading for the dorm. We prepared a kit of water and food and within minutes were on the road to some unknown location within Risnjak National Park, about fifteen miles northwest of Mrkopalj, where a phantom spring reportedly bubbled from the ground like magic. I couldn't imagine such a thing, but I didn't put it past Croatia to have something like it.

Inside Risnjak National Park, 1,600 acres of beech and fir undulated over hard waves of limestone and dolomite—the geological glue between the Alps and the Balkan mountains. "You'd think they'd have signs everywhere, right?" Jim murmured absently as he drove. "I mean, this place is a pretty big deal."

We'd set Charla the GPS on Razloge, the town near the river's source, and she took us off the paved highway to a gravel back road that spiraled darkly down a jungle-like gorge. There was no barrier to break our fall if Jim took his eyes off the road even for a moment. Down we circled, carsick and burping, passing rickety Dogpatch-style shacks and workers smearing tar on sections of road.

When the road dipped back up, it skimmed a sunny mountaintop, a dramatic panorama of peaks and green rolling out for miles, a handful of red-roofed hunter cottages like tiny birdhouses dotting the vast ocean of trees. We pulled over onto a tiny patch of gravel where a single park bench acknowledged that yes, this was a very big deal.

My family sat. Silence and distance roared on the wind.

"I have to pee," Sam said.

"Me too," Zadie said.

"I wish there were road signs," Jim added. "Or other people."

We relieved ourselves by the car—we had seen Croatians doing this along the highways and we'd deemed it acceptable, even wise, behavior—and drove the last few miles to a tiny broken-down village with an abandoned church. Charla told us it was Razloge.

Two unshaven men watched suspiciously as we cruised the half-dozen houses that passed for a town. We didn't see anything that looked like a river spring. When we reached the end of town, perhaps seventeen seconds later, Jim threw the car into reverse and backed up the length of Razloge. Then he rolled down the window and pointed at a small wooden sign, about the size of a human hand.

It read IZVOR KUPE, 25 M. There appeared to be a trail near this sign.

"Well," Jim began. "This could be the trailhead."

"What's an *izvor*?" Sam asked.

"Son," Jim said, "I just don't know."

The mountain men stirred uncomfortably on their porch as we got out of the Peugeot. We stood to allow the Croatian stare. Zadie pointed at them silently. One indicated the ground next to the sign, stacked with a neat pile of walking sticks.

"What do you think?" Jim said, turning to me. "Is this right?"

"Right enough," I said. "I think the 'twenty-five m' means twenty-five minutes. I can start the timer on my watch. We'll hike exactly that long and turn back when it hits time."

I was surprised that Jim and the kids went along with this idea. Sam and Zadie spent a great deal of energy trying to talk us out of making them exercise. They had to know from the look of things that this hike would be particularly strenuous. Jim, perpetually consumed with the fear that a natural disaster would smite his family, had suddenly become adventurous. And me? Well, I suppose I was just trying to roll with it.

We stepped into a clearing in the jam-packed woods. The trail ran like a small vein through it. We neither saw nor heard other humans. It was just my family and a stiff-legged descent down a rocky path. We were surround by blackberry bushes heavy with fruit, a testament to how few visitors had been here before us. We'd traveled to Mrko-palj, a place that felt to us like the middle of nowhere. We were now venturing into the middle of nowhere's own version of the middle of nowhere.

Zadie was oddly quiet. "You okay, kid?" I asked as we held hands.

"I like berries," she said.

Sam picked up a long stick and declared he was going on a bear hunt. He held out some fruit as a lure, twirling the stick in his other hand like a light saber.

"Here, bear . . . ," he called. "Come heeere. . . ."

The noise was just enough to scare away any possibility of an actual bear.

The temperature dipped as we descended into the forest canyon. We came upon a backwoods farm where a woman hung laundry, shooing away chickens as she moved. We strained to find the faint bull's-eye trail markers painted in red on trees and rocks along the way. I noted points of reference so that we could find our way back: an unusual tree; a washed-out gully forking in the shape of a V; that lady's laundry. We were covered in sweat. I didn't want to think of the climb back up.

Eventually the trail turned into a more distinct thing. We saw a picnic table. An actual set of stairs. A rope railing down the rock face. The trail ended at a dry riverbed overhung by great ferns and leggy lowland trees. Giant mossy rocks nudged from the carpet of the forest floor. Jim and Sam, who'd gotten quite a bit ahead of berry-picking Zadie and me, looked tiny moving through the Jurassic landscape.

"It's been twenty minutes," I called to Jim.

"I hear something beyond this bend!" he hollered over his shoulder.

Indeed, it was the Kupa River, flowing smoothly over worn stones, spanned by a wooden bridge and marked by an appropriately understandable set of signs. We picked quickly over the dry riverbed to get to it.

The Kupa was a meandering twist, dappled by sunlight that broke through the heavy canopy. Other families walked along the water, speaking German, Japanese, French. I had no idea where they'd come from; we hadn't seen a soul on the trail.

I worked my way to the river's edge, reached down, and splashed water over my face. The kids threw stones. We stared up at the canyon walls around us; we were in a very deep pocket of earth here.

"The source is over there," Jim called, heading down a path, ducking behind a jagged outcropping of rock. We followed him. Though the woods had been warm and close, it was ten degrees colder in this divot in the earth from which sprung a pool the size of a farm's fishing pond. A mist rose from the water's surface. Beneath it, the pool ranged in color from turquoise to indigo. Lake trout hung in this cloudy abyss that was almost 300 feet deep and somehow flowed clear and fast when it hit the river channel that would run for 184 miles beyond.

"Mommy," Zadie whispered, "what is this?"

"It's the beginning of a river," I said.

"Is there a Loch Ness monster here?" Sam asked.

"I am fairly sure there is not," I said.

To be certain, Sam slapped the water with his stick.

"Are there wizards in here?" Sam asked.

"Yes," Jim confirmed.

It was all silence and watchfulness by this eerie blue-green pool fringed with ferns. Every now and then one of us would get up and walk around it, to take a look from other sides. Sam and Jim waited for wizards and dragons. But mostly, we just stayed quiet in reverence of a mysterious thing.

When we finally retraced our path back through the dry riverbed, up the steep incline for an hour-long return, the hike wasn't as horrible as I'd thought it would be. We took it slow. We stopped at intervals to catch our breath. Jim and I alternated carrying Zadie on our backs when the climb exhausted her four-year-old legs, once stick-like but now showing hints of muscle. We steadily worked our way up the slope, perhaps fueled by the magic of that mystical wormhole that birthed the Kupa River, the heavy strain on our lungs and legs a reasonable price to pay for seeing the spectacular turquoise well. Sam jousted along with his stick, defending threats to the Jedi's rule over the Republic, hiking ahead of his laboring parents, lost in his own place in a galaxy far, far away.

We took the final step off the trail together, in unison, and threw our walking sticks back into the pile beneath the trailhead sign. We walked slowly to the Peugeot. In that moment of silence between the slamming door and the buckling of seatbelts, before the radio would blast us with a song of triumph, or a song by Triumph, I think we each felt a surge a pride. No one had thrown up, gotten lost, cried, or yelled. We'd faced a mystery and emerged unscathed.

In the car, we sailed through the forest that had been strange to us just a few hours before. Jim and I took off our shirts and hung them out the windows so the sweat would dry as they flapped in the wind like victory flags. We celebrated at Pizza Scorpion.

Later, I found this, from an 1898 book called *Gorski Kotar* by Dragutin Hirc:

> The path leads past an older house on the slope of the hill and then you arrive at the green source of the Kupa River. What a rare sight! The peak of Kupeški vrh rises up 300 m above the Kupa. When you look from hill to hill, there are no settlements to be seen, not a soul in sight, nowhere a human voice. The ear can distinguish only the sound of the dearly flowing water. How pleasant and lovely it is in this solitude. This is not the home of human evil, vileness, hatred, discord or envy, but is the home of peaceful souls, the home, according to the legend, of the mountain fairies. A man would leave the world, if that were possible, and move here, to live a blessed and peaceful life. The water in the spring at the source of the Kupa is dark green, turbid and completely calm. Only when a grayling jumps to catch a fly or a damselfly nymph, does its surface gently break.

chapter **nineteen**

For as long as anyone could remember, life in the Gorski Kotar revolved around *drvo*, or wood. The *šuma*, or forest, provided for the people of Mrkopalj through war and peace.

On any day in Mrkopalj, you could hear the sound of chopping wood. Whether they used the big communal wood splitter that made its rounds in the village, or a simple ax in the backyard, people stockpiled this essential fuel for the long winter ahead.

You could learn something about a person from the way he stacked wood. Meticulous types groomed a symmetrical stack with a little roof over the top to protect it from the elements. Some piled wood against the house, bookended by long supporting planks: casual, yet responsible. A dumpy heap of logs covered by a blue tarp hinted at a slacker at home. Others kept their wood entirely out of sight—secretive!

Robert's woodpile was weird. He was a house stacker with an extra pile in the backyard, out of public view, edging the concrete slab. That's the pile Jim and I used one time when we decided to make a fire out back after the kids went to bed. We ended up burning a Yugo-sized hole in the yard that Robert never did notice. The yard was sometimes a maze of drying laundry and firewood, giving it an air of a refugee camp, more so when Robert began sleeping outside on the swing, and a brown wool blanket and a pillow also appeared on the lawn and stayed there.

The finishing touch of Robert's wood storage was the great pile inside the back barn portion of the house. There were no lights in there, so you had to scale it in darkness, seeking a good piece of kindling without rusty nails, praying you would be spared an attack by vermin or an injury that might bring on a case of lockjaw.

The whole system was discombobulated, and therefore I couldn't easily psychoanalyze Robert based on his wood. He had so many styles—fairly tidy at the base of the house, sloppy on the concrete (not necessarily a bad thing, if you're trying to let it dry), a heaping mess indoors. I concluded that there were just different degrees of Robert.

Jim asked Robert if he could help cut the yearly firewood, and Robert explained that he always hired a crew of young guys who worked for the national forest office up the street. But Jim persisted. He needed a solid dose of manliness in his new life.

With all the competitive drinking, steely-eyed smoking, and slaughter and roasting of barnyard animals, Jim felt as if he was going soft. His days were spent cooking for us, driving us around, and following the kids as they monkeyed through the spectacular mountain scenery of Mrkopalj. He began plowing through my books. When I'd return from whatever research mission I was on each day, a common sight was Jim perched on the yard swing, reading while the legs of our children dangled up in the trees.

It was mildly bothersome to him that people openly wondered why he was living the life of a Croatian woman.

One afternoon when I arrived home from writing at Stari Baća, Jim was sitting on the bench in front of 12 Novi Varoš trying to explain to Robert and Mario what he did for a living. The explanation was more for Mario's sake. Robert thought every man's life should be like Jim's, sans the family duties. But Mario was a worker and a devoted family man, and it mattered to Jim that Mario understood his situation. Though Mario spoke no English to us, we were fairly certain he understood most of what we said.

"I am an architect," Jim said. "I work on old buildings. I fix them when they are broken. I put back the wood and the stone the way it used to be."

"So you are architect for the wood, like Mario?" Robert asked, swigging a *gemišt*. Mario perked up in his red lawn chair, hands tucked under his armpits.

"No, not really," Jim said.

"You are architect for the stone?" Robert asked.

"Well, no," Jim said. "In the States, we just call it an architect."

"He builds stuff, too," I said, joining the conversation. "We fixed up an old house together."

"Oh Jeem," Robert said, smirking. "You are architect for the wood, architect for the stone, and architect for the old house. You are a very important man. I have much work for you in Stari Baća."

"I'm sure you do," Jim said.

"Robert, we could be here for ten years and Jim wouldn't be finished with the work in Stari Baća," I said. He shrugged.

"Can I get you guys something to drink?" Jim asked. "I'm going upstairs to get a beer. Jen, do you want something?"

Robert looked at Mario and they shared a grin.

"What?" Jim asked.

"You are like woman," Robert said. Then he and Mario guffawed.

And so Jim persisted with this wood-chopping thing. Wood and the stockpiling of it dominated the Mrkopalj male psyche, and Jim didn't want to miss out. A few weeks into August, as Jim and I sat with the kids in the backyard, Robert approached him.

"We go to forest and make wood for fire," he said. "You come. Tomorrow morning."

My husband left the house in the morning, excited to be part of such tangible work, sure that he'd have a really fun day in the *šuma*.

He returned to me in late afternoon a defeated, soaking wet, sunburned pile of flesh who peeled off his jeans and left them in a pile of sawdust at the door.

"Sweet mother of God," I heard him whimper in the shower.

Goranka had dinner for the crew down at Stari Baća, but Jim recapped the day before he joined them. They'd driven to Robert's allotted plot of timber on an uneven grass field. Near some makeshift hunter's cabins, they came upon a clearing littered with a great stack of felled trees. They were big trees. About 125 big trees. And on that day, a crew of six guys—two of them over forty—sawed those trees down to size.

"There were so many of them," Jim said, dazed, eyes bloodshot. "It was like a battlefield out there."

He was a little hazy on the details, what with the sunstroke and all, but as far as he could tell, four of the guys wielded chain saws and chunked the trunks down into manageable pieces, like segments in a full-sized Tootsie Roll. A few weeks later, after the wood dried some more, Robert's crew would split these logs into stove-sized sticks.

Now, from what we'd seen, men in the Gorski Kotar owned three things: a slingblade, a cement mixer, and a chain saw. People did for themselves and their neighbors, and you could get a lot of surviving done with those three tools. A chain saw is a high-ticket item in a poor country, and the guys on Robert's crew treated theirs with respect. Goranka's soft-spoken brother sharpened and oiled his machine so tenderly that he could have been diapering a baby.

The young guys were methodical and bull-like in their work, tossing great chunks of *drvo* like balsa. Jim and Robert were the elderly shaggers, following directly behind to throw logs out of the way. Both were sunburned beyond recognition when they returned.

"This is Dream Team for Wood!" Robert said on the first of many *pivo* breaks.

Goranka packed an ample picnic of beer, homemade sausage, hard-boiled eggs, bread, and cold potatoes. "It wasn't anything fancy, but it was the best picnic I've ever had," Jim said.

"You should get down to Stari Baća," I said. "You coming back after dinner?"

Jim, all but weeping from sore muscles and sun damage, said, "I won't be out late tonight, if that's what you're asking." Then he turned and trudged out the door. I'd never seen him trudge to any bar, much less Stari Baća, and that was when I knew for sure that he wasn't faking his exhaustion.

I sent Sam to dustpan the sawdust that Jim left in his wake. "Why do I have to sweep the floor again?" Sam whined. "I do that work in the morning."

"Sweep the sawdust, son," I said. "And be thankful you weren't on the work crew that produced it."

Jim called me in an hour. "Why don't you come down?" he asked. "The summer kids are all here. Let's have just one drink and then we'll go home together."

"Like a date?" I asked.

"Sure, a date," Jim said. "Robert says to send the kids to play with the girls."

We left the kids during the morning walk, but somehow leaving them to go to a bar felt trashy. However, when the bar was the only show in town, I could rationalize it. I herded Sam and Zadie downstairs, passing the second-floor rooms along the way.

"Mom, is Robert done with our rooms yet?" Sam asked.

"Considering the giant pile of rubble in the doorway, I'm thinking no," I said.

"That's okay, right?" he said. "I don't want to move. I like it in the dorm."

"Sam likes it because his Legos have their own corner," Zadie said. "I want to move so we're closer to the girls."

"Consider the dorm home for now," I said. "The girls can visit whenever they want."

Robert's girls were in the yard, preparing to walk Bobi. Ivana immediately picked up Zadie like a baby, even though Zadie was almost five. I left for Stari Baća, reveling in the naughtiness of it. What kind of mother leaves her kids to have a drink at a bar? Me! It felt kind of delicious. Judging from the squeals of laughter coming from Robert's yard behind me, it felt delicious for the kids, too.

When I walked in, the Dream Team for Wood was finishing their meal. Stefanija cleared dishes as I bellied up to say hi and compliment her new short bangs. Stefanija and her sister, Marija, took turns cutting each other's hair. Unlike the majority of women who tried home hair care, they both looked super cute at all times.

"Ooh, Jennifer, you are at the bar with your husband tonight," Stefanija teased.

"I'm only here because I'm afraid I might have to shovel up Jim," I said. "What should I drink?"

"It is warm outside," she mused. "A Karlovačko would be nice."

"Yes!" I said. "But make it a small one, not one of those big bottles."

"A *mali* Karlovačko, then," she said. "Jennifer, my grandmother says she would like to meet you."

"Seriously? That's awesome!" I said. "When?"

"Soon," she answered. "I will call you. Now you must relax with your husband."

I looked over at the men. Robert's big nose was bright red with sunburn. Jim, slumped to one side, perked up slightly when I joined them at the table. He introduced me to the woodcutters, who nodded politely at my intrusion. The suave one leaned over to me and raised his eyebrows.

"I am Lepi," he said. "I am a very beautiful man."

"What does *'lepi'* mean?" I asked Stefanija when she brought over my beer. She said nothing, but slapped Lepi in the top of his head.

"Oh, hey, Jenny!" Robert said. "Your husband! He is Architect for the Wood!"

"I am very proud," I said, squeezing Jim's arm.

"He is good, working!" Robert said. "Jim is good for wood."

From that day forward, word got around that Jim was interested in the work of Mrkopalj. Mario picked him up with a tractor full of garbage to show him a typical trip to the dump, called the *smećer*, pronounced SMETCH-air. "*Smećer*" became part of the family lexicon, denoting all things negative. As in: "This coffee you made is for the *smećer*." Or "I would very much like to take a *smećer*, but there's no way to lock the bathroom door."

But mostly, Jim stayed home for us. Jim was a peaceful homemaker and by far the better cook. It felt natural, despite our breaking so many stereotypes.

As we sat enjoying our date, a tall and gaunt man walked in. Within minutes, there was a great row at the bar. It was Robert. He and the man had gotten into an argument instantly. Robert stood and put his hand to his heart. *"Komunista!"* he cried.

Then the guy got up and saluted Robert. "Heil, Hitler!"

Jim headed over to investigate.

Stefanija sat down with me at the table, rolling her eyes.

"What the hell?" I said to her, incredulous.

"Robert's family is Ustaše during the Second World War. That man, policeman for Mrkopalj, his family was Partisan. They come here every week to argue in this way."

"Mrkopalj has a town cop?" I turned to her, astonished.

"Yes, of course," Stefanija said. "You think we do not have police?"

"I guess I've never seen any police," I said. "The way people drive, I just figured there weren't any."

Jim had once seen a guy driving home so drunk that he stopped in the middle of Stari Kraj to take a nap. People just drove around him.

We watched Robert and the cop fight for a while. Then the cop leaned over to Jim. "I have gun in my car!" he said. "You want, I go get, and you can shoot Robert."

Jim stood back in surprise. "Shoot Robert? Why would I want to do that?"

"Shoot him! He is Nazi!" yelled the cop, pointing at Robert. "Shoot him, but not in head. In stomach! Stomach is more pain."

Jim put up his hands. "No, no, no. I definitely don't want to shoot Robert."

The cop nudged at Jim's chest with his index finger. "You want to shoot Robert! I will help you! We kill Nazis together!"

Then everyone at the bar erupted into laughter, as if this was the funniest thing they'd heard since Robert and the cop had their last arguing date. Everyone giggled except for Robert, who remained stone-faced, not so much because this odd humor failed to appeal to his sensibilities, but more because the joke had come from his adversary.

Jim stayed with Robert, who poured himself a halp-halp. I walked over.

"Robert, aren't you even bothered that that guy wanted me to shoot you?" Jim asked.

Robert turned to Jim, took a long swig, and shrugged his Robert shrug. "Is joke," he said. "Croatian joke."

"Why do Croatian jokes always involve maiming another person?" I asked.

"Is not true," Robert said. "I say to you about Obama when you come to Mrkopalj. You remember?"

"I remember what you called him," I said.

"I kid," Robert said. "Is Croatian joke."

Stefanija, a true diplomat, stepped up behind the bar. "Jennifer," she said, catching my attention before I reached over to smack Robert in a little Croatian joke of my own. "*Mali* Karlovačko?"

chapter twenty

On a lazy August morning, Jim and the kids swung by Stari Baća while I was writing. Zadie's hair was a tangled mess, and both kids' faces were smeared with ice cream. It struck me that my children had gone feral in Mrkopalj.

"We're driving to Rijeka," Jim said, pulling up a chair. The kids hung themselves on me, one on each side. Zadie picked up my pen and drew in my notebook.

"Voluntarily, you're going to Rijeka?" I asked, incredulous.

Jim nodded.

"What on earth for?" I asked.

"Robert said there's a store called Metro, like a Costco, for members only," he said. "They've got more food than Konzum, and I'm making hamburgers!"

"Hamburgers?" I asked. My mouth began to water.

Robert popped his head out from the back kitchen, his mouth loaded with what appeared to be boiled potato. "Originale American hamburger!" he called.

Jim shot him double ones across the bar. "Robert gave me his Metro card so we could get in. It's Burger Quest! You want anything?"

"I would love something like mustard on my hamburger," I gushed.

"Dad says we can get junky cereal there," Sam said.

"And maybe chicken nuggets!" Zadie added.

"They have both of those things," Jim confirmed. "I asked Robert."

"What else do they have?" I asked. "Peanut butter? Dr Pepper? Doritos?"

"I don't know." Jim laughed. "We'll see!"

Late in the afternoon, I found Jim in the dorm, adrift in a sea of grocery bags. "Shopping took five hours," he said. "Making hamburgers in Croatia is a daylong affair."

The gardens in Croatia were going nuts, and every meal we had included fresh carrots, cucumbers, and lettuce from our neighbors, who knew we had no garden of our own. I sliced onions, tomatoes, lettuce, and—here's the miracle—hamburger buns. Jim had unearthed an acceptable facsimile at Metro.

Jim patted together discs of ground beef, and directed me to take a look in the dorm fridge. There, wedged into a side compartment, next to the homemade raspberry juice Anđelka made us, was a jar of yellowish brownish substance labeled "*senf.*"

"What's that?" I asked.

"I'm not a hundred percent sure, but I've got a feeling that it's mustard," Jim said.

I unscrewed the lid and tasted. Indeed it was mustard. I did a happy dance.

We headed outside with the fixings. From old bricks and a grate that he found somewhere, Jim had built a makeshift grill in the area of the yard where we'd burned that huge hole. Mario and Jasminka came over, and Tomo pulled into the driveway.

Jim was in a frenzy, just like he was back home when he was

preparing a meal for friends, trying to get everything perfect. I sat down next to Jasminka and chewed on an onion. When it came to food preparation, Jim and I traded personalities. Cooking hamburgers over natural flame was melting his brain—we'd forgotten to pack his *Barbecue Bible*, and Jim didn't go for inexact science when it came to meat.

Tomo, Mario, and Robert shifted uncomfortably in their lawn chairs as they watched. Though I'm pretty sure they were critiquing Jim's fire-building skills in Croatian, they didn't say a word to him in English. I even saw Mario sit on his hands. It wasn't until Jim grabbed the plate of buns—clearly with the intention of toasting them—that all three men stood and eased toward the fire ring, gently crowding out my sweating husband and nurturing his coals into a tiny heap, then a concentrated inferno, and then turning to Jim to hand back the reins with quiet nods. He toasted his buns to perfection.

"Originale American hamburger!" Robert declared as Jim put the finishing touches on the table. Everyone sat down to eat, and Jim modeled the ideal burger design—bun, patty, lettuce, tomato, onion, ketchup, mustard—for his guests.

Jasminka sneaked in a few cucumber slices, and I congratulated her instincts.

"Back home, we put pickles on them," I said. "Jim couldn't find pickles."

The buns were hard, the meat dry and bland. Mario passed, claiming an aversion to "mixed meat." But mostly our friends wolfed down the burgers with enthusiasm, marveling that Americans certainly have big mouths to be able to manage such a giant sandwich. For some reason, this made us proud. We had big mouths!

Robert, more than anyone, seemed to sense the gravity of Jim's Burger Quest. East met West in one big greasy package of gratitude delivered from a visitor who had embraced Mrkopalj from the very beginning. The Originale American Hamburger was the first thing we'd forced Robert to eat that he actually enjoyed. He'd run away in alarm when Jim offered the chili. He'd covered his face in horror when I showed him my peach cobbler. But he stuffed so much of that hamburger in his mouth that he shot out chunks of it when he complimented the chef and gave an enthusiastic thumbs-up. Jim looked so pleased that I thought his chest would burst. He had communicated love in his own meat-centric way and our friends in Mrkopalj had copied the message.

Sam and Zadie served jelly beans and Twinkies from a care package my parents had sent. This offering Mario accepted. It turned into a game between him and Zadie, with him asking her for just one more, and her digging into the bag to hand him jelly beans throughout the night.

I busted out a tin of Jiffy Pop popcorn, another care-package goodie. Tensions mounted as the Jiffy Pop expanded and erupted. When Jim cut open the foil to reveal popcorn, everyone seemed visibly relieved, and we ate the whole thing in minutes.

As the sun began to set, we noticed Željko Crnić sitting at his backyard picnic table, looking skyward. Jim hollered across the fence, asking him to join. Željko went into his house and returned with an old straw hat full of delicate pears from one of his trees. Željko gave Jim the pears, nodded in thanks, and took a burger. He had been outside, he explained, because he was waiting for the Perseid meteor shower.

And so we built up the fire, brought out more chairs, and waited for stardust to fall from the sky as Tomo, Jim, and Robert floated away on a sea of *gemišt*, which culminated in Tomo's passionate declarations about the large heart of Mrkopalj. I think this was the local equivalent to "I love you, man."

And that night, for all of us assembled around the fire, the feeling was very much mutual.

chapter twenty-one

I'd hit an impasse on my genealogical mission in Mrkopalj. The more comfortable we got with life in the village, the closer we felt to its people, the more distracted I became from finding my blood connection to the place.

Plus, it turns out, I don't really have a head for genealogy. (I feel like an idiot even admitting that.) I'd made a list of ancestors from the Book of Names. I'd tried drawing maybe twenty charts illustrating how we all were connected, every effort thwarted as my brain was overtaken with some rare form of dyslexia, scrambling when I tried to understand who had been related to whom, and how. It was like playing Tetris, and I'm bad at that, too.

I wondered if it might help to get another look at the Book of Names, now that the new priest was in town. Barely in his thirties, he couldn't have the historical baggage of the Owl and those book-burning Communists. So I headed on over after a Sunday mass in mid-August. Robert and Jim came with me. I can't remember why I let them. But for whatever reason, they were right by my side when the new priest handed over the Book of Names with all the breeziness of an anti-birth-control pamphlet and shut us in a small meeting room with it.

"You've got to be kidding me!" I said excitedly as the priest closed the door. "He just gave us the book!"

But I realized within moments that I had new barriers to contend with. Their names were Robert and Jim.

Robert grabbed the book and sat down at the long conference table. Jim stood over him with a notebook. I sort of nudged between them, reaching across Robert's gut to open to the first page number I'd found with the Owl.

Robert read off the names of Valentin's family. Jim wrote them down. I just stood there. "Now wait a minute—which Marija is that again?" I'd ask. "I get it confused. There are a lot of Marijas."

Robert blew me off. Eventually they just pushed me aside altogether. Every time I tried to help them as they paged through the Book of Names, I'd notice something irrelevant to their hard-core fact-finding. "Hey look! It's Mario and Jasminka's names!" I'd exclaim, and Robert and Jim would sit, pens poised, as if waiting for my stupidity to pass so they could get back to work. What it probably boiled down to was that modern-day Mrkopalj just interested me more than the paper trail of the dead.

This made Jim impatient with me, and annoyed at how little I now cared about that big dusty book. But I was finally enjoying life in this place where my ancestors had lived. When it came to family, I was walking in their very footsteps. I ate from the same soil that fed them. I was fairly certain that I could trace an ancestral line to each and every person I passed on the streets of Mrkopalj. I was learning more every day about what my family left behind, the good and the bad, rather than learning more about *them*. Maybe it was one and the same. I just didn't know.

Either way, I hated when Jim was mad at me. He was the first person who'd ever had complete faith in me, and I felt rattled to the core when I thought his faith was shaken.

So after a sleepless night fretting that I was botching my ancestral calling, I walked to the Church of Our Lady of Seven Sorrows, my sandals slapping against worn slate tiles as I made my way to the front. I eased onto the kneeler and sank my forehead into my hand. I breathed a heavy sigh, and though it was late summer, I thought I could see my breath in the cold of the stone church. I offered up my worries into the cool air. Should I be seeking my family more diligently in Mrkopalj? Or had I already found them?

Almost instantly, these burdens lifted from my mind. The quiet of the sanctuary always calmed me, though I no longer had the faith of my youth, when I wore a brown scapular and arranged the Stations of the Cross in my bedroom next to the Duran Duran posters. In Mrkopalj, where the silent pleas of men and women seemed palpable in the air, I felt steady companionship for my heavy heart.

The church bell tolled eleven times. I noted that the sculptures of saints in Mrkopalj were particularly well muscled under their metallic robes—church was the village refuge, and the heavenly guards were ripped. It made me feel stronger myself; I supposed this was the intended effect. I walked outside to take another spin around the cemetery to find the graves of the people Valentin and Jelena left behind.

Tombstones sprawled forever toward the tree line of the mountain. I put my hands on my hips and looked around.

"Well, where is everybody?" I asked out loud.

I looked to my left and then to my right. The first grave my eyes rested upon read Josip Iskra. Doubly heartening: The one next to it bore the name Marija.

I called Jim on the cell phone—his was the only number I could dial with ease; we still hadn't fully figured out Croatian cell phones and were starting to suspect it wasn't entirely a user error. I checked the dates on the headstone with him.

"You've got the wrong Josip and Marija. Sorry."

"Hm," I said. "I was excited there for a second."

"Well, don't give up already," he said, testy.

"I'm not! Gah!" I said, and clicked the phone shut. That *man*.

Looking out over the crowded stones, faded flowers, and flickering red hurricane lamps, I wondered if maybe there was an old grave map existing somewhere in the church. For a village that tended its cemetery with such care, this seemed like a real possibility.

I concocted a sentence to communicate to the priest that this time, I wanted to know if perhaps there was a Book of Names: Cemetery Edition. I scribbled my sentence onto a piece of scrap paper so I wouldn't screw it up.

Vidim kniga cuvajmo red na groblju. Or, in mangled Croatian: "I would like to see the books of the lines of the cemetery."

I crossed the street to the priest's residence. The nun answered the door. Before I even had a chance to hand her the note, she winked at me, whirled me down the hallway in a flap of black vestments, grabbed the Book of Names, presented it to me, and pushed me into the back room.

"*Neh, neh!*" I protested. "*Kniga cuvajmo!*" Graveyard book!

She smiled as she shut the door.

I stood for a moment, blinking. Then I fished my cell phone from my purse to call my first neighbors, who also happened to be devout members of Our Lady of Seven Sorrows. I looked up Mario's number in my phone as Jasminka had entered it for me, and after three or four attempts I successfully called him. He answered, I started babbling, and he handed the phone to Jasminka, who promised to send Jakov, who happened to be on break from Olympic training.

I clicked the phone shut. Good. Jakov spoke fluent English. Plus, he was hot.

I watched out the window. Within about eighteen seconds, he drove up in a little silver car plastered with Olympic sponsorship stickers. He bounded up the steps, and I heard him talking his way into the priest's residence.

I emerged from my sequestered room and stepped up behind Jakov. He seemed to be explaining my purpose here, but the new priest and nun were grilling him. Jakov was a local celebrity. Everybody wanted a piece of the guy. He'd stand in the street, all bronze and blue-eyed, sheathed in shiny bike shorts, and girls and boys alike would flock to him to ask questions and request autographs. The fact that he spoke politely to the clergy impressed me even more than his finely tuned calf muscles. Well, just as much.

Jakov turned to me, almost imperceptibly rolling his blue eyes. "He is reminding me that I must put Bog and prayer before the Olympics," he said.

"Bog?" I said.

"God," Jakov explained.

"Okay," I said. "What else?"

"He is also telling me that there is no Book of Graves."

How in Bog's name would I find Valentin and Jelena's parents?

The nun spoke up. "If there is such a thing still in existence, it is at the municipal building," Jakov translated. "This is where the office of your friend Mr. Cuculić is." Then he winked. *Hot.*

Jakov drove me the block to the municipal building—seven seconds, including a brief wait for a goat herd—where a guy named Marin was hustling out the door.

"That is the man you want," indicated Jakov.

We stopped Marin, who was in charge of county records. He was also the tax man, the fire chief, and a fairly decent boccie ball player down at Šume Pjevaju. Jakov asked Marin about the Book of Graves. Cuculić appeared in the doorway, a standard grimace on his mustached face, and maneuvered around behind Marin, trying to get into my field of vision.

Marin confirmed that the Book of Graves no longer existed. Even worse, many of the oldest graves had disappeared over time, the plots sold to other families. The village mapped out a new guide to the cemetery in 2004, but graves were included only if families were present in Mrkopalj to pay a tax. The government had effectively stolen Mrkopalj's oldest history.

"No way!" I turned to Jakov. "They sold the old graves?"

"Yes," Jakov said. "I am sorry."

"This is true," Cuculić said.

Marin shrugged, then hurried away, casting occasional worried looks behind him.

Jakov turned to me and nodded once. "There is no book. It is gone."

Cuculić stepped forward. "He says there is no book! It is gone!"

I turned to Cuculić, who was feeling expansive. "During Communist times, the books were confiscated because all property became public, including the cemetery. This book you search for was never seen again," Cuculić said. Tito's men had destroyed it.

Cuculić saw my face fall. "It is our problem, and not your fault," he said, and I do believe he was trying to comfort me.

"So, unless some miracle happens, I won't be able to find the graves of Jelena and Valentin's parents," I said, mostly to myself.

That evening, Jakov sat on a stationary bicycle in the Fak driveway. He'd pedal furiously, halt, take his pulse, and go back to pedaling like a man possessed. He'd been at it for an hour and a half before I walked over to ask what on earth he was doing.

"I raise my heart rate to its limit," he said. "Then I stop and force my heart to calm down." This came in handy for an Olympic biathlete in training, he explained. If he was going to hit those shooting targets in between rounds of skiing, he couldn't be panting. Part of biathlete training was gaining control over one's respiratory functions.

"That's pretty cool," I said. I thanked him again for helping me with the Book of Graves, or lack thereof.

He stopped his bike and mopped his face with a towel.

"You are disappointed," he said.

"I am," I said. "I've been having a hard time staying focused on the search for my ancestors. I thought this was a way to connect with them, without paging through old books or surfing the Internet. But if those graves are unmarked, I don't know how I could possibly find them."

"Maybe it's a mystery," Jakov said. "Maybe figuring out how to find these graves will put you near your ancestors somehow."

"Half the time I don't even know what I'm searching for," I said, chuckling. "How will a couple of unmarked graves change my life, right? Why are we here anyway? I guess that's always the question, though."

Jakov thought about this for a moment. "There is a word in Mrkopalj," he began. "It is called '*init.*' This is when you want something so bad, and someone tells you that you cannot do it. Tells you that it is not possible. Then you say 'Yes I can. It *is* possible. And I *will* make it.'"

He pressed his fingers to his neck and breathed in, long and deep.

"It's this sort of mentality that came from Mrkopalj. That came from your people," he said. "*Init.*"

Later that day, when I went out to enjoy the sunset from Robert's front-yard bench, Jakov was still pedaling in his driveway, staring straight ahead into the evening sky.

I watched as the sun tinted the green overgrowth of the land with a holy shade of gold. Mrkopalj in summer was a wildly fruitful place. Gardens rioted with vegetables and vines to the point that they appeared to be encroaching on the households that tended them. Wildflowers flew their last banner of color for the season in deep tones of yellow and purple and red. A second bloom of tea flowers burst forth, and two old women made slow passes through the meadow in babushkas, dropping handfuls of blossoms into their aprons. Apples and plums rained into Robert's yard from Željko and Anđelka's trees. Jakov's brother Stjepan pushed a wheelbarrow by to harvest the fruit for a friend in Rijeka who made *rakija* in the fall.

"Jennifer!" Jasminka called from her balcony. She waved and jogged down her steps, passing her son on the stationery bike.

I rose and we met halfway in the road.

"Mario and I have tourism for your family," Jasminka said. "Tomorrow, we drive to pick berries! New berries for fall."

A rare mix of blueberries and mountain cranberries simultaneously fruited during a narrow window of time in late summer. On a Sunday in late August, we followed Mario and Jasminka's van up a steep mountain road that eventually dipped back down into a bowl like a dense forested volcano. In Mrkopalj, they called this place Okruglica (oh-KROOG-leets-uh).

Though it was hayfever-and-humidity season back home, fall iced the air in the Gorski Kotar. I bundled Zadie into a white cardigan and tied a flowered scarf on her head. I pulled a ski cap over Sam's noggin, which was a task because he had taken to wearing his hair in a self-styled Mohawk. My son was a vegetarian with punk-rock hair. I was raising Henry Rollins.

"How does nature even develop berries in the woods?" Jim wondered aloud. "We see them everywhere. Raspberries, blueberries, strawberries. . . ."

I thought about this. "Bears eat berries. Bears poop seeds. There are lots of bears. There are lots of berry bushes!" I reasoned. "Oh, look how much we've learned!"

The kids giggled in the backseat. It didn't solve the question of how the berries had gotten there to begin with, but wondering passed the time in the car.

Zadie even joined in. "In this world, the government of the woods invented them so the animals can use berries for money."

We spent our Sunday afternoon in the vast Okruglica heath. Many people were out with their families picking along the hillside, where tufts of wildflowers mingled with the low dark-green ground-cover where both berries grew, side by side.

We hiked up, and Mario scouted a patch that looked promising. Jasminka handed out empty yogurt cups. We moved aside leaves in search of blue and pink fruit. Each success was followed by the satisfying *plonk* of berry hitting cup. Mario crouched next to Zadie, dwarfing my tiny daughter, gently handing over his cranberries and blueberries so she'd have the most treasure.

Eventually, Zadie crept over to Jasminka and whispered into her ear. Jasminka nodded gravely and said something in Croatian to Mario, who smirked and began putting the berries in his own cup.

"Zadie tell me to make Mario stop giving blueberries," she told me. "Only pink! Pink is pretty."

Zadie nodded to herself. "Only pinks," she repeated under her breath.

Jim and Sam worked over a small section of bushes for the better part of an hour, Jim lounging on the ground watching his boy with an easy smile on his face. I pulled on Sam's discarded ski cap, wrapped my sweater around me, and spread out in the sun, listening to the hum of my children's voices, to Jasminka encouraging them, and to Mario visiting with a man who'd brought his grandkids here, and who sounded mildly grouchy that Mario had invited outsiders like us. In my mind, I imagined Mario explaining that we, too, were family.

That night, Jim made his mom's recipe for peanut butter-oatmeal-chocolate chip cookies. We shared with Mario and Jasminka and the other neighbors and he received two recipe requests, which we delivered with the caveat that chocolate chips cost about $10 and you had to drive all the way to Rijeka to find them.

The early autumn breeze was fantastic as we lay awake that night. "I love making my mom's cookies," Jim said. A few years ago, he'd baked twelve batches in a row to perfect the recipe. I gained four pounds; the cookies were worth it.

Cesar the Hunting Dog of Indiscriminate Origin started barking. I got up and looked outside to see the shadow of a cat standing just a few feet away from him. The cat bolted, and Cesar returned to his tiny chalet, a miniature pot of red geraniums over his doorway swinging gently. Our street looked so pretty just then. My eyes welled up.

"Everybody loves my cookies," Jim mused, drifting off to sleep.

I had not yet found my ancestors, but surely I was getting close. All genealogy and bookwork aside, our friends and neighbors felt a lot like family in Mrkopalj, this place where even the simplest neighborly gesture of baking peach cobblers was received with such a flood of maternal kindness. The last time I'd made my signature recipe, Anđelka had returned her pan filled with plums surrounding a jar of jam she'd made from them. Pavice brought over another pitcher of milk and *kolaći* for the kids. You could stock a Konzum with all the garden produce Jasminka perpetually showered upon us.

God knew what they'd give us in return after Jim's mom's cookies. Medo the cow? A parcel of land? A baby?

chapter twenty-two

If I couldn't find the graves of Valentin and Jelena's parents, I figured there were other ways to channel my ancestors, starting with doing what was probably the same work they'd done a hundred years ago. So in the morning, I walked over to Pavice and Josip's house and pantomimed my way through a request to help with chores. They both laughed at me.

I tried to explain that I wanted to experience, in some small way, the daily life of my great-grandparents. But all that I could say in Croatian was: "Grandma. Grandpa. Cow."

Still, Pavice and Josip told me to come on over at the crack of dawn the next day.

I rose at 6:30 from the red futon, stiff and disoriented from another night's sleep on a mattress only marginally more comfortable than pavement. I looked out the window at Pavice and Josip's place. Cesar jumped and pranced in the dawn mist, the chain around his neck jangling as Josip released the turkeys to peck in the yard.

I dressed quickly. The fog that settled in the valley overnight hung low to the ground, draping Novi Varoš in a ghostly veil. I walked across the yard to where Pavice was smoothing down her terrific explosion of bed-head. A pair of dainty rubber boots awaited me at her feet. I sat in a plastic lawn chair next to her and pulled them on.

Josip hauled a dark green wooden milking stool from the shed. Pavice brought a basin of hot water. We ducked into the first-floor cellar with the three cattle chained to a wall. Šarića kicked at flies on the left. On the right, Medo's calf, Kuna, nuzzled Josip and licked his hand with a long, thick tongue. Josip's face melted and he smiled as if to say, *They totally love me.*

Medo stood patiently in the middle. It was her business that I'd be working that morning.

The air was hot and moist, fragrant with the new layer of sawdust on the floor. I washed Medo's udders (Sam and Zadie called them "weenies"), careful to remove every bit of hay and mud. They felt unnaturally warm and alive in my hand, and for some reason, this made me feel faint, the way I get at the Red Cross when I feel the bag of blood growing against my arm. Josip indicated that I rinse my hands. I did so, and he directed me to sit down on the stool.

I sat. I reached. I pulled on the first weenie.

Nothing happened.

Josip gave me instructions in Croatian.

I pulled again.

Nothing happened again.

Josip gave me more instructions.

I milked to no avail.

I must've looked bewildered in the murky cellar light because Josip nudged in and took over. In Josip's grip, Medo's udder emitted a stream of warm milk so strong that it nearly blew the pail from between my knees. Josip's was the type of body that, when brushed against in any way, communicated the immovable solidity of a linebacker.

I tried again with Medo. She wasn't happy to be deedled by a novice in this way. She stomped and shoved me. Josip gave her a loud slap on the back of the neck, the kind that didn't seem to hurt because she didn't flinch, but the message was clear: Allow yourself to be deedled.

I worked the udder again. A feeble trickle stood testament to three generations of weakening Radošević constitution. After ninety seconds of fruitless squeezing and pulling, the hand of this ineffectual great-granddaughter of Mrkopalj was getting kinda sore. Again, Josip moved me aside and drew forth that great propulsion of milk. Then he laughed and brought out the big guns: a milking machine that sucked right onto those weenies at the flick of a switch. Within minutes, we had a full vat of milk. The drops I'd eked out were thrown into a pan for a patient audience of cats gathered at the barn door, all of which seemed disappointed in me.

I hayed Medo, Kuna, and Šarića. A few moments later, I heard a great squalling coming from Robert's yard. Zadie came zipping around the corner to tell me that she and Sam had gotten up early to play outside and Sam had been stung by a bee.

My life as an eighteenth-century farmhand ended at just shy of five minutes.

As I scratched an angry little stinger from my screaming son's foot, Jim came down the steps in his jammies.

"How'd it go?" he asked.

"The milking or the bee sting?" I asked.

"The bee sting is awful!" Sam moaned.

"The milking was similar," I said.

Jim sat down on the bench.

"So much for living the life," I said. "I can't do genealogy. I can't milk a cow."

"Well, you're trying," Jim said. "That counts for something."

That night, we walked to the mountain as a family. It was potato-mowing time, a very big deal in a village where everyone had at least one large patch of *krompiri*, even Robert, who could take care of no living thing without assistance.

One of the local lumberjacks moonlighted with a potato chopper on the back of his tractor. A few days later, he'd come through the fields again to turn the earth and expose the potatoes for harvest. Potatoes traveled from the dirt to red mesh bags to the cellars of Mrkopalj for a long, harsh winter. The routine of village life was comforting.

Josip and Pavice's son, Josip Dva, brought us over a load of *krompiri*. We took them because he pressed them on us, but we both worried that the neighbors' generosity would put a dent in their winter stores. In Josip and Pavice's case, the bounty of their small farm made them self-sufficient, but when they needed staples like flour or oil, or when the winter supplies ran out, they tapped Josip's small lumber-mill pension.

Josip Dva beckoned us over to where his parents watched the potato tractor, arms crossed in satisfaction. As soon as Pavice saw us, she set about busily picking at something in a clump of weeds nearby. When we'd made our way over to her, she was bearing a fistful of *kopriva*.

"Jeem!" She ran at Jim, flicking him with nettles. "*Kopriva!* Woo! Woooooo!"

Jim ran just out of her reach, and a surprisingly spry Pavice continued to chase him, waving *kopriva*, trying to whack him with it. It's worth noting that Pavice was carrying the nettles in her bare hands, which were so callused that she couldn't even feel them.

"Yenny!" she said, holding out one stalk, shaking it at me as if I should touch it. For some reason, I did touch it. I'd barely brushed the thing when I was stung so hard that I couldn't feel two of my fingertips for days. Pavice exploded into laughter. This was all very funny! She had paralyzed the fingers of the writer!

At times like these, I wondered if there was even the faintest trace of family genetics left in this village.

Pavice pointed at the field of potatoes.

"Oh, Yenny! Jeem! *Krompir!*" Pavice cried. Then she added, with a big grin: "No GMOs!"

"No GMOs?" I repeated.

"*Hrvatska je organska!*" Pavice crowed. Croatia is organic!

It seemed so out of place, listening to my gruff old-world buddy brag about organic produce. But Croatian farmers couldn't afford the chemicals we used in Iowa, and because of that, everything we put in our mouths there was pristine, like their sea. Mrkopalj had a way of changing our ideas about prosperity.

The tractor kicked up a halo of dust in the sunset, shearing the stalky potato plants and throwing chunks of roots and leaves through the air in silhouette.

Then a young woman joined us. Pavice introduced her as her grandson Hervoj's girlfriend. I turned to greet her and then froze: She looked exactly like my sister Stephanie. Great brown eyes, thin eyebrows that curved upward as if she were perpetually worried. Olive skin. Wide smile.

Hervoj came up and introduced himself in English.

"You are in the village to find your ancestors?" he asked.

"I think so," I said.

"How are you doing this?" he asked.

"Well, I milked your grandparents' cows," I said, rubbing my two numb fingers. "I think I found my great-grandparents' houses. I saw the Book of Names at the church. That's it so far."

Hervoj's girlfriend looked at me with a smile and then spoke. "You should talk to the old ones," Hervoj translated. "They remember."

Maybe it was just a coincidence. But probably not. I felt as if it was a sign from somewhere, carried, as always, by the women of Mrkopalj, who saved me every time I faltered.

chapter twenty-three

On the Monday of the last week of August, I was at Helena's house, where she, her sister, Cornelia, and her mother were translating a recipe for *želudac* (ZHEL-oo-dots), a haggis-like dish that meant "stomach." We were at an impasse. My grandma Kate and I made it during Holy Week—Grandma used a pressure cooker, but she swore her mother cooked it in a sheep's stomach.

"It had cornmeal, raisins, ham, eggs, and green onions," I explained. "We had to wait until midnight on Good Friday to eat it, because we were fasting."

Helena translated. Her mother shook her head vehemently.

"My mother says you are describing Sunger *želudac*," Helena said. "We can't understand how you have Sunger recipe in Mrkopalj family."

In the one-kilometer distance between Mrkopalj and Sunger, the recipe for *želudac* morphed from the savory loaf of my grandmother to a culinary superfund site that required forty eggs. I could feel my arteries hardening just talking about it.

"I am *not* from Sunger," I said. "I might not be the best genealogist, but I'm positive I've got the right village."

My cell phone rang. Jim was on the line, in a tizzy.

"Come home," he said. "I've got something for you."

It was a good excuse to pack up.

I rolled open the dorm door in late afternoon as Jim was putting the finishing touches on a pencil sketch. Photos of the Book of Names were pulled up on my laptop screen in front of him.

"What's up?" I asked.

He stood and held up the drawing: a color-coded family tree. "I think this'll make things a little easier for you," he said, grinning.

He'd spent the whole day decoding the chicken scratches in the

Book of Names, using my computer to magnify the photographs of the pages, then copying down what we'd found, translating my family history into a legible (and pretty!) family tree that even I could read.

"You rock!" I said, putting on water for tea as Jim examined his drawing, pleased with himself. "Now we can at least trace the lineage properly, and see if I might have some direct relatives here in the village."

"That's right," Jim said. "And I've got news for you: If the information I found in the Croatian phone book online is right, then your grandma Kate's first cousin lived in Lokve. And if he's lived as long as the old people around here, he might still be alive."

"You're kidding!" I said, looking over his shoulder.

"I think she might have a few more cousins in Rijeka," he said. "Grandma Kate's first cousins, Jen. Those are the closest relatives we can hope to find."

The chance to meet Grandma Kate's first cousins meant seeing my grandma—if only a hint of her—for the first time in ten years. I hugged Jim.

We hustled from the dorm in search of Robert. We found him in the second-floor rooms, napping. In another Mrkopalj miracle, the rooms were nearly finished. We hadn't known it.

"Oh, hey, Jenny. Hey, Jeem," Robert said, stumbling forth. "I am now sleeping."

"I see that," I said. "Looks like these rooms are really coming along."

"Maybe you move in, two or three days," he said, scratching his head. "Or maybe you stay on third floor. Whatever you like."

Jim and I glanced around. In the red-tiled bathroom, the one with the time machine, the sink shelf held several toothbrushes and somebody's retainer. The kitchen counter was piled with food. Blankets and pillows were heaped on the couch in front of a television set. The Starčevićs were moving in instead of us. Well, I'll be.

"What's going on, Robert?" Jim asked, suppressing a laugh. "Looks like someone's been living here."

Robert shrugged. "Is good rooms," he said. "Maybe your family come here. Maybe they like instead to stay on third floor. With good window. Nice bed."

Jim and I tried not to laugh. Every person in Mrkopalj had heard me complain about the futon. I walked with a limp thanks to the damage it had done to my coccyx.

"You guys might as well just stay here," Jim said, looking at me for confirmation. "We're settled in the dorm now."

"Is okay? Is not a problem?" Robert asked. "I feel bad. It takes many weeks to finish rooms. And now we stay! I am sorry for this."

His words were those of a sheepish man, though Robert didn't seem all that sheepish. He stretched with a mighty inhalation of what would have been Mrkopalj air, had the architecture of the second floor not sealed it off from the outdoors.

It was true that we liked the dorm now. People saw our windows thrown open night and day, and commented that Americans didn't have the sense to shut out the cold. But we didn't have air like this back home, so fresh and pungent as it circulated down from the mountains.

I nodded. "We actually like it on the third floor. We've had plenty of time to adjust, it having been two months and all."

Robert lit up a cigarette and shrugged.

"Hey, Robert, can we ask a favor?" Jim began.

"What is favor?" Robert said, leaning toward Jim, cigarette dangling, ready to rumble.

"Do you know a Franjo Crnić in Lokve?" Jim asked.

Robert plucked his cigarette from his lips and rubbed his hand across his mouth. He looked toward the ceiling and exhaled smoke.

"Franjo Crnić," Robert mused. "Is father of Boris?"

"I don't know," Jim said, looking at the family tree he'd drawn. "I didn't draw those branches yet. Can you come upstairs and check with us?"

"Yes, I come," Robert said. "In one, maybe two minutes."

"See you up there," Jim said.

We headed up the steps and waited. The kids came in for a snack, then went back out to play. An hour later, Jim went back downstairs and found Robert sleeping again. Jim sat on the second-floor couch and waited him out. When Robert woke again, Jim dragged him up the steps. Together we studied the computer images of the Book of Names. Sure enough, Franjo Crnić was the father of Boris.

"Boris, he work in *pilana* in Lokve," said Robert. "Yes. I know."

"Is his father alive?" Jim asked.

"I don't know," Robert said. "I think."

I rubbed my face in excitement.

Jim picked up the phone and handed it to Robert. "Can you call his house for us? If he's alive, then he's Jen's closest relative in Croatia."

"Yes, of course," Robert said.

Robert dialed the number Jim found on the computer. He spoke fast Croatian into the phone. He explained that Franjo and I might be related. At least that's what I think he said. I should've asked Stefanija to do this for me.

I heard a woman's voice talking excitedly on the other end of the line.

Robert listened for a second, one hand on his hip. Then he said, "*Hvala!* Bog!"

He turned to me. "Yeah," he said.

"Yeah what?" I asked.

"Is Franjo still alive?" Jim said excitedly.

"Uh-huh," Robert said, grinning.

I stood up and hugged him. He smelled like a recycling center.

"Franjo is alive?" Jim asked again.

"Mm-hm," Robert said. "But no remember Valentin."

Valentin had been in America for twenty-four years when his nephew Franjo was born.

"Grandma Kate's first cousin is alive," I marveled.

"Yes, first cousins, Kate," Robert said.

"So that's first cousin, twice removed, to you," Jim said.

Robert and I stared at Jim blankly.

"First cousins, twice removed," Jim said. "You know. Twice re-moved?"

Robert and I continued to stare.

Robert broke the silence. "Okay, I ask Franjo, one day we go into Lokve."

"Yeah, yeah, yeah!" I said. "Let's do it now!"

"I ask," Robert said, picking up the phone again.

Jim stayed silent, rubbing the back of his neck as Robert arranged a visit the following day. When Robert was through, he had a question for Jim.

"What does this mean, removed cousin?" Robert asked.

Jim, who gets loud and insistent when he's excited about something, showered Robert with complex sentences in English.

"Twice removed means you're cousins, just two generations away," Jim said. "Jen's mom, Paula, and Jen's aunt, Terri, would have been Franjo's first cousins, once removed."

Robert poked an index finger in the air. "First cousins, Franjo and Kate. Second cousin, Aunt Terri and Paula and Boris. Jenny and children are Boris's three cousins," Robert said to me. "Franjo and Kate. Kate is your grandmother. Is good speak Croatian?"

"Um," I said. Genealogical dyslexia settled like mist over my brain.

Jim read the definition from the computer. "Your first cousins are the people in your family who have the same grandparents. Second cousins are people who have the same great-grandparents. Third cousins share great-great-grandparents. The word 'removed' means that two people are from different generations."

Here I chuckled. I knew Jim wasn't going to let this go. He couldn't bear it when people didn't understand things exactly as he did. Robert coughed uncomfortably and lit another cigarette.

"So," Jim concluded, "Franjo is your first cousin twice removed. Boris is your second cousin once removed."

"Second?" Robert said. "Boris?"

"Yeah," Jim said.

"Franjo and Kate is the first cousins," said Robert.

"Right. But to Jennifer, he's still a first cousin. He's just twice removed. Two generations away."

"Yeah, two generations," said Robert, grappling with the English. "Hoa! No first! Who is first cousins?"

"These two, Franjo and Kate," Jim tapped the family tree on the table. I poured a cup of tea and sat back. "So that means Franjo is still Jennifer's first cousin, but twice removed."

"Yeah, yeah, yeah," Robert said, as Jim rambled on. Jim talked some more. Something about space and time and chaos and string theory. Or maybe about cousins.

"I don't know," Robert said, trailing off, defeated.

Jim talked on. Twenty minutes later he concluded the conversation by announcing that in the family-tree department, he was "lining 'em up and knockin' 'em down!"

Which confused Robert further, so Jim began an exhaustive lecture about American slang and its subtler meanings.

The next day, we wound through the mountains toward Lokve. Jim and Robert were hunched in the front seat of the Peugeot while I warded off carsickness in the back. Goranka, realizing the gravity of the meeting, loaded up Roberta and Zadie and Sam in the Kangoo for an afternoon playdate at Goranka's mother's farm.

The old masonry two-stories of Lokve hugged the road in a march of pastels. Robert directed Jim to pull over on a winding back road that followed a slight rise toward the mountains. Robert gripped a piece of paper bearing Franjo's address in one hand, a cigarette in the other. As he walked far ahead of me, I noted that he was broad in the shoulders and small-waisted. I hadn't noticed much about Robert's physique before, since his front was dominated by a broad beer belly. But if I squinted, I could see the young rocker in him who'd snagged the babes after the final encore of "Layla."

An old woman pushed open the shutters of an upper-story room and leaned out the window to watch us pass. The street was so quiet that the rocks grinding under Robert's huaraches echoed off the smooth faces of the houses. When I turned to look at Jim, he was smil-

ing up at the sky, ambling slowly. I walked halfway between Robert's
rush and Jim's stroll, wondering how all this would turn out. Would
Franjo Crnić seem like family to me, considering I hadn't known he
existed until yesterday? Would he look like Grandma Kate? Meeting
this man would be my very first contact with a flesh-and-blood ances-
tor. This was why we'd come so far. My heart beat against my chest as
I prepared for the branches of my family tree to come together again
after having parted so long ago.

We turned a corner, and Robert disappeared through a small
gate. We followed him into a tree-filled courtyard in front of a two-
story stucco house where a short, squat man stood on a step, staring
blindly into a sky as blue as his eyes.

Franjo turned toward us as we ascended the steps of his walkway. Slowly, with a certain sadness, he put out his arms to me. I stood
before him, and he kissed both my cheeks. I searched his face, looking
for my grandmother, finding traces in his high cheekbones and wide
chin. We stood there like that, looking but not smiling, for a long
time, an unabashed Croatian stare between lost relatives.

He had a wife, Vera, a soft powdered woman in a flowered shirt
and a gray skirt who fluttered close by and hugged me and kissed me.
The murmurs of greetings filled the courtyard around us.

"It's good to meet you," I said.

Franjo just nodded.

Vera led us into a drawing room right inside the door. She seated
me at a large table covered by a tatted cloth, across from Franjo and
Robert. Jim sat next to me. Vera took her place at the end of the table, near the doorway. She rose and went to the kitchen periodically.
We'd asked Robert to tell Franjo that we'd worked so hard to find
him, and here we were at last, face-to-face with family I'd never
known.

I started my tape recorder. Robert spoke.

Of this, there was much to tell, Franjo began. He spoke stoically,
his eyes wet with tears.

Why was he sad? Jim and I, who'd spent the last year of our lives with the goal of this very moment in mind, waited for Robert's translation.

We waited.

And waited.

And waited.

Robert carried on an intense conversation with Franjo Crnić, which from the sounds of it was nuanced and passionate. I say "from the sounds of it" because Robert translated maybe twenty words from the entire experience, pausing only to brush me off when I tried to squeeze in a question. I suspect this had to do with Robert's not knowing as much English as he liked us to believe. He wanted to help us, but he couldn't quite, and by the time he realized it, he was in over his head.

But Robert knew how to put on a show. He played the part of the genealogical sleuth in a way that made this meeting in which Jim and I did not comprehend a single thing seem absolutely revelatory. The clock in the room ticked loudly as Robert learned about my family, making the occasional exclamation of surprise and casting knowing looks at us. Jim butted in with a question here and there, stubborn in his pursuit of filling out the family tree he'd drawn, but I just sat there, once again lost in the talk between men as Franjo Crnić peeled back the layers of time.

The only reason I can relate any of what happened in the fancy room of a modest house in Lokve, Croatia, is that I later turned the tape of the interview over to Stefanija, who coaxed from its raspy recording the spoken timeline of my family in Mrkopalj. Robert relayed only the most basic of details on that day, so I had just a rough idea of Franjo's story at the time.

When I walked into his courtyard that day, Franjo had been waiting for me. In fact, Franjo had spent his entire life waiting for family. I was the first relative who had cared enough to come back for him since the day he was deserted as a very little boy.

Franjo slid on a pair of thick glasses that didn't quite wrap around the backs of his ears. He dug out from his Camel cigarettes wallet a piece of paper that had been folded and refolded so many times that it had grown soft like a petal. This was his parents' marriage license, which he reverently smoothed out over the tablecloth, then presented to me with gravity. He had carried the only remaining physical evidence of his parents with him since he was a boy, perhaps for comfort, and clearly it was a treasure to him.

Twenty years after Valentin Radošević left Mrkopalj, his sister Ana married a man named Anton Crnić. They had two children. When Ana became pregnant with the third—Franjo—Anton Crnić abandoned his family to find work in Canada. Eventually he remarried. "When my father left in 1928, I wasn't even born yet," Franjo said.

"Did he ever come back?" Robert asked.

"No," said Franjo. "Never."

Before Franjo was two years old, his mother died of tuberculosis.

"My mother is buried in Mrkopalj," Franjo said. "But for a father, I don't know."

Franjo was bounced around among his grandparents, then went to an aunt, who gave him away to people outside the family. An uncle heard about this and retrieved him, giving him back to his grandmother. Then this grandmother also died, and another batch of relatives took him in. There was more shuffling around until he grew to be a young man in a house in the fields between Mrkopalj and Tuk. But as a child, Franjo barely got to know the last home before he was moved to another.

Franjo stopped here, not weeping, but tears fell. I thought of my own children, and my heart hurt for this old man. Vera stood.

"Would anyone like something to drink?" she asked. "Some juice or beer?

"I would like some beer," Robert said.

"And you?" Vera asked Jim.

Jim looked over at me, recognizing the word for *beer*.

"You can have one," I told him.

Robert rolled his eyes, then said to Franjo, "He must look at his wife first."

"First she has to say yes," Franjo joked.

Vera brought drinks and heaped the table in front of me with food: cheeses, meats, an enormous plate of cookies. It dawned on me that I was an honored guest here. It meant so much to me to see Franjo, this blood relative I hadn't even known I had, a connection that had pulled me across the clear sea. But I hadn't given any thought to what it might mean to Franjo. He was frail and near the end of a life spent waiting for someone to care enough to come back for him, which had happened at last with my arrival. I hadn't expected this at all.

"What do she and her husband do for a living?" Franjo asked Robert.

"She is writer, he is architect for buildings," Robert answered.

"Well, Robert, you speak very good English!" Vera congratulated him.

Robert shrugged. "Not really."

"What did Franjo do for a living?" I asked. I wanted to conduct an actual interview—I had so much to ask Franjo—but Robert literally cut me off every time I tried to steer the conversation even the slightest bit.

So instead of relaying my question to Franjo, Robert turned to me. "I told you in car, he was cooking the bread. He was a *pekar.*"

Jim laughed quietly.

"Why you laugh?" Robert asked Jim.

"Because *pekar* in English is slang for something else."

Robert turned back to Franjo and continued his conversation. As for Valentin Radošević, no one heard from him after he left Croatia. It was as if he'd disappeared. "I didn't even think about him," Franjo said. "He didn't write to anybody."

"But to whom could he write?" asked Vera.

"From my family I didn't hear from nobody," Franjo shook his head. "There was nobody from my family."

"Do you know where Petar Radošević is buried?" Jim asked Franjo.

"Petar Radošević?" Franjo harrumphed, as if startled. "Who is that?" Then he thought a moment. "Oh. He is my grandpa."

"Do you know where his grave is?" asked Robert.

"At the cemetery is only my mom," said Franjo.

Vera pointed at me. "Jennifer looks like his mother," she said. "You can see the picture on her grave."

Of course, I was oblivious to this bomb at the time. Robert wasn't translating. But it probably would have freaked me out.

"Before, our graves, the Radošević family, are very nice. All in one line, near the pathway," said Franjo. "But over the years, they just vanished. Disappeared. There was nobody out of our family who would care for those graves."

Vera passed Jim the cookies. "Take some," she said. "You aren't fat at all."

"Do you remember anything about where your grandparents are buried in Mrkopalj?" Jim asked Franjo again.

Robert translated to Franjo. Franjo sat up, surprised. "He says there is something wrong," Robert said.

"Did anyone ever talk about your grandfather?" Jim asked.

Franjo jumped again. "Who?" he said, alarmed. "Who has been talking?"

Franjo rubbed his eyes. I thought he was crying. He said something to Robert that I assumed was an emotional soliloquy about his family home.

The reality: "You know, I'm eighty-one years old. That's a lot of years. I've got heart problems, lung problems. And they sure ask a lot of questions."

Mercifully, Franjo and Vera's son Boris came in, breaking up the static of confusion. Boris lived upstairs, and he and his parents described where we could find the grave of Franjo's mother—Ana Radošević Crnić, the one who looked like me. I think to help his father, who was looking worn out, Boris suggested we walk to the tourism office and meet his daughter, Diana.

I hugged Franjo and Vera and thanked them for the honor of the visit. Before I left, Franjo wanted to tell me something else: He had two sisters.

"Josipa in Zagreb. Katarina in Rijeka," he said.

"They are living?" Robert asked.

"Yes," said Franjo. "Josipa is widowed and in frail health in Zagreb. She cannot have visitors. But Katarina is healthy and living with her son's family in Rijeka."

Valentin's brother, Matej, also had a daughter living in Rijeka. She, too, was named Katarina.

"You have two more cousins in Rijeka," a smiling Robert told me, the benevolent interpreter now.

I pressed a hand against my cheek. I touched Franjo's arm. "Really?"

Not only would they like to meet me, they were expecting us the following day.

I hugged Franjo again, and we posed for family pictures. In them, Franjo is staring off into the sky, a look of satisfaction on his face. His family had come back for him, at long last.

We drove in uncharacteristic silence to the cemetery in Mrkopalj to find the grave of Ana Crnić, each of us overwhelmed by our own emotions—Jim and I from having finally made contact with such a close relative, Robert from thinking about the facts of Franjo's story that he never did pass along to us. The meeting had ignited in all of us a sense of urgency to track down the graves of my last relatives who had lived in Mrkopalj. If Franjo recalled his people being buried in a tidy line near the grave of Ana Crnić, then the Radošević family, including Valentin's parents, must be nearby.

When we arrived, the three of us waded through weeds and stones, and we quickly found the tall white pillar of Ana Crnić's marker. An old cameo photo of her, young and pretty, stared out at me. High cheekbones, a bow of a mouth, a prominent chin—there was a resemblance. I passed my hand over the letters of her name. At that time, I still had only a scant idea of what Franjo had said or what any of it meant; I only sensed that something powerful was shifting within me.

"Valentin and Jelena's parents must be in here somewhere," I said to Robert and Jim.

Robert patted my shoulder. "Is okay," he said. "Baby steps, right?"

On the drive home from the cemetery, Robert leaned over to Jim. "What is *'pekar'* in English?" he asked.

"The word *pecker* is slang for this," Jim said, indicating his crotch zone.

Robert cackled. "Is dick? Is cock?"

"And also pecker," Jim said.

Robert mused. "I like this word. This *pecker*."

"Me, too," Jim said.

They drove in thoughtful silence. Though they were radically different men, Jim and Robert had been kindred spirits from the start, and unequivocally loved each other in that dude kind of way. The two of them together lightened up a situation, and I was grateful for them on a day that was turning out to be pretty heavy.

I stared out the window. I had found a living relative—as close as I could ask for. The whole landscape of my family had changed in an instant. It was surreal.

At bedtime, usually reserved for my own thoughts or late-night talks with Jim, I had the deep urge to cry, but I couldn't. I thought about the little boy Franjo, my own flesh and blood, being passed from person to person in Mrkopalj. He'd grown up to be a good man anyway, though he spent his childhood adrift, his mother dead and his father gone.

It struck me that Franjo had been searching his whole life for the same thing I was: a solid and reliable family. But as I had roamed to find my own answers, he'd struggled to simply find home. Of course we were blood, expressing in polar ways the very same need for love, for family. He'd been searching just as I was. He just had a lot less to start with.

It made me reconsider what I did have. My mother—Grandma Kate's daughter, Valentin's granddaughter—seemed trapped in her housewife existence. She wasn't equipped with the sensitive New Age vocabulary that might have communicated her isolation. My mom had never gone to college; she'd barely completed high school. She married my dad and moved to a small town. Dad went to work at Maytag; Mom raised four kids. She stayed home all day, every day. Sometimes nights, too, as Dad labored through years of night school. She kept an immaculate house. She managed a lean budget. She picked through garage sales so we had nice things and stocked up every week at Aldi's with off-brand SpaghettiOs and five gallons of milk.

From the time I was seventeen years old, I've been traveling. With my first detasseling check, I bought a plane ticket to Washington, D.C., to visit the capitol. From that time forward, I built the life I wanted. Even by the time I was born, times had changed significantly from my mother's era. Bras had been burned.

If my mother's blood runs through my veins—I look like her; I sound like her—what sort of life was hers? How cooped up and trapped did she feel? She must have fought it all her life, until finally, she just gave up and never really left the house at all. In Des Moines as a young woman, she'd worked as a department-store model and a telephone operator. Then she met my dad and her own life ceased and ours began. My life and my choices had been different from hers, and yet I'd felt traces of the same isolation when my own family was forming.

How many times had she been tempted to run?

She could have abandoned us the way Franjo's father had abandoned him. But I always had a home with two parents in it. When Maytag shelled out the yearly Christmas bonus, Mom stood in line for my first Cabbage Patch doll. It might not sound like much—mere presence does not a healthy family make. But I knew the urge to roam. And it's no small task to stay.

I was sure, lying in the dark in Mrkopalj, that my life would have turned out much differently if she hadn't. As it stood, I have a very good one. My mother had some part in that outcome, no matter how mangled the process might have been.

And she stepped up when I needed it most. When Sam was born, I was inconsolable. There is perhaps no greater life change for a woman than having a child. Some women thrive on it. I had friends who lived and breathed for their La Leche League meetings and spent hours shopping for the latest baby slings. I loved Sam from the moment I peed on the stick, but one small nub of my soul felt this was a setback of sorts. At thirty, I was just coming into my own power. Then along came motherhood and the sleepless nights and that cooped-up feeling and the endless worry that somehow I wasn't doing things right. The realization that my life was no longer my own hit hard. My career was just gaining momentum—I'd moved from rock writing to city news to travel writing, and I was exhilarated by all of it. I worried, as I spent whole days watching Sam coo and breathe and nurse, that my life was over before it had even really begun.

Then my mother knocked on my back door, walked in, took my son in her arms, and became his Grandma Kate. She adored him immediately and without reserve. For the first two years of his life, my mom came to our house regularly to sit with him while I desperately wrote stories, hunched over the dining room table, sometimes with a breast pump attached to my chest. They sat for hours on the couch in our tiny house. She talked to him quietly all day, pointing out neighbors, pushing away our huge dogs when they'd sniff him too much. The dogs triggered her allergies to the point that she looked as if she was weeping when she left.

And maybe she was weeping. It's a great gift for a mother to have a worry-free break from her kids. I'm not sure she had that from her own.

Things faded for us again when I had Zadie. She's not the uncomplicated kid her brother is. Zadie is inquisitive and intense and independent. In other words, she's like me. Plus, Mom was getting older. Keeping up with two kids was tough. She receded from the picture. But I never forgot what she did for me during my initial growing pains as a mother.

I had met families in Mrkopalj shot through by the self-absorption of alcoholic fathers. Kids who lived at home well into their thirties, adrift in a bum economy where $2,000 a month was rich-man's money and $300 was usual. I'd seen put-upon mothers leaning on church and neighbors for comfort. And yet they all lived together in messy harmony in Mrkopalj. In addition, for all our American advantages— jobs, industry, good malls—they felt sorry for me. No one in Mrkopalj could fathom what it must have been like to *not even know my great-grandparents*. To have to sleuth down clues about my relatives. I tried to explain that this was the norm in America. People barely knew their own grandparents. But Mrkopalj understood what we'd lost, and the gravity of it was dawning on me, too.

Sometimes, as a bar trick, Robert would make Jim recite our combined lineage. "Jeem," Robert would begin, "tell my friends which country your family is from."

Jim would patiently repeat the same thing he always said. "On my Dad's side, from the fjords of Norway. On my Mom's, from Alsace-Lorraine and Germany."

"Okay," Robert would say, pumping up his audience. "Now tell where Jenny family from."

"Dad's side, Ireland and England and some Cherokee Indian. Mom's side, Croatia and Italy."

Robert would hold up both hands, the big finish. "Now tell me, what country is blood from Sam and Zadie?"

"Norwegian, Alsatian, German, Irish, English, Cherokee, Croatian, and Italian."

And the drinking men would shake their heads in disbelief.

"American families," Robert concluded with a squinty-eyed philosophical face. "Like United Nations, but knowing none."

But we were trying to know. Everything we'd been through in Mrkopalj so far was part of that knowing. What I was finding in Mrkopalj wasn't as simple as good herbal remedies for cramps, or my kids learning how to shoot pool in the bar, or the best way to milk cows. I was finding gratitude for what I had, rather than a low simmer of anguish over what I didn't. I missed my family back home with a basic longing, missed that familiarity, that mysterious connective tissue. When you've lost that, you've lost something important. You feel free, sure. Americans like the lone-wolf illusion. But you also feel disconnected from something primal and essential.

If I doubted any of these revelations, I had only to think of Franjo Crnić, standing blind and alone in his courtyard, looking up at the sky and waiting for family he didn't know and couldn't possibly remember.

chapter twenty-four

I was walking down the concrete steps of 12 Novi Varoš to hang out the laundry when Robert, in wraparound sunglasses, a cigarette hanging from his lip, skidded into the driveway on a yellow bicycle.

"Today we go to Rijeka to find the Katarinas!" he said. I think Goranka browbeat him into arranging the visit, because we'd asked him on the way home from Lokve and he'd said he was too busy.

"I call," Robert said. "They wait."

I clothespinned the wash before gathering Jim and the kids. I was getting good at hanging out laundry. If I got started early enough in the morning, I could finish a whole load in one day. This was a tricky maneuver, considering that the average Croatian washing machine takes approximately three hours to cycle through (slowly wringing the color from all fabric until everything we owned morphed into a weird shade of lavender). Still, the smell of line-dried clothes made the extra effort involved in doing laundry in Mrkopalj well worth it. Except for the scorpion-like pincer bugs we found nestled in our underwear elastic—Pavice assured us they were harmless, but then again, I still couldn't feel my fingers from the *kopriva* incident, so what did she know?

Within the hour, the kids and I were in the backseat of the Peugeot while Robert and Jim commandeered the front. Robert drummed his fingers to the rhythm of one of our road-trip CDs. His sunglasses

bounced as he head-banged with an imaginary bass guitar while staring at Jim. Robert complained bitterly when Jim's weepy Nick Drake
music came on. We found common ground when Robert embraced
one of my favorite underrated bands and found them "not good like
Bon Jovi, but good."

We stopped in Belo Selo, a tiny dot of a village with a natural
mountain spring. We knew about this spring because at the edge of
the village was an old stone fountain that trickled into a giant stone
trough. Robert told us the water ran from the fountain all day every
day for as long as anyone could remember. Jim and I made a habit of
filling up empty bottles with Belo Selo water every time we passed
through, often waiting in line behind other locals doing the same. We
weren't entirely sure where the water came from or what it was exactly, but it had a taste similar to the smell of someone who's just
come indoors on a cold winter day. We concluded that it had filtered
through the mountains for one hundred years, and thus we were drinking snow that had fallen in my great-grandparents' time.

Jim filled his bottle first, followed by Robert, though I'd never
seen him drink water, and his bottle boiled in the Peugeot for weeks
after. The kids and I went last.

We pressed on to Rijeka, stopping along the way to say hi to Jasminka, who usually worked in the Number 3 tollbooth. She waved
and slid open her window.

"You go now to Rijeka to meet cousins?" she asked us.

"Yep!" I hollered from the backseat. "How did you know?"

She threw her hands up in the air. "Everybody in Mrkopalj know
everything about everybody in Mrkopalj!"

Robert directed us with surprising precision through the head-
achey, pencil-lead-gray maze of downtown Rijeka. Communist-era
tenements towered over the city, blocking the view of the Adriatic. We
took a wrong turn in an effort to locate the side street Franjo Crnić
had given us as his sister's address, and leaked into an outlying area
where makeshift homes from pilfered construction materials squatted
under a bridge.

Jim stopped to ask for directions from a bone-thin man with a pyramid of a nose. He shrugged at us and stared.

Robert suggested we get back on a main street. Fast.

"Gypsies," I whispered.

Robert looked at me gravely and nodded.

Gypsies picked through the *smeće* on the outskirts of Mrkopalj, and families camped out behind the Konzum on some nights. Anđelka let them pick from her fruit trees. A crinkly-skinned grandma materialized at my side one morning as I was on my way to get a new jar of Nescafé, her hand outstretched, intoning words that didn't sound familiar, but I got the drift. I begged off as an *američki*, but truthfully I was scared. What I knew of gypsies came from books and Cher.

I was relieved when we were out of the shantytown and back among the looming tenements. "I don't understand," said Robert. "Franjo tells me she lives in house, not apartment."

We parked and walked around a cluster of buildings, past battered compact cars and young people in slacks and long-sleeved shirts, overdressed on another unemployed afternoon. And then, suddenly, right in the midst of all these tenements, we came upon a two-story villa-style house at the end of a pleasant, shaded stone walkway. Narrow brown shutters opened upward toward the sky. It was as if modern Rijeka had grown up around this place that might once have been a country estate, and time had simply passed it by.

A gray-haired woman in a sleeveless black housedress answered our buzz. She was as pear-shaped as Franjo Crnić and my grandma Kate. She greeted us with a tentative kindness as we descended upon the airless, quiet sanctuary of her home, and directed us into a spotless living room with peach-slipcovered furniture and a gray area rug designed like a peacock's fan. Family photographs lined the wall.

She motioned me toward a plush chair as "guest of honor," explained Robert. I was again surprised to be thought of as such. I stole a look at the kids, who were getting the picture that they were about to be forced to stay seated and quiet for a long period of time. Zadie squirmed noiselessly as if trying to escape her own skin. Sam twiddled his fingers, looking pale and worried.

"Mom? Can we go outside?" Sam asked. They'd seen a grim play set by the tenements.

"Not yet," I said. Both kids winced. "If you can make it through this, we'll stop at McDonald's on the way home."

They nodded seriously.

Katarina left us to settle in the living room while she made a few calls. Within the next half hour, we were crowded by relatives. Her son, Celio, and his wife, Vlatka, a lawyer for Croatian Railways, came from their upstairs apartment to help translate.

The room was warm and still. I fished in my purse and found a pack of crayons and paper, arranging them for the kids at the coffee table. This occupied them as the adults stared at one another.

Robert cleared his throat, causing everyone to jump. "Jenny, I must see family tree. Can I have, please?"

I dug into my purse again, moving things around in search of the family tree. I was sure I'd packed it. I'd packed the empty water bottles for Belo Selo. I'd packed the kids' art supplies. I'd packed fruit snacks sent by the grandparents. I'd packed the directions to the Rijeka McDonald's.

But I hadn't packed Jim's family tree.

"I didn't bring it," I said to Robert sheepishly.

"Jenny!" Robert exclaimed, smacking his own forehead. "How you forget?"

Jim rolled his eyes. "You are kidding me."

"I'm sorry!" I pleaded, putting up my hands. "I forgot! I just—forgot!" For as much stuff as I remembered to bring along every time my family walked out the door—sunscreen, wipes, snacks, art supplies, gum, reading material that spanned three generations of interests—they sure weren't very forgiving when their personal Sherpa forgot something. Sheesh.

Both men stared me down. Wordlessly, I shrugged.

After a long pause, Robert rolled his eyes toward Katarina. "So, you have heard of Valentin?" he asked her.

Katarina sat quietly and thought.

"I have heard that he leave and he never contact anyone here, never," she said, Celio translating. "That's what I have heard."

I asked Katarina if she remembered Petar and Katarina Radošević, her grandparents, Valentin's parents. She said her grandmother died before she was born, in 1918, but she remembered Petar.

"We were always going to visit his house," she said.

"Do you remember where your grandparents are buried?" I asked.

"No, I have never known that," she said.

Katarina's story was the same as her brother Franjo's. She'd been passed from family to family as a small girl. But in Rijeka she met and married a nice man, a successful shipping magnate, and she'd had a comfortable life in adulthood.

The door buzzer rang again. Katarina rose to answer it. A lovely dark-haired woman, also in the shape of the Radošević pear, stood in the doorway, dressed up for this occasion in a gauzy black outfit and perfect makeup. This was Katarina Blažević, daughter of Matej Radošević (Valentin's brother). For those of you keeping track at home: Katarina 1, Katarina 2, and Franjo were the children of Valentin's brother and sister, all first cousins to each other and to my grandma Kate. See? Genealogy is *hard*.

Katarina 1 left for the kitchen, to fix drinks for all. Robert and Jim ordered *gemišt*. Katarina 2 stood looking at me, her dark eyes nearly black, like my aunt Terri's and my mom's and my sister's. She walked slowly to me and hugged me tight, speaking gentle words in Croatian. She was so soft she seemed like liquid in the heat of the living room. She walked over to Sam and kissed him. As she spoke, Robert translated.

"That is one nice boy," she said.

She turned to Zadie and approached her.

"That is my daughter, Zadie," I said.

"Very nice girl," Katarina 2 said.

The kids looked panicked, anticipating more kissing, but Katarina 2 returned to my side. She hugged me again, then pulled away to look me over. I wasn't prepared for all the emotion, being Iowan and all, and I didn't know what to say, but I let her poke me and hold my face and gaze at me, probably seeking the same recognition that I was. We were blood relatives who had never known each other.

"I am your aunt," she said, tears spilling down her cheek.

"Well," Jim corrected, under his breath, "technically she's not your aunt. She's your grandma Kate's first cousin, which makes her your first cousin, twice removed."

I cut Jim a look.

He shrugged. "It's true."

Robert said: "In your family, every other woman is Katarina, Katarina, Katarina."

Katarina 2 and I were locked in on each other. "The blood in our veins is the same," she said. Suddenly, the whole room seemed to be spinning. I started crying, too. I was hot and afraid I might pass out. This all took place in absolute, carpet-padded silence while the whole room stared at us.

Then Zadie, as if psychically mirroring my own thoughts, whispered urgently: "Mom! I want to go home!"

I excused both of us to a small powder room at the back of the apartment so we could have a little privacy. "I don't like all these new people," Zadie cried as I stood against the bathroom door, breathing hard.

"It's tough for me, too, but we're going to have to stick it out," I said. "This is our family. We've just never met them before."

"Then why are they our family?" she asked, settling on the edge of the tub, her little sandaled feet dangling.

"Because my great-grandpa and their parents were brothers and sisters," I said.

"But we don't know them," Zadie said, to which I had no answer.

When we emerged, Jim placed in front of me a new sketch of the family tree that he'd made during this break in the action. I sat down to study Jim's drawing, which saved me from the agony of having to ask "Now, who are you people again?"

Then Katarina 2 told us her story.

Like his brother Valentin, and like Franjo's father, Matej Radošević had abandoned his family. He left his wife, Matilda, and two daughters when he moved to Le Havre, France. Matilda died in 1944 and he didn't even know it, because mail didn't run in Croatia during World War II. Matej's first letter home arrived in 1948, more than ten years after he'd left, addressed to a dead wife and daughters who were all but orphans.

Katarina 2 pulled out a picture her father had sent in that envelope. Matej looked happy and healthy in Le Havre. Meanwhile, because there was nowhere for her in Mrkopalj, where families had barely enough to feed their own kids, Katarina 2 and her sister had been sent to live with the nuns in the convent that was just two doors down from Robert's house. The convent was a warm and happy place, and life was acceptable, though it didn't pass for real family. Katarina 2 married and moved to the island of Krk with her husband, who died in 1985.

She blotted her eyes. Valentin, or "Tine," had disappeared and never returned. When she was fourteen or fifteen and living in the convent, she told me, Sister Paula had written to her, inviting her to come live with the Radošević family in the United States.

"She did?" I sat forward, incredulous. "Do you have the letters?"

"I can't remember how all that ends or how we stopped our letters," she said. "I get married later, and we lost every contact."

Since then, she explained, the Radošević family line had been broken. Until today.

Why, I wondered aloud to the Katarinas, had Valentin cut ties with his Croatian family? They didn't know for sure. So many of his relatives had died or moved, it probably just didn't seem to matter anymore.

"People left because they were hoping to find a job in America, but

the same things were happening there. No money, no jobs," said Katarina 1. "They were just normal people, and having no education made
things worse."

"Did you know your grandfather Petar?" Jim asked.

"Yes," said Katarina 2. "There exists a grave in Mrkopalj, and my
mom is buried there, too."

"Eee!" Robert said, jumping up. Jim did the same. "You know
where is buried, parents of Valentin Radošević?!"

"Yes, I do know," Katarina 2 replied passionately. She reached for
my hand.

Both men crouched next to the weeping Katarina 2. Robert
grilled her for details as Jim sketched on the kids' drawing pad. Petar
and Katarina Radošević were buried with her mother, Matilda, the
one who died when her husband left for Le Havre.

"On grave is only one small board where is written 'Matilda
Radošević,'" she said.

Back then, family members could be buried in the same grave
after ten years had passed between burials. Jim and Robert worked
furiously on a cemetery map.

Katarina 2 looked up at me. "Something in your eyes looks like
family."

The living room was hot, close, and still. Sam and Zadie were
flushed and restless and, after Vlatka served them cake and two plates
of cookies, Sam passed me a note informing me that their tummies
hurt. As the men finished the map, my mommy radar indicated that
the kids had approximately ninety seconds until meltdown.

"It's time for us to go," I said. Everyone jumped up in visible relief; apparently the kids and I weren't the only ones feeling uncomfortable. The Katarinas and I embraced and took photos. I herded my
pack toward the door, scooping Zadie into my arms, and she quickly
fell asleep even as we filed into the hallway.

Outside, Celio and Vlatka took us behind the villa to an overgrown garden, lush with lemons and kiwi and neglected flowers. Celio pointed out the grape arbor they harvested for wine near a charred

outdoor fireplace. It was gorgeous and decrepit and the sun revived us all. This side of the family had done well for themselves.

Once again, we drove home in moody silence. The kids were just happy to be out of that living room. Robert and Jim basked in the mutual satisfaction of having ferreted out the grave of Valentin's parents, even without the aid of the original family tree!

As for me, I was thinking about what had happened to the family that stayed in Croatia. Jim and I were a hundred years and three generations away from the difficulty of that turn-of-last-century life. How much had I been spared because Valentin had so abruptly cut ties with his home?

Since coming to Croatia, Jim and I had blessed America on every crappy unpaved road that dropped off a sheer cliff into a rock-strewn abyss. Every time someone ladled sour cream onto our pizza. Every time we opened our dorm-sized fridge or lay awake on a bone-crushing futon, wrapped in a sleeping bag, head resting on a pillow as soft as a bag of hammers. It was great to meet relatives I never knew existed. But Zadie was right. We didn't know them. I didn't find anything in Lokve and Rijeka that I didn't already have.

I've spent years inventorying things about my childhood that could have been better. Add a freethinking feminist (yep, even from the start) to one quiet, dutiful Catholic family, and you can do the math yourself. But there was nothing in that equation that could match the strain, the trials, and the heartaches I'd just witnessed. The Radošević children were physically abandoned, left to their own devices to grow up. From what I'd seen, they'd made decent lives anyway. Even prospered. They were living proof that pain didn't preclude happiness.

My own parents raised four good and hardworking human beings. My dad, Harold "Bud" Wilson, kept a stable job all his life to provide for us. He didn't lout around in the bars. He didn't do anything to make us less than proud of the gentle country man he is. He took me fishing and he taught me how to shoot a gun. Though I was the type of person to yell "Run!" to the first squirrel I had a chance to shoot, I still got the lesson that girls have as much right to the outdoor life as boys. Dad taught me to drive a stick shift. He played my first records: the Spinners, the DeFranco Family, Al Jolson.

In my memory, he and Mom never missed one of our school events, even when I went through that awkward show choir stage.

I am 100 percent certain that a complicated, wandering girl was not an easy daughter for my parents to raise. I'm pretty sure I'm raising one of my own. But Mom did what she could to make a good home, in which chocolate sizzle cake or rhubarb crisp was always cooling on the stove.

Because Valentin Radošević left and never looked back, I was spared the calamities that Franjo and the Katarinas had been subjected to. So were the American generations before mine.

Had Sister Paula grown up in Croatia instead of America, she could very well have been killed by Partisans. Instead, she traveled widely and lived to be almost a hundred years old. The husbands of the Radošević sisters went to war, but they stayed home safe, never knowing the horrors that their Croatian relatives witnessed. In my generation, I'd seen the look those horrors left behind. I've mentioned that many refugees from the Yugoslavian Wars landed in Des Moines. Men and women who had been doctors and lawyers and professors in Yugoslavia were now bagging groceries, looking humbled and stunned but grateful to be alive. I was so far removed from my Croatian heritage that I barely knew about the war that had brought them over; and my own brother had been in it.

In leaving without a trace, Valentin led us all to safety without even knowing it. Or maybe he did know it.

My family had a hundred years to forget how lucky we were to be in America. A country that, while maddeningly imperfect, still held the torch of possibility. After all, a small-town kid like me could work hard to make my wildest dreams come true.

That evening as I brushed Zadie's hair before bedtime, we discussed what we might tell our friends back home about Mrkopalj.

"I think I will tell people about how old this place is," I told her.

"Old in good ways, like how it remembers the past. And old in bad ways, like not having a good Mexican restaurant."

"And putting pigs in fire," Zadie said.

"I kind of like the pig cooking," I told her. "What will you tell people?"

"I will tell them that there are no Popsicles in this world. The girls, for Popsicles, they say it's ice cream," she said.

"In this world?" I repeated.

"On this planet," Zadie corrected herself.

Mrkopalj seemed such a strange place to my daughter that she thought we'd entered an entirely different universe. I was about to ask her more about this when my cell phone rang.

"Molim?" I answered, like everyone else in Mrkopalj. Please?

It was Stefanija, calling to tell me it was time to meet the old people of the village. She'd spoken to Viktor and Manda, and they'd agreed to talk with me. To walk me through the Mrkopalj of their earliest memory, which would be much like the Mrkopalj of my great-grandparents, as little had changed in the village during that century.

chapter twenty-five

Viktor Šepić kicked the gravel on Novi Varoš on his way home from school. The year was 1933. The time was noon. He was six years old and happy because he got to leave school early. His main job was not reading and mathematics, which was good because he was bad at them. Viktor's main job was to feed his family's six cattle and herd them through the field behind his house at the foot of Čelimbaša. When he turned seven, he would look after the horses, too.

Viktor sniffed the air. Soon it would snow. It snowed in Mrkopalj from October until late April, and it piled so deep that everyone in the village wore skis all the time, even to go to the mercantile to buy sugar, cloth, oil, and corn. Viktor's family shopped Golik's store across the street from the Radošević family. The Goliks were so rich from that store! The village got electricity in 1929, and the Goliks' house was very modern in that way. But even they still had an out-house.

Before the first snow, little Viktor had to go to the pilana *and get a few scraps of wood to carve new skis that he'd attach to his old shoes with a belt. Viktor's mama had been angry and had broken his old skis. It was worse than being beaten, the breaking of skis. He cut over to the* pilana *to look at the scrap pile. It wasn't hard to find perfect wood in Mrkopalj. There were five* pilanas *in Mrkopalj and Sunger. When Viktor was a man, he would work in the woods with his* tata. *Maybe he could save enough money to buy a bicycle. Everybody wanted one, but no one could afford it.*

Working in the woods was dangerous, but Viktor could not wait until he was old enough to do it. With as much as eight feet of snow on the ground every day, there were snowslides on the mountain. Men would climb the mountains for wood anyway. Sometimes they cut themselves on their axes. Viktor knew three men who died when logs rolled over them. Because Mrkopalj had no doctor, one worker died of a burst appendix because nobody knew what was wrong with him.

The men in the šuma *worked for six months, then the* pilana *closed and fired all the workers each year. Viktor's family and their neighbors, all with at least five children, had to work very hard on their farms to make their small bags of* pilana *money last so that nobody would starve. There were five thousand people in this village now! Still, lots of children would die from* fras, *especially in winter. When a baby had* fras, *it would be so hot and it would shake. Viktor had seen it. Babies died from* fras, *but grown-ups and kids died from* tuberkuloza.

Viktor did not find good wood in the pile on this day, and so he walked home. His mama had served the usual breakfast—polenta with milk—and it was now time for lunch. Viktor got the lumberman's lunch of one piece of bread and one hunk of slanina, *or raw bacon. For supper, Viktor would have polenta and milk again, and he hoped this was enough food to make him grow taller someday.*

A group of woodsmen sang "Malo po Malo," the song of Mrkopalj, at the edge of the forest. Viktor's chest swelled with pride. Their village was the best village! The people sang all the time! When they were hungry or bored or worried about family who went to America. But Viktor did not remember seeing any people leaving for America, so he did not know this to be true.

"What? How could you not remember something like that?" squawked a heretofore quiet Manda Šepić from under a black babushka to her husband, Viktor.

Immediately, we all snapped out of the last century. It was a Sunday night at the end of August. Stefanija, Manda, Viktor, and I were sitting in the Šepić kitchen together. Viktor, in a white cotton buttondown shirt, sleeves rolled up to his elbows, and wool pants, firmly tapped a box of mints against his kitchen table. This was the only indication that Viktor ever gave of being rattled about anything.

The difference between Stefanija interpreting and Robert interpreting was the difference between taking a smooth ski lift up a mountain and trudging up the thing wearing shoes with no tread. Being able to talk freely and ask questions was such a heady feeling that I felt nearly drunk, and I would have felt this way even if we weren't drinking *gemišt* made with a bottle of green wine labeled with tape and a marker-scrawled date.

Viktor and Manda met when she was the cook for the priest in Slunj, where she grew up. That priest was Viktor's brother, who noticed that both Viktor and Manda were single, so Viktor's brother picked him up from the *pilana* one day and drove him straight to the church, where Manda was waiting at the altar. They married and that was that. There were no children.

Manda motioned to Viktor. "He complains all the time. His brother never complained," she said. "If his brother didn't like what I was cooking, he'd just say he wasn't hungry."

And she could not believe Viktor didn't remember people leaving for America. "Each of us had somebody in America," Manda said, through a mouth full of handsome dentures. Her eyes were the brightest blue I'd seen.

"Why did they go?" I asked. "Why would my relatives leave a happy Mrkopalj?"

"They couldn't work here," Viktor said. "There weren't enough jobs."

It was simple as that. Mrkopalj lived off the land, and land could only support so many. Because of this, Mrkopalj experienced waves of emigration at the turn of the last century, then after both World Wars.

Manda rose to walk to her stove. Her kitchen was a pretty shade of aqua that was popular with the vintage hipsters back home. When I told her this, she put a hand to her cheek. "This old kitchen?"

"It's a beautiful kitchen," I said. Compact, with a linoleum floor and shelves lined with pretty canisters for tea, flour, and spices. Rosaries were draped above the table.

"Would you like tea?" she asked me.

I said yes, though I was also drinking with Viktor.

After World War II, Manda said, there wasn't much of anything to put in a kitchen. The shelves at the mercantile were bare, so the people of Mrkopalj culled their closets and drove in oxcarts to Rijeka, where they traded clothing for sea salt. Then they'd get back in the oxcart and rumble the seventy-five miles to Karlovac, where they sold the salt to buy corn and staples.

An easier, but less reliable, source of money came from relatives abroad. "When someone went to America, everyone was happy," Manda explained. "Now they would send money."

Well, most of them would. I told them about Franjo and the Katarinas, how their fathers had abandoned them.

"Only men could work at that time," Viktor confirmed. "It was a terrible time for the woman, because she must be home then. Nobody wants a woman for a worker. Many, many women lived like that in Croatia."

"A woman managed how she knew," Manda said. "She sells milk from cows. She works in garden. She fights to save her children from starving."

"Did people think poorly of the men who left?" I asked.

Manda thought for a moment. "Anyway, it wasn't good," she said, finally. "The worst was for the children."

We sat and drank for a while, me double-fisting it with both tea and wine.

"What did it look like, when someone was leaving for America?" I asked. "Were they walking down the road with suitcases and everyone waving, like in the movies?"

Viktor chuffed a laugh. "No suitcases," he said. "A few clothes. Maybe some food. But they are walking. Walking all the way to Rijeka."

"My great-grandfather didn't even have fifteen dollars when he left," I said. "How could he have afforded a boat ticket with that?"

Viktor let out a long "Pffffff!" and slapped his hand in the air. Manda threw her head back and laughed.

"Nobody is paying on that ship!" Viktor said. "They were hiding on that ship! They hide for four or five days. If they are found, ship turns around, they go to prison. They wait in prison. They come out. They run back to ship again."

I said I remembered Aunt Terri telling me that there had been some strange family rumor that Valentin had been a pirate. "That's probably the thing," Viktor said. "He got caught. He was in jail. He had to try a few times."

Once a stowaway successfully hid for half the transatlantic journey, he'd present himself to the crew and they'd usually let him stay on. "They have to pay for the ship crossing somehow," Viktor said. "He does work on ship nobody wants to do, maybe. Or when he get to America, he work on the dock and first pay goes to government because he was sneaking on the boat."

"Surely some people crossed legitimately," I said.

"Yes," Viktor nodded. "Then they need passport."

"That probably cost money, too," I said.

Viktor let out another *bwah-ha-ha* laugh. In those days, Croatian people bought their cattle from Germany. Germany issued cow passports—no photo, just the name and lineage of the cow. Each family from Mrkopalj with a German cow had this version of a German passport.

"They were running then!" Viktor said. "Oh, they were running!

Your family was running, too! All the families run to America! Running with their cow's passport!"

"You people with your cows." I smiled.

"My friend was running. He worked a while then sent another friend his passport," Viktor said. "One cow sends so many men to America!"

"Did you ever try to go to America, Viktor?" I asked.

"Never," he said.

"Why?" I asked, amused.

"Because"—he spread his hands before him—"I like it here."

At that moment, Pavice rapped on the kitchen window. She came around through the side door. Stefanija explained that Viktor and Manda were telling me about old times.

"If you ate just a piece of bread back then, you'd eat it happily!" said Pavice. "Now we are different. Now we throw away the crusts."

Stefanija rolled her eyes.

Pavice had news for me.

"Yenny, what is the name of your granny?" she asked.

"Jelena Iskra," I said.

"Uh-huh!" Pavice nodded once, with gusto. "Josip's sister married an Iskra man. Her mother was Jelena's sister! They live in Germany now. Everybody in Iskra family is gone from Mrkopalj."

"See?" Stefanija said. "Pavice knows everything."

"Now you understand!" Pavice slapped me on the knee, hard. That would leave a mark. "Now you understand what it was like for them!"

Viktor leaned a cheek on his hand. "With most of them running on the passports of cows."

I filed away Pavice's revelation and turned back to Manda and Viktor. How could Jelena have had so much money for her passage—$100 according to the ship manifest.

"Usually people from America send money for their woman," Viktor said. "The man was running, but the woman gets money sent to her family. Later, the man had money to pay for that ship."

I asked them what life had been like for those who stayed in Croatia, those who'd lived through the poverty and chaos around World War Two, when the Communist secret police terrified everyone, and the Ustaše built concentration camps. They said it had been a nightmare.

"First was Italians, then Ustaše, after that Partisans," said Viktor. "They all march in to Mrkopalj, and people must decide what side they are on. You change over time."

Each new political alliance was suspicious of the others. During the 1940s, the Fascist Italians actually *fenced in* the village with chain link topped by barbed wire, a barrier that ran the length of Mrkopalj, from Stari Baća westward.

As Viktor had told the story of his life, now Manda spoke. Her voice, which I'd barely heard before that day, emerged loud and full of passion: a wailing. She told me that many small villages were forcefully overtaken as the Communist Partisans fought bitterly against the ultranationalist Ustaše for control of Croatia. "During World War Two, everybody left my village," she said. "Partisans tell everyone in Slunj we must go. With nobody to look after the houses, they were ruined. Where I lived, there were seven villages. Seven villages were abandoned."

I tried to imagine what it would feel like if the entire county where I grew up suddenly emptied out. The closest I could come was the deserted feel of when the Maytag factory closed down. Still, my people moved by choice. This was a whole different ball game.

Manda continued. "In that war, from my family, four people died," she said. "Father, brother, sister, uncle."

"The Ustaše killed them?" I asked.

Manda shook her head. "Partisans."

She was eighteen when her father was shot. After a skirmish with the Ustaše, the Partisans counted up their losses and killed ten civilians for each of their dead soldiers. "They were innocents, but never mind."

"Her sister was killed behind her own house," added Viktor. He tapped his mints.

"Fifteen years, she had," Manda said, looking straight at me, eyes full of tears.

Those who survived in Manda's family ran for a full year, sheltered by churches or other sympathetic souls. For weeks they lived in a ruined and roofless house, where they were perpetually rained on. Once, she'd been herded into a group of people as Partisan soldiers prepared to shoot them all. Manda held her breath, waiting to die. But a man rode up on a horse bearing a white flag for reasons she never knew. He saved all their lives. They ultimately waited out the war in Zagreb, where Catholic families adopted many refugees.

Manda had spent a vast portion of her life peeking from windows—at first too scared to go outside, then, finally, too old to venture out.

"*Moj meni*," Manda said. "Who could even say all that has happened to me."

I covered her hand with my own. I didn't know what to say; I was humbled by her hardships. Pavice had gotten up and left somewhere along the line. I hadn't even noticed.

"I don't know which side was worse, Ustaše or Partisans," Manda said. "They were all doing against the people."

I held up a hand. "But I thought the Ustaše were the bad guys."

Much of Mrkopalj, Viktor and Manda and Stefanija agreed, had sided with the Ustaše.

Wait. What? My ancestral village on the side of Nazis and Fascists in World War Two? This isn't the kind of uplifting revelation one likes to make when researching family history.

"Partisans were Communist," Stefanija said. "Ustaše were from the people."

"Italians were the best," Viktor opined, holding up one bony finger. "At least the Italians were feeding us. They were chickens, actually. They fenced us in because they were scared of us. Partisans were just schmucks. And the Ustaše: They were fighters!"

It surprised me that Viktor would feel this way. Especially after what he told me next: The Ustaše, a bizarrely disorganized bunch, had nearly destroyed Mrkopalj entirely. In fact, I came pretty close to having no ancestral village at all, thanks to the Ustaše.

It all started, Viktor said, when somebody reported to the Nazi Germans and Fascist Italians that Mrkopalj was full of Partisans. They told the Ustaše to burn the houses along Muzevski Kraj and Stari Kraj. Italian forces set fire to the village of Tuk, razing the whole place.

"Funny thing is, all those houses belonged to Ustaše families," Viktor cackled, shaking his head. In 1944, the Germans bombed Mrkopalj on Good Friday, destroying the Catholic church that once stood at the crossroads of the town. The villagers used the rubble to build a stone fence around the cemetery at Our Lady of Seven Sorrows. The fence was still there.

"Even then, nobody changed their minds about the Ustaše?" I asked.

Viktor harrumphed, his blue eyes squinting. "No," he said. "All Mrkopalj was in Ustaše. There was just a few that wasn't. Hundred fifty Ustaše from Mrkopalj were killed, all of them married with three or four children. So they were getting theirs anyway."

"A lot of widows," Manda added, wringing her hands.

"The history books say the Ustaše were Croatian Nazis," I said. "Is that how they were viewed here?"

"Partisans call it that way," said Viktor. "But the Communists were even worse than the Ustaše."

"What do you mean?" I asked. "They were fighting against the Nazis and Fascists. Where I come from, that's a noble cause."

Manda smiled gently. "If you weren't there, you couldn't imagine it. *Catastrofa!*"

(I asked historians about this later, and the point remains murky to me. Apparently, the actual number of Ustaše fighters in Croatia was quite few. It would have been unusual—and highly unlikely—for such a small village to have a large population of Ustaše soldiers. One historian also told me that the Communist Partisans had a tendency to label anyone who opposed them as "Ustaše," so there may even have been some misunderstanding locally, and indeed some of the villagers insisted later that being Ustaše simply meant you wanted Croatian independence. Many more men throughout the country enlisted with the Croatian Home Guard, known as the Domobrani, whose main job it was to keep war out of the villages. It's my best guess that if Mrkopalj truly did lean Ustaše politically, it was because this was the one of its two rotten political choices that seemed least likely to endanger their beloved Catholic Church.)

When Germany lost the war, the Communist Partisans in Mrkopalj stepped forward. Neighbor turned on neighbor, informing about anyone who'd opposed the winning party. People disappeared in the night. Viktor and Manda hid in their house most of the time, wanting nothing to do with any of it.

"There is one hole here in Mrkopalj. Fifty people died in there," Viktor said. "Partisans killed them."

"Fifty men and one girl," Manda corrected. "That girl was killed because they couldn't find her husband to kill him. This left four children without their mother. But we couldn't say anything! You must be frightened of *everything*."

Viktor nodded and tapped his mints.

"We had an expression, 'The night will eat you,'" said Manda. "The church keeps us all together and keeps us strong. But the Communists are killing the priests and they want to destroy our church and our religion."

This sense of lawlessness remained in Croatia until about 1947, Viktor said. At the end of World War Two, Mrkopalj was bombed out. Tuk was burned. Partisan soldiers dismantled wooden houses and sent them to Serbia by train as rewards for soldiers there. After Marshal Tito took power, his men set up secret police and they acted as judge and jury for anyone whose politics were suspect. Which, my hosts told me, was most of Mrkopalj.

"If you went with them," Manda said, "you didn't come back. Ever."

"It was a violent time," I said.

"Yes, it was," Viktor agreed. "If you were on this side, it wasn't good. If you were on that side, it wasn't good," he said. "On any side, it wasn't good."

"These days, the truth is in the middle."

Stefanija breathed out, hard. "I have to smoke," she said, rooting around in her giant purse. She found a pack and lit up shakily, pulling so hard on a cigarette that her face nearly went concave. "This was very disturbing for me."

No wonder people were still arguing in the bars about World War II. It had ripped this village apart.

"Are Croatians done with war now?" I asked Manda.

"They say that Croatians will not go to war anymore, but who knows," she answered.

"There will be war, definitely," Viktor said.

"Why?" I asked.

"We usually fight for our land. Our territory," Manda said. "To be Croatian."

"Italians want part. Slovenians want part. Serbians want part," Viktor said. "We have the sea. They want the sea. Not for anything else."

"And you have all the good-looking women," I said.

"And some who are not," Manda tilted her head to the side and lifted her eyebrows. "Good and bad and smart and stupid. We have every kind."

"I am sorry for your troubles," I said.

"It is past, it is past," she said, patting my hand. "What you have passed through in life, you must forget."

But they hadn't forgotten. No one in Mrkopalj had. It was their blessing, and their curse.

I was desperate to know one thing before I left.

"Were the bad people, the ones who killed others in the night, were they Iskras or Radoševićs?"

Viktor thought. "Radošević people, there are good and bad ones." He laughed a slow, rumbling laugh.

"Which Radošević are you?"

chapter **twenty-six**

It was my turn to head to Stari Baća alone. I had some thinking to do, and I wasn't going to lie on the leaden futon to do it.

Only a few of the dedicated drinkers were in the bar on a Sunday night. Marijan, the young and dapper tenor from church, was among them. He seemed to be mulling something over. I sat down next to him at the bar. There had been a controversy that day at Our Lady of Seven Sorrows, he said.

"I also decorate the church," Marijan said. "My family was Partisan in World War Two."

"What does that have to do with decorating the church?" I asked.

"Did you notice the flowers on the altar? They are *red*," he said, tipping his face toward me. "*Communist.*"

I just shook my head.

"I know, it is absurd," Marijan said, rolling his eyes. "More absurd when I don't even buy the supplies. They are purchased by someone other than me and then I decorate. Anyway, you are who you are. If I shut my mouth, my ass will talk."

Suddenly, it seemed impossible to escape politics in Mrkopalj. And I was humbled by my lack of knowledge. The previous night, after everyone had gone to bed, I sat up into the late hours, surrounded by a pile of books and magazine articles about Croatian history. I read and read until I could only rub my eyes and cry as everyone else slept. What had these people done to each other over the years? And why didn't I know any of this stuff?

"I just don't understand the politics here," I said. "I had no idea I was such a stupid American, but I am."

"I don't think that's a bad thing," Marijan said. "It could be good or bad, I don't know. But to have a cross to bear on your back all the time? I think it's not good."

I ordered my new favorite, boiled wine, a cheap red served steamed by the explosive cappuccino maker. I headed to the bathroom for safety while the summer girl behind the counter made it. When I returned, Marijan and I drank in silence and I thought over the things Manda and Viktor had told me.

"You know, it seems like the more I drink here in Mrkopalj, the more I feel I've I become part of the place," I said absently.

"To know Mrkopalj, you must drink, of course," Marijan said. "The people here are hard workers, and they've had a hard time."

He was quiet for a moment.

"Well, maybe not now. Now, most of them are drunkards," he said. "Even me! I must go."

Marijan pulled on his tailored gray wool coat and wrapped a cashmere scarf around his neck. He had to return to Rijeka early in the morning and told me good-bye. A few of the college kids came in, crowding the bar near me, but I stayed on my own.

Some time later, Cuculić entered the bar.

"Hello, Gospodin Cuculić," I said, looking over at him.

"Hello, Mizz Veelson," he replied, sitting next to me.

The kids snickered. He was the only person I had met in Mrkopalj who looked consistently and entirely miserable.

Viktor and Manda had told me that not everyone in Mrkopalj joined the Communist party after World War II. However, those who did received good jobs and cozy lives, as did their families after them. (In Mrkopalj, on the other hand, the government closed all the lumber mills except the one near Čelimbaša, and jobs pretty much evaporated.) Only one guy in town exuded the scent of cronyism Manda and Viktor had spoken of. Someone who held a plum job, and who showed no fear of losing it, despite never really doing that job. That guy was sitting right next to me in the bar.

"Gospodin Cuculić, can we talk about history?" I asked.

"No!" he said loudly, plainly, staring straight ahead.

"Why not?" I asked. "Everyone in Mrkopalj picks on you. It's because of your family's politics, isn't it?"

He shook his head, more in refusal than denial.

"Can I get Cuculić a beer over here?"

I heard Mario and Jasminka's son, Stjepan, say something in English, and therefore directed at me: "He will not talk, so she buys him beer."

There was more snickering. I didn't really care. Cuculić didn't seem to either. He took the beer. We drank together, outsiders.

"You have been here three months?" Cuculić asked finally.

"About that, yes," I said.

"You could spend three years trying to understand this place," he said.

"Shouldn't I try?" I said.

Cuculić looked over at me. "In our country, here is reality: one brother is Ustaše; one brother is Chetnik, one brother is Partisan. They are carrying knives against each other. Knives! And that fight never ended. It has been going on for more than seventy years now."

He took a sloppy pull off his beer, dousing his nicotine-stained mustache in suds.

Cuculić did talk to me, with the caveat that his simple English could never encapsulate Croatia's turmoil. He told me his father was high up in the Partisan government just after World War II, that bloody time that had terrified Mrkopalj.

"Do you know who is Aleksandar Ranković?" Cuculić leaned in to ask.

I did not. I do now. Aleksandar Ranković was the minister of the interior and head of military intelligence in Tito's Yugoslavia after World War II. In other words, he was the guy who *invented* the secret service.

"My father was what you call his right-hand man," Cuculić said. They'd had a falling out in the 1960s over Ranković tactics—which included bugging Tito's own vacation home in the Brijuni Islands—and Cuculić's dad quit his position.

"We were neighbors in Belgrade with Tuđjman," Cuculić said. "I was born there. I grew up in Sarajevo."

I told him that it seemed as if he was tortured by his father's life.

Tortured by the fact that his dad had helped create an organization that left Croatia with some of its deepest scars. I was feeling very philosophical, with all my hot wine.

"He was a good man," Cuculić quietly insisted.

He looked up from his beer. "I am a child of the flowers. I am for peace! For love! I just do not like the present days," he said. "Everything is so rough."

I told him that I'd been scared of him when I first arrived.

"Why?" he exploded, typical Cuculić: head cocked, hands out, shocked.

"You were so angry," I said. "You were yelling at me that I was late!"

Cuculić nodded. "This is true," he said.

"Plus, I'm pretty sure you'd been drinking," I said.

"This, too, is true," he said.

"I was lost, I needed help, and you were my only contact here," I said.

He nodded.

"So why wouldn't I have been scared?" I said.

He looked at his beer. "I don't know of this."

I suggested that perhaps the drinking was part of his problem, too.

"From my generation, there are many men like that," he said. "We drink too much. But we hurt no one."

Jim had once asked Cuculić if he planned to retire any time soon. "I don't think about that," he'd told Jim. "I will be dead in a few years."

Cuculić's Partisan father had written a private history of the village that was still considered the best. Even ultra-right Robert thought Cuculić's dad's book was good. I asked Cuculić if he'd share it with me. I could use the historical help.

"No," he said simply.

"You're not being very helpful again," I said.

"It will be a hundred years before we understand the wars of Croatia. This is how long it takes for people to gain perspective.

Europe is different than America. You've forgotten your history. We remember ours. We remember our cousins. We remember our wars. In 1944 this place was burned—*destroyed!*—by Germans." He shook his head and took a drink, not finding the words again. "See? That's the problem in talking about that."

He said there was no way an American, with my country's wimpy two-hundred-year history, could possibly appreciate the complexities of Croatia. "In any country in Europe, we are destroyed three times in a hundred years. Five times! Everywhere in Europe. Everywhere!"

He told me that the monument Jim and I and the kids had seen, the twenty-six stones in the field by Summer Rocks, actually commemorated the deaths of Partisan soldiers in the 13th Primorsko-Goranska Division, who'd all died in a forced march in the middle of winter during World War II. The Mrkopalj cemetery contained a common grave for seventy-six Partisan soldiers. They'd died fighting Fascism and Nazism in the Gorski Kotar. In Mrkopalj, there had been a lot of blood.

Cuculić was bereft of hope. Terminally sad and lost. And he knew it.

We continued to drink together, speaking the common language of nothing at all. History and drinking made up so much of Mrkopalj. I was thoroughly soaked in both that night. Viktor recalled singing in the Mrkopalj of his boyhood. The party sure had ended. I walked home with only one clear thought: Their loss was my loss, too.

From that day on, Cuculić was fine by me. The guy didn't need any more enemies. And anyway, what did I know about the past? It was just now a hundred years since Valentin and Jelena left. I was only beginning to understand what that meant. Just as Cuculić had said, it had taken that long to gain any sort of perspective.

chapter **twenty-seven**

It was a crisp Saturday morning, the first weekend of September. Jim and I sat at the kitchen table drinking Nescafé in flannel jammies. We could faintly see our breath from the chill air coming in through the windows along with the morning sounds of Novi Varoš: the guttural clucking of Josip and Pavice's turkeys; a rooster crowing; Cesar's random barks; Jasminka vacuuming the inside of her car.

I grabbed Zadie to put her hair up, tugging through tangles, finding a sucker stick on my first pass through. Her hair had grown so much over the summer it was remarkable. It had been shoulder length when we left Des Moines, and now it almost hit the middle of her back.

"What time is the phone call tomorrow?" Jim asked, only half paying attention, studying a European road atlas. We were getting ready to spend some time driving through Italy.

"Six in the evening," I said.

A techie niece was Skyping us in to the surprise anniversary party for Jim's sister and brother-in-law. It was going to be our first real contact with anyone back home, other than care packages and e-mails. Funny how we didn't miss it as much as we thought we would. I felt nostalgic about visiting with neighbors on our porch. I missed peaches-and-cream sweet corn and the Des Moines farmers' market. But living in the bubble of Mrkopalj, I felt for the first time that I could parent exactly how I wanted to and be whoever I needed to. We didn't have obligations. We didn't have to be anywhere, ever. This could be excruciatingly boring, but it was also liberating. I was connecting every day with Sam and Zadie, but giving them the independence and freedom I believed in. Jim had started homeschooling them. He was making his own discoveries that he would reveal to me later. I had asked myself, so long ago it seemed, if I could get away from it all and take my family with me. And here I was, doing just that.

I drained my coffee and stood. "I think I'll head down to the church to look for the graves," I said.

"We'll walk you out," Jim said, rising too. "See what's happening in the 'hood."

We all wandered outside, past Manda's laundry waving in the breeze like prayer flags, where Robert and his daughters picked through their potato patch. Robert had already filled a wheelbarrow with silk-smooth, caramel-colored *krompiri*. Cuculić, who had once claimed the field as partially his, was nowhere in sight.

"Oh, hey, Jeem!" Robert called. "Look here!"

Robert had been saving the weird potatoes in a bucket. He held up a giant mutated one shaped like a Mummenschanz mask. Jim laughed.

Then he held up an elongated one. "Like pecker!" Robert called.

"Oo! Let me get my camera!" Jim said.

The kids and I wandered over to the Starčevićs. Bobi lounged nearby, gnawing a potato. The meadow was deep green under the cluster of houses with crimson rooftops crowding around the open field. It was tailgating weather. Eventually, I pulled my sweater closer and walked the road to Our Lady of Seven Sorrows, leaving behind the kids smashing pecans with bricks, and Robert and Jim setting up photos of misshapen potatoes.

The church was unlocked as I entered. I walked toward the front and sat down. Silence washed over me like cold water. It was exhilarating to be alone in the dark sanctuary on a quiet morning. I knelt and prayed for my family, for peace in Mrkopalj, and that the world would leave Croatia alone with its sea, as they had done such a nice job of taking care of it.

I unfolded the piece of paper in my pocket: the cemetery map that Jim, Robert, and Katarina 2 had sketched. It seemed fairly simple to just walk outside and find the graves of Valentin's parents, hidden beneath that of their daughter-in-law, Matilda. I was pretty sure that all I needed to do was ask Pavice to figure out where Jelena's parents were, too.

But for some reason, I wasn't quite ready to do it yet. If I found the graves of my ancestors, what was left for me to do in Mrkopalj? I knew our time would end before long; we couldn't stay forever. And the way our American lives seemed to swallow us whole, there was a chance we'd never be this close as a family again. I wanted to savor the mystery for just a while longer. I folded up the paper and put it in my pocket. Out of habit, I crossed myself. I left the church and walked home to my family. I would find those graves another day.

On the way back, I saw Željko Crnić and Viktor sitting in Željko's backyard at the picnic table shaded by a grape arbor. They'd been working on a stone fence Željko was erecting between his house and Robert's. I think they'd moved maybe three stones before starting on the wine. Željko's precocious granddaughter Lucia buzzed around me as I walked. As we visited, Jim joined us.

"Are you studying your Croatian?" Lucia asked me, smirking.

"Sort of," I said.

"Say something in Croatian," she said, tugging on her purple cardigan.

"*Kopriva,*" I said.

"Pecker," Jim offered.

Željko asked us to sit down. Viktor removed his newsboy cap and nodded to me.

Željko was a big man, not tall, but stout like an old barkeep. His eyes wrinkled at the edges before his loud, Santa-like laughs, which were usually followed by a fit of wet coughing. He wore suspenders, and he and Anđelka puttered endlessly in this backyard, which was my favorite in Mrkopalj.

I said I'd just been to the church, and Željko told us about its history. It was built on the site of what had once been a roadside shrine honoring Our Lady of Seven Sorrows. We'd seen similar chapels all over the back roads of the Gorski Kotar, flickering red candles illuminating plastic flowers and a Virgin Mary inside. In the time of *kuga*, or cholera, in Croatia, the people came to Mrkopalj's shrine to pray for Mary to cure them. They promised that if she ended the plague, they'd replace the shrine with a church, and they did so in 1854.

I'd seen the small statue of Our Lady of Seven Sorrows on the altar. Mary cradled her son Jesus after he'd been taken from the cross, her eyes turned to heaven. Seven swords pierced her heart. Jesus wore gold pants.

Željko noted that one of the popes—and I never figured out just which one—had decreed that anyone who made a pilgrimage to the September festival of the Church of Our Lady of Seven Sorrows would be forgiven of every sin.

I told Jim to make a note of this date.

"Done," said Jim, writing it on his hand.

"Sister Terezija runs that church very well," I said.

"She doesn't run the church; she just works there and cleans it," Željko corrected. "The nuns did everything from when the convent began in 1928." They cooked for the priest, they rang the church bell every hour on the hour, they taught domestic skills to girls—like my cousin Katarina, whom they'd taken in as an orphan. The sisters farmed and raised cattle.

"Like normal people," Lucia assured me.

Nuns started the Mrkopalj choir. Children sang before school, during school, and after school. Adults sang in the evenings.

"We're from Mrkopalj! Mrkopalj sings well!" Željko said with pride.

The convent closed in 1977 when its numbers dwindled. With the proceeds of the sale, Mrkopalj bought a new electric bell ringer.

"When you come to church, you don't have to stay downstairs. Come up and sing with us," he added, smiling.

"We'll do that!" I promised.

Jim and I headed over to the meadow where the kids played. He threw his arm around me. "Thought you were going to look for graves," he said.

"I guess I'd rather spend my time with my living family instead," I said, giving him a squeeze.

We decided it was a good day to take a beach drive together. Just as I'd felt those first pangs of wistfulness about our time in the village, we both noticed there wasn't much summer left to wring from the days before the frosts. Jim grabbed the atlas from the Peugeot and we searched for the place along the Adriatic waterfront that Pavice's grandson, Hervoj, had told us about. Hervoj was a breath-diver—that's deep-sea diving without a tank, baby—and he'd recommended the secluded village of Brseč, an art community back in medieval times that even then boasted zero illiterate residents. Only about a hundred residents remained.

Sweet cottages with sky-blue shutters overlooked a sea shining back in a similar shade of blue. Hervoj had directed us a kilometer from town, where we eased the Peugeot down a dirt path to a deep cove ringed by sheer rock faces. There was no official parking lot—this wasn't an official beach—so we stuffed the Peugeot between cars on a high precipice. The path to the beach was so steep that we sometimes slid on our butts.

But the payoff was heaven. I had never seen water so blue and clear, and it lapped the curves of this tiny protected canyon. Sifted white gravel served as a beach, where women wore no tops and teenagers clambered up tall cliffs to dive, their silhouettes soaring through the sky into turquoise water.

There were some lower rock perches, and so Jim and Sam performed a bit of cliff jumping too, at which time Sam switched his climatological allegiance from Iowa's winter snow to Croatia's summertime sea. Zadie and I sunbathed.

"Mommy," Zadie began, lying prone on her foam mat next to me, pink Dora sunglasses dwarfing her little face, "I like it when we're fancy girls together."

"We're like fish baking in the sun," I said. "If you taste your arm, it's all salty."

I looked over and saw her tentatively stick her tongue to her forearm.

"I wouldn't eat fish," she said. "They pee in their own house."

Sam came up and dripped cold seawater on us. "Dad says to look at him."

I sat up on my elbows and scanned the water for Jim. He floated out a ways, nodding toward two fifty-something biker types making out furiously against a rock.

"Wow, those people really love each other," Sam said.

"They're just tasting each other's salt," Zadie corrected.

Brseč was a dream, but getting out of there was not. We'd wedged the Peugeot between cars on the edge of a cliff about five hundred feet above the sea. Our departure required an approximately thirty-eight-point turn, executed on the precipice. We spent thirty sweaty minutes with Jim behind the wheel and me calling out "Okay, forward!" "Now back up again!" "Stop! Stop! Stop!"

Driving away, we laughed with astonished relief. How had we done that? What a crazy thing! If Jim had made just one false move, the Peugeot would have plunged to its death in a shallow sea!

Suddenly, Jim stopped laughing.

"What?" I asked.

His voice shook. "We had the kids strapped in the car the whole time."

Neither of us had even realized it. We'd been so afraid they'd screw around and fall off the cliff that we'd buckled them into the car while we tried to get out of that impossible parking spot. Had the Peugeot rolled off the edge, as it could have any number of times, it would have taken the kids with it.

Jim and I fell silent. I rested my hand on my cheek, stomach churning. Jim slipped his hand into the backseat to rest it lightly on Sam's leg.

We'd had enough gut-wrenching excitement for one day. We drove back to Mrkopalj, thankful to be together, and alive.

"Remember the first time we saw that?" Jim pointed at Kalvarija, its three monolithic crosses on the hill above Mrkopalj lit by spotlights in the night.

I nodded. "Viktor told me that the Communist government actually moved Kalvarija to the churchyard. The first thing the Croatian soldiers did at the start of the war in the 1990s was to get those crosses and carry them back up the hill."

We watched Kalvarija as we passed. I couldn't understand all the trouble that Mrkopalj had known. The most violence I'd ever experienced was the silent treatment. But I would never again think of any war as storybook simple—good guys versus bad guys. Life was just more complicated than that.

That theory proved itself ever more true when, a few weeks later, Stefanija took me to meet a Serbian family in Tuk. I'd been asking her if there was someone who could tell me firsthand what it was like to be Partisan here and she introduced me to an elderly couple and the husband's crippled sister, ethnic Serbs and all faithful Partisans. Shrunken Ankica's leg had been crushed when the stage collapsed at a dance in the 1940s, and the Italians who invaded soon after fixed it in a prisoner hospital. Her brother Milan, in round plastic-framed glasses, had earned patches like a Boy Scout in Tito's Communist work crews as a young man, when everyone in Yugoslavia had a job and a little spending money to vacation by the sea. His wife, Marija, was a heavyset woman with the cleanest house I'd ever been in, save my own mother's. The home was so close to the street that when they hid inside during the Nazi invasion, they could have reached out the window and touched the swastikas on soldiers' arms.

I would relay their story right here—their family had suffered unspeakably; Milan and his father had once crawled through open graves in search of a sister, hoping not to find her in the faces of the dead—but it would be like repeating the ones I've already told, with only the names changed. The Serbian village of Tuk is almost a physical mirror of Mrkopalj (just substitute the steeple for a spire), once known for its raucous weekend dances just as Mrkopalj was known for singing, and now similarly silent.

When the Italians burned Tuk, Milan and his family found refuge in Mrkopalj. With the family that lived in House No. 262, no less. I was connected to them, too. The ghosts I had felt in 262 could have been the ghosts of the dead in this very family.

Who knows what I would have done, if I had lived in this place during all its bad times. Probably Jim and I would have been like

Viktor and Manda, hiding from the soldiers, hoping that this, too, would pass. We would have sheltered Milan's family when the Italians had burned down Tuk. And we'd probably be joining the ranks of people filing in to Our Lady of Seven Sorrows every Sunday, when this dying village made the most joyful noise we'd ever heard.

There was something to that. Despite the darkness, Mrkopalj sang.

chapter twenty-eight

So what kind of Radošević was I?

I wondered as fall wound down. After the dizzy lushness of the growing season, Mrkopalj bore so much fruit in fall as to seem lewd. Tiny makeshift tractors putted down Novi Varoš piloted by stoic men with old farmwives sitting on mounds of potatoes. When apples came on, even men without a decent tooth in their head didn't leave a seed uneaten.

Jim and I had dreamed of simplicity when we left home. Of time and space and filling an emptiness inside our family. When we'd first arrived in the village, I worried that our act of bravado would somehow damage us. And though it did stir up more questions about the world than ever before, in our updated version of the American Dream, we knew this to be a good thing. Mrkopalj showed us that it didn't matter what we *had* (although I still wished I hadn't left behind my super-cute chocolate suede clogs). We'd been eating cheese and crackers for at least one meal every day and could now pack all our belongings into five suitcases, yet we didn't feel as if anything was missing. This feeling only got stronger as the night chill turned into flat-out cold, and the children of Mrkopalj returned to school.

Our outlook had changed so much that on our walks to Tuk, Jim and I openly wondered how we would return to a place where people had everything and appreciated so little. Sometimes, we just wanted to stay. For people in Mrkopalj, life had been bone-hard. But there had been singing in the streets, and sudden electricity between two people who'd known each other all their lives. They'd built their own houses, planted their fruit trees, perked their own liquor for God's sake. They needed their family; they needed their neighbors; they needed a piece of land. Most of them needed that church over there.

We had become part of this fabric, in the twilight years of an old village. Nothing was here to keep the kids home except the bars and each other, so they left, like my great-grandparents had. Another exodus. Croatia had earned its freedom, and yet it didn't seem to know what to do with it. As an American, I could relate.

Little by little, Mrkopalj told me its story. We'd been drawn together. I had grown to love Jasminka and Ana Fak and Pavice and Anđelka and Manda and Stefanija and so many others in our ever-widening circle. I hadn't even found the family graves yet. Did it matter? I had a month left to figure it out, if the snow held off for that long.

We took our final beach drive to a stretch of shoreline from Opatija to Mošćenička Draga, the Croatian Riviera, a winding seaside necklaced by old resort towns. We'd brought Roberta along with us. Our little Peugeot skimmed past the old villas fronting the towns of Lovran, Ičići, Medveja. The kids and I stared dreamily at the sparkling sea with international yachts like quills poking out of the surface. Jim drove slowly, looking around with almost athletic interest, his love for shabby architecture piqued by the old-timey tourist towns. Stone pathways wound from the shore drive to meat-centric taverns called *konobas,* ice-cream shops, resort-wear boutiques. White Christmas lights were strung from the trees above cobbled ancient downtowns. The oldest resorts still held moonlight dances on patios overlooking the water.

We pulled over for coffee at a little restaurant perched on a hill, an Adriatic overlook with stone tables and chairs.

"I feel like a character in a Merchant Ivory film," I told Jim.

"Except that we're not miserable," he said before heading inside to hunt down a server and put in our order.

Zadie and Roberta vibed on the place. Zadie took out a paper fan and demurely looked over its edge at the water. Roberta slid on a pair of sunglasses and tipped her head back, soaking up the morning rays.

Sam brought out his new favorite toys, knowing Jim and I could languish forever over coffee. He held up four fingers on each hand, then upended them on the stone table. These were the Little Guys: Warrior One and Warrior Two. My son had gone from being the prime toy consumer of the family to playing with his fingers. The Little Guys were built-in soldiers, light and mobile. Two fingers of a hand served as legs, two fingers as arms. The thumb behind the palm? A jet pack. Today, the Little Guys moved to the old stone patio railing, chasing each other through a jungle of a bougainvillea vine.

Zadie sighed over her fan, making a twirling motion at her temple. "Sam is *ludi*."

Roberta, not even moving from her lounging position, giggled.

"I love *ludi* Sam," I said. "*Ludi* Zadie. *Ludi* Roberta."

Roberta sat up now and slid her glasses over the crown of her head. "*Ludi*," she said to me. Then, plain as day: "Crazy."

I hugged her suddenly and hard, American style. I knew her sisters had been drilling her in English. Zadie clapped. "Good job, Roberta!" she cried.

I'd been honing my own Croatian in preparation for having Roberta alone for the first time. If she needed something from me, she couldn't ask for it, and so the night before, I sat in my rocking chair and studied important phrases, such as "Are you hungry?" and "Are those Italians bothering you?" I wanted things to go smoothly so Roberta would have good memories of the day. Roberta was a tough little girl who wheeled around Mrkopalj on a tiny bicycle. She was shy, which made her appealingly quiet, and she kept Zadie entertained. This meant I spent significantly less time in public restrooms. I loved Roberta.

Jim returned to our table with drinks and surveyed our group. "Looks like everybody's peaceful," he said. "This is probably our most low-stress beach trip so far."

As such, this realization was our first triumph of the day. We'd gotten at least as far as our first coffee break without incident. Though we'd passed through dread Rijeka, we hadn't even gotten lost.

We left the café and arrived in Mošćenička Draga (I couldn't even begin to tell you how it's pronounced), where we whipped into a parking spot, only mildly scraping the Peugeot's bumper against a small boulder. Between the lot and the water was a long, tree-lined promenade, set up with kiosks. I held hands with the girls and we slowly made our way down the shady path, browsing tchotchkes. Roberta, Zadie, and I looked at one another with big eyes when a group of young Italian men in tight Speedos tried to order ice cream. There was much gesturing as they argued over flavors and pricing. One of the men walked away in disgust, brushing past Zadie. The girls watched him go, pointing at his tiny swim suit, dissolving into giggles.

Jim and Sam hurried away from us, toward the beach. By the time the girls and I caught up to them, they'd rented a beach umbrella and chairs from an enterprising guy on the boardwalk. We staked our claim on a patch of white cinder shore. Jim and Sam waded into the water, snorkeling around in search of fish that in America we'd have to drive to Petco to see.

The girls stripped down to their swimsuits and wandered a few steps away to where the water lapped the shore, picking through the rocks to find the perfect one.

And then . . . I sunbathed.

I stretched out my toes at the end of the lounge chair. My skin prickled in the late-summer sun. I closed my eyes and basked. I thought, *This is the kind of thing I'll daydream about when I'm in the retirement home, smoking Camel Wides and drunk on gin.*

Yes, I sunbathed on that beach for more than ten minutes. Less than fifteen, but definitely more than ten. Every now and then, the girls would need a potty break or an ice-cream cone. But mostly, I tanned.

This was the second triumph of the day.

The third triumph was Sam's. After we'd dried off, gathered our things, and piled back into the Peugeot, the kids announced that they were starving. I had to concur.

It would take us about a half hour to get to the beachside restaurant we'd read about on the Internet. It was my habit to interview the children to pass the time in the car. I'd ask questions like "If Earth faced total destruction, what would you miss most, our dog or our cat?" or "If you could forcibly dominate any planet, what planet would that be?" The usual lighthearted Mom stuff.

"Sam Hoff, first question," I began, just as the whining in the backseat threatened to ruin our good day.

"Yes!" Sam perked up.

"What are your favorite activities?" I asked.

"Number one is taking Bobi the dog for walks," he said. Jim and I exchanged looks. Number one had always been a television-related activity.

"Number two is snorkeling."

Jim gripped the steering wheel. Number two had always been a toy of some sort. This was getting good.

"Number three is swimming. Number four is reading *Diary of a Wimpy Kid* books."

Both a mental and a physical activity! Crazy!

"Five is riding my bike. Six is when me and Zadie roller-skate in the driveway with Roberta."

Jim and I exchanged a silent high five when Sam finished his list. I looked back at Roberta, who was holding hands with Zadie and grinning at Sam with her white kernel teeth. "*Ludi,*" she said.

I'd count the dinner on the pier overlooking the Adriatic in a restaurant that bordered on nice as a triumph, but I didn't get to sit through my whole plate of pasta with fresh scallops because the kids kept wandering over to the lobster tank. Since Jim lives in constant fear of our children being stolen by pedophiles, we had to take turns keeping vigil over them, though that tank was only about nine feet away.

Still, I think a nice meal with both cloth napkins *and* kids makes for a solid bonus point, if not a full-on triumph.

chapter twenty-nine

As the first frosts iced the Gorski Kotar, Robert entered a Blue Period.

All summer, we knew that if we got up early, we could look out the third-floor window and see him sitting on the bench in the yard, staring into the ether, sweating out the halp-halp as Bobi sniffed the ground around him.

But during the first week of September, Robert developed a violent and tubercular cough. (Unfortunately for everyone, he didn't cover his mouth when he coughed, and his great hackings sprayed upon the people in Stari Baća. Soon, many people had the same illness, and Robert sat virtually alone at the bar, smoking joylessly. Jim still went down at night with Stefanija and Pasha. They did not get sick, because they sat far away from Robert.) The doctor in Delnice prescribed strong antibiotics, and Robert could not drink while he took them. Drying out turned Robert inward. He spoke little. His face appeared deflated. He shrugged more than ever.

Robert still sat on the bench outside our window. But New Robert was even more oblivious to his surroundings. One morning, Jim noted a grasshopper sitting on Robert's massive head of curls, a few inches above his eyebrow. Jim didn't mention it to him, figuring Robert would feel it soon and looking forward to watching the frantic panic that would follow. But as the day progressed, the grasshopper stayed there, moving little, just like Robert.

Jim began hearing rumors that Robert was going to close Stari Baća. He decided that things had officially gone far enough and went looking for Robert on a sunny Monday afternoon after sending the kids for a walk in the meadow after lunch. Jim found him sprawled on the yard swing, covered by the wool blanket, face buried under a water-stained pillow.

"You okay, Robert?" Jim asked, poking him on the shoulder.

Robert slowly moved the pillow aside. "Oh, hey, Jeem," he said, then sat up and doubled over in a spasm of gape-mouthed coughs.

"You okay?" Jim repeated.

Robert swung his legs around and faced his house, rubbing his face.

"I am old man," Robert said.

"Aw shit, Robert, you are not," Jim said.

"Yes! I am!" Robert beat at his chest, producing another round of hacking. "I look at my life, and what? Yesterday, I am boy. And then I am old man."

"Robert, you're not much past forty," said Jim.

Robert shook his head, returned to a reclining position, and covered his face with the pillow. Jim left him there.

I felt myself rooting for Robert. It was either that or punch him. I saw him as a true nonconformist, wildly creative and likeably charismatic but colossally lazy. He'd let Stari Baća go to hell. Just walking into the women's bathroom required rolling up your jeans because a leak in the plumbing caused an ever-present inch of water on the floor. The hostel rooms upstairs were filled with big mounds of clothes that the summer girls were supposed to wash and iron for the silent Goranka, who couldn't keep up between working at the tollbooth and maintaining the bar as Robert languished.

Mario mentioned to Robert every so often, jokingly but a little serious, that he knew a good rehab on the coast. As Robert's first neighbors, they knew more than anyone that Robert's family needed him to step up. Mrkopalj needed him, too; he had all the characteristics of a leader. His father had been an adviser to all, according to people in the village. Robert had a similar gravitas, but he was ruining himself.

Robert's Blue Period both fascinated and saddened Jim. I've said before that the two men really got each other, and I think Robert's midlife reassessment made Jim start reflecting on his own life and how it had changed while we'd been in Mrkopalj.

"How's the homeschooling going?" I asked, one fall morning on our way to Tuk. He and the kids worked in the mornings while I went to Stari Baća to write.

"Good," Jim said. "We study for a hard four hours. I switch back and forth between them, giving lessons. Pretty smooth so far."

At night, Jim thumbed through the homeschooling books we'd brought from home, surfing for ideas before heading out to Stari Baća for his own routine: a nightcap with Stefanija and Pasha.

Within a day, Jim had taught Sam to tell time. Zadie had been toying with sounding out letters since Iowa, but she and Jim played intense phonics games.

"Zadie's got a surprise," Jim said. "When you come back for lunch she'll have a little book for you."

"That's sweet," I said.

"No, she's not just going to *give* you the book," Jim said. "She's going to *read it* to you."

I stopped walking.

"You taught Zadie to read?"

"I did," Jim smiled.

"That's amazing, Jim," I said, hugging him. "She's *four*."

Jim and Sam had designed a video game from scratch, based on Internet tutorials. They had based it on a Shel Silverstein poem, despite the objections of Zadie, who thought the author's jacket photo on *Where the Sidewalk Ends* was creepy.

"So what comes after this?" I asked him. "What will happen when we go home? It would be tough to go back to your old job, I bet."

"I guess I'm not really thinking about it," Jim said. "I'm just focusing on my family."

Jakov Fak passed us on the street, his long ski skates making smooth rolling sounds as he glided by, waving.

"Nobody would believe me if I said the hardest part about this trip is not working," Jim said. "Not having a purpose. You think all you want to do is get away for a break, and then when you're not working, you feel useless."

"You taught your four-year-old to read in a matter of a few weeks," I said. "That's so far from useless."

"I know I'm doing a good job. I'm not looking for a pep talk," he said. "But I'm an architect. It's what I studied in college and it's what I'm good at. I'm not cut out to be a permanent stay-at-home dad. I love the kids, but it's hard."

"It's temporary," I said. "When we get home, you'll start doing the work you were meant to do. And then you'll figure out how to get the balance right."

"I'm over forty years old now. I'm an old man, just like Robert said," Jim continued. "I don't want to let things just happen to me anymore. I want to make my life what I want it to be. Whatever feels right when I get home, that's what I'm doing."

Back in the dorm, I lingered before going to Stari Baća to write. I wanted to be near Jim and the kids. To listen to them work. To hear Zadie read. It was a lovely sound, my husband and my kids turning over new things in their minds together.

Maybe Jim didn't see it, but his best qualities were getting stronger and more defined in Mrkopalj. He was the guy who found joy in gathering and nurturing the people he loved. Whatever might happen once we returned to Iowa, if he followed the same jovial path he'd taken the minute we entered the village, he would be just fine.

I hoped Robert would find similar happiness, but I wasn't so sure. One need only witness his degenerating coffee-making skills to see how far he'd fallen.

At the height of his Blue Period, Robert made the absolute worst cappuccinos. Lukewarm, without the slightest hint of froth, no sprinkle of powdered chocolate. Sometimes, Jim and I avoided Stari Baća in the mornings altogether. The summer girls had mostly gone back to school, so there was no one to bail us out of this one. A few times, we'd committed the faux pas of visiting other café-bars, but people always talked when we did that, and we didn't want to make Robert feel worse. So mostly, we were loyal to the familiar murk of Stari Baća.

Though Robert talked to Jim during his Blue Period, he did not speak to me. He said he'd lost his English. He could barely string together a sentence. I couldn't stop wondering what was going on with him. It struck me that in a village where I'd talked to just about everyone about their personal history, I'd never spoken so deeply with Robert. Of course I had no idea what was wrong with him. I barely knew the guy.

"Robert," I said one morning as I sat sipping a strawberry juice, "tell me about your life. You know more about my history than I do at this point. Now I want to know about you."

He'd been standing there, apron wrapped around his middle, staring into space. He sighed heavily and looked at me. "Why do you talk?"

"I've been getting to know people since we first got to Mrkopalj," I said. "But I hardly know the guy who lives downstairs from me."

"Aw," he said, sucking his teeth. "I am no interesting."

"You are, Robert," I said. "You are a rock star."

"I am no," he said, dead-eyed.

"Let's get together and talk tomorrow morning," I said. "It's a Saturday. I'll see if Stefanija will be home from school so she can translate."

"No Stefanija," he said. "No morning."

"I'll see you at four-thirty, then," I said brightly. "The bar is pretty quiet at that time."

Robert sighed. "Yes," he said. "Okay."

I showed up at four-thirty to Stari Baća. Only a few old guys sat in the dining area. Robert sat with me at the bar for a few seconds before getting up and nervously pacing the floor after I asked the simple question of when he was born.

Goranka hovered in the kitchen, grousing at him in Croatian. Robert rubbed the back of his neck. "I have no words," he said.

"Can we try again tomorrow?" I asked. "I'll swing by at four-thirty or five."

"Is okay," he said, leaving.

So I've mentioned before that when somebody blows me off, it only makes me want to talk to them more. But on top of that, considering my own family history, my obsession with the newly sober Robert was also fueled by the desire to understand what makes an alcoholic parent tick. The more Robert eluded this conversation, the more I wanted to have it.

I showed up to Stari Baća the following day. Robert did not. I checked the second-floor rooms on my way back to the dorm. When I knocked, no one answered. I stepped inside and found Robert on the couch in long johns, sleeping.

Later that day, Robert called and suggested I come to Stari Baća at ten o'clock Monday morning. I did so. The door was locked. I peeked in the window. Empty.

He called later. "Your family come. My house. Tomorrow night."

When we all arrived, Helena was there. And so, it seemed, was every other relative he'd ever known, as he'd filled the second floor with a real crowd. They cooked a huge *pole* and poured drinks, and I didn't get the chance to ask Robert even one question.

We tried again the following night.

This time, there were fewer family members, but Robert had piled so much wood into the stove that it was unbearably hot and everyone was soon soaked as if sitting in a sweat lodge. I became disoriented from the heat. By sheer force of will, I asked several questions, which Helena translated, but baby Magda was crying, probably cooking in her own skin. I was clearly taxing Helena's patience. I knew this because she kept pouring drinks and yelling at me: "You're so boring!"

Before long, Robert took a smoke break. Jim followed close behind. "What's up, Robert?" I heard Jim laugh as they walked out to the breezeway. "You seem a little uncomfortable talking about yourself."

"Helena, please tell Robert that I want to try one more time, tomorrow, with Stefanija, in Stari Baća," I begged. "Please."

"Why do you want to talk to my uncle?" she asked, peeved.

"Because he *is* Mrkopalj," I answered.

She huffed out of the room, baby under her arm, and whatever she said to Robert worked. The Robert that showed up the next day was resigned and reflective. Stefanija translated for us, steady and patient. The privacy of the empty bar seemed to help.

Robert grew up a wild child, his mother's youngest and favorite. When he turned eighteen, he was called to serve in the Yugoslav army. Robert always had trouble with authority, and his military service was made even worse by the aversion to Communism he shared with Ronald Reagan.

Besides, Robert didn't want to fight. He wanted to rock.

So in 1986, he deserted.

To catch an Iron Maiden show in Zagreb. (Opening band: Waysted.)

Seeing that band was more important than any stupid army, he said. He was gone for two days before the police found him in a bus station, drunk and high on hashish. He'd lost his uniform and stood before the cops, woozy, in nothing but a T-shirt and pants.

Robert was sentenced to sixty days in jail, but his friends told his sergeant he'd gone crazy. Robert was moved to a psych ward and banned from carrying a gun, which was fine with him. Then his girlfriend in Sunger broke up with him in a letter and married someone else. He'd always been prone to depression, and this one was a doozy. Robert cried for months. Finally, the army discharged him.

"I have three sister and one brother who worked. They gave me some money," he said. "For one year, I lay down and do nothing."

But he wasn't done with the military. In 1991, during the Yugoslavian Wars, he left to fight like many Mrkopalj men. He said he spent one ten-day stint on the front. His platoon patrolled a border in Lika. The Serbs eventually figured out their patrol pattern and snipers shot six of his friends.

Robert and his peers recovered all the dead but one. Two months after the battle, the Serbian and Croatian soldiers arranged a body exchange.

"We carry that body for five kilometers to the military tent," Robert said, rubbing his hair. "At first, it doesn't change me very much because I don't understand what is happening. In that moment of war, you don't realize a lot. But some months later, the dreams start and they don't stop."

Robert didn't know what to do with himself after the war, so he decided to dedicate his life to his band. "When I was very young, I didn't see myself," he said. "I only know that I need to drink, to eat something, and have one pair of jeans for the year. And when I have *kriza,* crisis, I have a woman. At that time, women were only numbers to me."

His life on the road with the band was pretty wild, until he met Goranka while he was moonlighting at Helena's family pizzeria. Goranka was young and gorgeous, and she wasn't easy like the other girls. They'd been married nearly sixteen years, and he considered himself a settled-down family man now. That sideways finger of his ensured that he'd never play professionally again.

"I still can't believe that surgeon sewed it on wrong," I said, touching it.

Stefanija spoke up. "You should see the arm of my brother," she said. He'd broken his elbow in such a way that it too required reattachment. To this day, his arm jutted away from his body, also sideways.

"Same surgeon," she said.

"Remind me never to go to the Rijeka hospital," I said.

I asked if he planned to stay sober when he was finished with his round of antibiotics. When Robert was on a bender, we'd hear Goranka yelling at him downstairs. Their unhappiness seemed to rise up right through the floors, and I told him it seemed that his family wished he would stop drinking for good.

"Who?" he asked.

"Um, well, your wife and kids would probably like it," I said, caught off guard. "And your sisters are always giving you a hard time."

"Go fuck them. They're stupid," Robert said of the sisters who'd supported him for a year.

"You just drink a lot, Robert," I persisted. I sensed I was crossing a line, but I couldn't help myself. "It doesn't make any sense to me."

Robert pointedly stirred the cup of tea in front of him. "I don't like it so much," he said.

Then he shrugged, owning up a little. "You haven't control of yourself. The last part of drinking time? That is the best part. I just want to have more drink and more drink. But then I am depressed the next day when I can't remember how I get home."

I assessed Robert with the Croatian stare. During his Blue Period, he'd even cut his giant explosion of hair. It was short and tame, reduced by at least 65 percent, as if he didn't want all that hair in the way between his brain and the world around him.

"Robert, is there anything you would have done differently in your life?" I asked.

He squinted through the gingham curtains of Stari Baća. Jakov Fak whizzed by on training skates, lean as a greyhound.

Robert lit a cigarette and pushed away from the table. "I wouldn't have smoked at all," he said. "I hate it. I smoke two packs a day since my mother died."

I sat there, astonished once again by the Brown Bear. Our friend Robert was an alcoholic, an army deserter, a rocker who'd quit the band—and his only regret was smoking.

Stefanija looked at me as he walked away, equally amazed. I rounded up our cups to put behind the bar, which stunk of old wine and stale beer.

"There is still a child in me. A boy," Robert called from the kitchen. "I hope that the boy will grow up before I die."

I walked home, thinking of Robert. I'd chased him down and examined him, maybe seeking some clarity about my own alcoholic parent. Shoot, Robert was probably my mother's second cousin, once removed. Or first cousin, twice removed. I'd ask Jim later.

Anyway, I'd harassed him enough. Robert's burdens weren't my own and maybe I'd been wrong in asking him to share them. Although that story about deserting the army to catch an Iron Maiden show was totally righteous.

Robert was who he was, and it had nothing to do with me. I was never going to understand him, and I needed to stop standing outside of our friendship until I did, as I'd stood outside of Mrkopalj at first. As perhaps I'd stood outside my own life and family, waiting to master it all before I could actually sit back and enjoy. I was beginning to suspect that nothing would ever fit my tidy mold of how things should be. Mrkopalj was teaching me to appreciate the whole lovely mess anyway.

As I rounded the bend into the driveway of 12 Novi Varoš, Lepi drove up in a tractor to deliver the wood cut by Robert's Dream Team. "I am a very beautiful man," he reminded me.

An enormous mountain of *drvo,* or wood, soon dominated the side yard in front of Viktor and Manda's place. Sam scrambled on top of it and busted out the Little Guys. At last, a galactic fort to protect Novi Varoš from Count Dooku's men.

Robert came home, and when he and Jim had finished unloading the firewood with Lepi, they headed down to Stari Baća to meet Pasha and Stefanija to celebrate. According to Jim, Robert was supposed to work that night, but he sat at the bar silently instead, serving no one. Finally, Jim started taking drink orders. He tidied up, with Stefanija directing him how to do this task or another.

Bit by bit over the next hour, Jim put Robert's bar back together until it was clean and tidy again. He took care of things, the way he always did for his family, joining the ranks of neighbors in Mrkopalj who helped Robert keep his world together until he could do so for himself.

Robert watched, watery-eyed, coughing all over everyone. Eventually, after depositing great chunks of what appeared to be lung tissue all over the counter, he got up.

He tossed the Stari Baća keys to Jim, declaring the words that my husband has recalled in glory maybe one hundred times since: "I am sick. Now I go home. Drink what you want. Lock up around midnight."

I can hardly imagine what this must have felt like for my husband that night. All I know is what he told me, which was this: The moment

Robert threw him the keys to the bar was perhaps the greatest of his whole life.

I did not take it personally that he neglected to qualify this statement with "besides when I married you" or "except when our babies were born."

chapter thirty

In the morning, the bells of Our Lady of Seven Sorrows rang as usual. Cesar yapped somewhere between dark and dawn—I didn't know exactly when because Cesar's barking was always lodged in my subconscious whether he was actually barking or not. Every day, Pavice and Josip let their turkeys out of the tiny cage wedged between Cesar's perky villa and Pavice's summer kitchen. Though I often plotted the death of Cesar, I could always count on the pleasant guttural clucking of turkeys to calm me down.

"That's nice of Pavice and Josip," Zadie said one morning. "They let those turkeys out every day to practice flying."

But I noticed the day after Jim's barroom triumph that the clucking was gone. Cesar barked without interruption. With no turkeys, I was worried what I might do about the dog. After dinner, I poured my tea and went outside.

"*Gdje je pura?*" I asked Pavice, who was perched on a lawn chair, shredding *ripa*, or turnips, to pickle. Inside the house, Josip milked the cows.

Where are the turkeys?

Pavice dragged a finger across her neck.

"Frigidaire!" she yelled.

I sat down next to her on a log stump.

"You killed the turkeys?"

She rubbed her chest with sticky hands. "Nom nom nom!" she said, laughing.

"Why didn't you kill Cesar instead?" I asked.

"*Neh*, Cesar," she corrected me, ticking one finger back and forth. "*Pura*."

I put my head in my hands.

Ana Fak crossed the street and sat with us and smoked. Zadie bopped over. Pavice pinched Zadie's cheeks, and Ana petted her hair. Sam rode by on his bike and asked Pavice if she had any *kolaći*.

"*Neh!*" Pavice answered. No powdered-sugar dough balls today! Sam rode off and parked at the woodpile, where Robert and Jim sat staring at it.

Since Lepi had delivered it, Robert's firewood remained untouched. It had been days now. Sometimes I'd see Mario standing over it, shaking his head. Seeing good wood exposed to the elements drove him nuts. Maybe Robert thought that if he ignored the woodpile long enough, Mario would get worried and stack it himself. Mario walked and fed Robert's dog, repaired Robert's house, and hauled Robert's junk to the *smećer*. But he would not stack Robert's wood. When it came to wood, Robert was on his own.

I walked over to the men.

"Maybe we can stack this now," Jim was suggesting.

Robert looked at Jim, slack-jawed. I got the feeling this was one of Robert's less productive nonconformist moments. He stood arms akimbo as he considered the enormity of the woodpile—125 trees' worth, the size of three cars.

No, Robert would stack wood when he thought it was wood-stacking time. I could almost hear him thinking it. Jim could, too. He rose and put his hands on his hips just like Robert. Robert sucked his teeth, and so did Jim. Then Robert sat down in the lawn chair again, looking bushed from all the thinking. Jim did the same. They both crossed their legs and waited. I fetched them beer. I returned to my old women. We all sat and waited.

Robert watched the sun go down from his roost. Then, when it was fully dark, he called to his children, who emerged from the second floor wearing work gloves as if they'd been waiting there all along. Jim called Sam and Zadie.

I came over to observe. Mario crossed the street and we stood together. Jim and Robert directed the troops as they all stacked firewood against the base of the house. Every so often, I'd grab a few pieces and at least pretended to help, but Mario, whose wood had been stacked for weeks, never did.

The night deepened. Chimneys belched smoke. Mrkopalj smelled like one big campground. I experienced great satisfaction watching the pile of wood turn into tidy rows. They even stacked around a first-floor window in a perfect square, to allow in light. With Jim's help, Robert's house had joined the orderliness of fall at last. His family and his customers would huddle around crackling fires in a darker season. We'd already started our own stove in the dorm, its pulse of heat a beacon of the essential abundance of Mrkopalj.

"Your family is best at helping with wood," Robert announced in a husky voice. I think Robert stole a glance at Mario, who stood with his hands in his fleece pockets.

The main activity the next day was admiring Robert's tidy new wood stack. Jim and I sat on the yard swing for a very long time, soaking it in, this signal that winter was nearly upon us. As we rocked, I noticed two skinny legs poking out from the canopy of Željko and Anđelka's apple trees. It was Viktor, picking apples. I hadn't seen the ladder that supported him.

I looked at Jim. "Do you think this is when people make *rakija*?"

"I don't know," Jim said. "I've seen an awful lot of people hauling apples."

"And you never see anyone putting away apples in the cellar, like they do those big bags of potatoes," I said. "The apples just disappear. Into a still, I bet."

We'd asked all summer for someone to show us how to make *rakija*, but the mere mention of bootleg liquor turned people curiously mute, as if they'd never heard of this staple of the Mrkopalj diet that was more vital than water. They'd share their most intimate secrets with me. But I got nowhere with a *rakija* recipe.

Viktor stepped down from the tree as Željko pulled in to the driveway. Jim and I stopped rocking, hoping to remain undetected. Željko disappeared indoors, then returned to set up big brown glass jugs along the picnic table. Viktor fetched some plastic tubing from the cellar.

Jim and I crept up to the dorm and called Stefanija to see if she might help us get to the bottom of this *rakija* business. By the time we were back downstairs again, spying around the corner, all the machinery was gone. Viktor and Željko sat at the bare picnic table, serenely sharing a drink of wine. When Stefanija showed up, we joined them.

"So," I began, "what are you guys gonna do with all those apples?"

A low laugh rumbled from deep inside Željko's chest. He fished a pack of cigarettes from the pocket of his work shirt. He shook one out and lit up, exhaling smoke and squinting at us.

"I don't know," mused Viktor, swirling his wine. "Maybe we will give away to other people."

"Are you making apple pies?" Jim asked.

"Apple cake?" I asked.

"Ha!" Željko laughed.

"Apple juice?" Jim fired.

"Yes, yes," Viktor said. "Sure."

Željko took a languorous draw on his cigarette. Viktor leaned his face against his hand.

"Apple muffins," I suggested. "Nom nom nom."

"We hear that you are sad Pavice's turkeys died," said Viktor.

"Pavice *killed* all her turkeys," I corrected.

"Yes, Jennifer. She put them all in the refrigerator to eat," said Anđelka, emerging from the house with wineglasses.

"Pavice and Josip are the top meat eaters in Mrkopalj," added Viktor.

"You're trying to distract us," I said. "I'm here about the apples."

"Vinegar," said Željko. "We are making vinegar from apples. For salad."

I looked at them both, hands on my hips. "Vinegar."

The two men chuckled. "Wine?" Željko asked, holding up a bottle of red.

Anđelka looked innocent. I'd shared enough *rakija* with her to know that she either had a direct supply or was going into debt buying in bulk.

"Some people make *rakija* out of apples, but I don't," Viktor said sweetly.

"Do you know anyone who does?" Jim asked.

Željko began humming under his breath. Viktor shrugged.

"If someone were to make *rakija* out of apples, how would they do it?" I asked.

"Well," Viktor began, "you'd put apples in a large box and crush them and put in some stuff and then you'd cook it and then you'd get *rakija*."

"Have you cooked yours yet?" Jim asked.

"Where do you store it?" I asked.

"Some people make *rakija* from figs, too," Viktor said to Željko.

"*Da, đa,*" said Željko, nodding.

"But I haven't cooked it myself," Viktor said.

"Nor have I." Željko shrugged.

Anđelka nodded, hands clasped together as if in prayer.

Željko backed him up. "Maybe someone makes *rakija* in Mrkopalj, but we don't know this," he said. "We don't have grapes, so we don't make wine either."

I looked over at the giant grape arbor. I looked back at them. Anđelka looked up at the sky, as if finding something very fascinating up there.

"The grapes are just for decoration," Željko indicated, stubbing out his smoke.

"Stefanija, can you find me someone who makes *rakija*?" I asked, exasperated.

"I don't know of anyone," she said.

"That's a load of shit," Jim said, laughing.

Stefanija avoided my eyes, suddenly absorbed with her nail polish.

When my people left Mrkopalj a hundred years ago, they'd dodged its sorrows. But they'd also lost their right to the recipe. When it came to making *rakija*, not even Stefanija could help me.

With *rakija*, I was on my own.

chapter thirty-one

I might not have been getting that *rakija* recipe, but Stefanija's grandmother Ana finally invited me over to her house. Stefanija had long insisted that the old woman would be able to tell me everything I needed to know about Mrkopalj once and for all, and though I couldn't guess what that meant, I was eager to find out.

Jim and I left the kids with Robert's girls and walked down Novi Varoš to a familiar place with a channel-glass door we'd seen many times on our walk to Tuk. Outside the house, I saw another entirely novel method for holding up the outdoor woodpile: a washing machine propping up the whole stack, a surreal setup that once prompted Marijan the tenor to describe Stefanija's grandmother as the Croatian Marcel Duchamp.

"Come in! Come in!" Stefanija said as she rose from the kitchen table and introduced us to Ana Tomić: stout in a brown housedress, with short-clipped hair and a face creased by sun and time.

The kitchen was small, dominated by a wooden table and chairs on a worn linoleum floor. For decoration a crucifix draped in rosaries hung near a picture of Jesus with a lamb. Baka Ana, or Grandma Ana, offered us the contents of her refrigerator: salty Mrkopalj prosciutto and the remains of an old ice cream cake. A stocky drill sergeant, Baka Ana spoke in a continuous demanding bark punctuated by bursts of cackling laughter that showed a mouth full of gums. She manhandled us into chairs and directed us to eat.

"Eat, or she won't stop telling you to do it," Stefanija said, lighting up a cigarette.

We ate.

Baka Ana asked me what I wanted to know about old Mrkopalj. I told her that I'd learned a lot already, especially from Viktor and Manda.

"I was born 23 July, 1928," she said. "Viktor is 1928 also. I went to school with him."

"I'll bet he was trouble," I said, smiling.

"*Ya! Ya! Ya!*" she jabbed a thick finger at me. "He wasn't a very good student. Do you want some juice?"

"*Neh,*" I said.

"*Kavu?*" she asked. Coffee?

"No, thank you," Jim said.

Baka Ana looked at us, puzzled.

"Your granddaughter is our favorite person in Mrkopalj," I told her.

"*Dobro!*" she cried, smiling big at Stefanija. "Ha ha ha!"

Baka Ana got down to business. Now, what were my great-grandparents' names? When had they left for America? Where had they lived?

I told her that Robert had taken us to House No. 262 after we'd seen the Book of Names.

Baka Ana cocked her head. She worked her jaw for a few seconds.

"Uh-oh. Here it comes," Stefanija said, taking a drag off her cigarette.

Baka Ana said she knew the family in 262. And they weren't Radošević. She directed Jim to go back to the dorm for the family tree he'd drawn. She told Stefanija to call her friend Zora Horaček.

"Zora was your family's first neighbor," Baka Ana said. "And she also—" She stopped. Zora must be here for this, she said.

What was going on here? What was the big mystery? Baka Ana sensed that something was wrong, and it was making me nervous.

Jim left. Stefanija called. Zora was in church. Stefanija hung up. Baka Ana made Stefanija call again immediately, and this time leave a message to get here as soon as possible.

Baka Ana told a story to pass the time until Zora came. She grew up in a house across the street from Stari Baća, and Mrkopalj was such a sheltered village that she didn't even hear of a banana until she was eighteen. The first building on the land where Stari Baća stood was built in 1940, the swanky home of a rich woman who ran a high-end restaurant-bar. During World War II, when there was a fence around Mrkopalj, Italian soldiers turned it into a mess hall. Children brought them eggs in cups and the soldiers would exchange the eggs for soup.

"We all speak Italian," Baka Ana said. *"Ciao, bella!* We didn't like Italians because they were fucking around with everyone. They liked the women."

"Ha! My grandpa Gino was Italian," I said, teasing her.

Baka Ana buried her head in her hands. "I'm embarrassed now." She laughed.

Stari Baća was later a *kuglana,* or bowling alley.

She hefted her body from the table and went into her bedroom just beyond the kitchen. She returned with a tall bottle of *rakija* and held it up.

"Rakija?" she asked us.

"Da!" I said.

"Dobro!" she said to me, and gave me a closed-mouthed smile so wide her eyes disappeared into her cheeks. *Rakija* sloshed over the rim of my shot glass.

I asked her what she missed most about the old days.

"Moj muz," she said. My man. "He was afraid when he died that I would marry again. But I didn't. I was faithful."

She missed their parties. Mrkopaljcis danced the polka, the waltz, the mazurka. I told her Grandpa Gino and Grandma Kate had thrown living-room polka parties with accordion players back in Des Moines. Baka Ana laughed and laughed. "You can't take the Croatia out of a Croatian!" she said.

Even more than the partying and the dancing, Baka Ana missed the special feeling on Christmas, in a poor village that saved up for holidays. Sausage called *mešnjače* on Christmas Eve. *Sarma* on Christmas Day. The only sweets they had was *povitica*.

"Would you teach me to make *sarma*?" I asked. I loved cabbage rolls.

"*Da,*" she said, quick and sharp.

"Does it take a long time?" I asked.

"*Da!*" she said. "Just cooking takes two hours."

"Wow," I said. "At what temperature?"

She waddled over to the stove. I hadn't noticed there were two of them in the kitchen. She opened the older one. A fire burned inside.

"You put in two sticks of wood, then burn down. You put in two more sticks of wood, then burn down. Put in two more sticks of wood, then cook for two hours."

"She cooks with a woodstove?" I looked at Stefanija.

"She always uses the wood stove," said Stefanija. "We buy her a new electric one and she won't use it. She says it's too expensive."

"When you cook with wood it is also warm," Baka Ana said.

"What do you do with the new oven?" I asked.

"I store my bread in there." She pulled out two loaves to show me.

"Kind of like the washing machine holding up the woodpile?" I laughed.

"*Da!* I wash by hand," Baka Ana said, energetically mimicking the motion of the washboard. "Electricity is expensive!"

She slammed the oven doors shut and labored back to her bedroom. She emerged with a plate of raw bacon, and unless Baka Ana had a refrigerator in there, which I doubt, she was keeping that bacon on her dresser.

I looked at it.

"Eat, Geri!" Baka Ana ordered, confusing my name. To Pavice I was Yenny. To Baka Ana I was the cousin on *The Facts of Life*.

We heard a knock. It was Jim, back from fetching the family tree.

"The kids are doing okay," he noted. "They're all just playing."

Baka Ana grabbed the paper and held it close to her face. I leaned in. "What's the matter?" I asked.

And that's when she told me: House No. 262 was not my ancestors' house.

Baka Ana shook her head once, vehemently. "It wasn't your family in 262. Uh-uh. No-no," she said. "Isn't the right house. Uh-uh. *Ni.*"

"So if 262 wasn't Valentin's house, where did he live?" I asked, desperate. Robert had *told* us that 262 was our family house! I'd spent whole days picking around that place, trying to commune with the dead. No wonder I'd just gotten static: I had the wrong number!

Stefanija rose preemptively to call Zora's family again, before my head exploded.

"Zora will be here in a few minutes," Stefanija assured us when she hung up. "Her granddaughter is walking her over now."

I asked Baka Ana if she knew anything about Jelena Iskra's house, House No. 40, on the other side of town. Had the Book of Names gotten that right at least?

Baka Ana shrugged. "Gypsies were living there," she said. "A few of them weren't. But mostly: Gypsies."

My eyes bugged. "Gypsies?"

"It was state ground," she explained.

Was I descended from gypsies? That would explain a lot.

Jim sketched out a map of Jelena's side of town and circled House No. 40.

"Was this the Iskra house?" Jim asked.

Baka Ana held up the paper to her face. Yes it was, she replied.

"So were they gypsies?" I asked.

She traced the street with her finger, reciting family names under her breath. Then she pushed away the map.

"Nah," Baka Ana said. "Your family wasn't one of the gypsy families."

I sat back in my chair, exhaling. She pointed at me. "Geri is sorry they weren't gypsies."

"I'm a little sorry," I said. "It might be cool to be a gypsy."

Baka Ana lowered her voice. If the Iskras had been gypsies in Mrkopalj, they wouldn't have made it out. Around World War II, the soldiers killed them all.

Baka Ana asked if I wanted a glass of red wine or a shot of *rakija*. I chose the hard stuff.

"Look how good she drinks *rakija!*" she said to Stefanija. "Oh, she's a good drinker!"

"*Živjeli,*" we said to each other, then beat our chests in fiery pain. Baka Ana's hootch was wicked. One of my arms went numb.

"Want some water?" Baka Ana asked.

"Nope," I answered.

"*Dobro!*" Baka Ana stood back a little. "*Rakija* gets a mother through the days."

"Good to know," I said, nodding.

She poured another, then browbeat us into eating more raw bacon.

"Trichinosis be damned!" I toasted, and we all drank again.

We heard another knock at the door, and Stefanija leapt from her chair to usher in Zora, who'd been delivered from church by her granddaughter.

Zora Horaček was built similarly to Baka Ana, but her eyes were a gentle blue. She wore a delicate plastic hairband and spoke softly.

The two women embraced and exchanged pleasantries.

"*Kako si ti,* Ana?" Zora said.

"*Kaki,* Zora?"

"Together, we have one hundred sixty years," said Zora, putting an arm around her girlfriend.

Zora Horaček lived in the house directly north of House No. 262, with her hardworking son Dražen and his family. Since Robert had told me of the Horaček family the first time I saw House No. 262, I'd come to know Dražen Horaček a bit better. He was a regular in Željko's backyard and the only truly handsome man in Mrkopalj, with cobalt eyes in a face that had all its parts intact and harmoniously arranged, including straight and present teeth.

Ana debriefed Zora on what I knew—and what I did not know—about my family. Then Zora recited the same history that the Katarinas had told me in Rijeka. She knew my family well because her family had bought my family's land.

"House 262?" I asked.

No, she explained. "Your family house no longer stands."

Long ago, just north of 262, sat two houses just like it, one behind the other. As time reeled forward through each wave of immigration, my family members had moved in or out or on to the next life. Eventually, the houses sat abandoned, paint fading, ceilings caving in, after the Radošević family left Mrkopalj. Katarina 2 had sold that property to Zora's family in the 1970s. Today, all that remained were traces of the foundation, which Dražen had let stand, as an homage to my family's roots, the home of the Horaček's long-gone first neighbors.

"You're kidding," I said.

Stefanija pointed over at Zora with her thumb. "She knows *everything.*"

I settled into my chair. Jim draped his arm across my back. "Well, how 'bout that?" he asked, laughing. "Robert showed us the wrong house!"

I just shook my head. "Well, I'm not sure what I think about that," I said. "But I'm sure the *rakija* will bring some clarity."

"Zora and I will teach you *sarma*," Baka Ana said, pouring me another drink. "And there is one original food from Mrkopalj we must also teach you. Polenta and cabbage!"

Baka Ana rummaged in her room again, this time producing a little wooden masher. She and Zora announced together: "*Kamusnicu!*"

Then they taught us a song, the main chorus of which was "*Rakija, rakija,* I love you so much." We toasted to the mysteries of Mrkopalj.

As Jim and I hobbled home, incredulous of all this news, disoriented by Mrkopalj as usual, Marijan pedaled by on his bicycle.

"Drunkards!" he called over his shoulder, waving.

chapter thirty-two

We woke to the sound of shouts and loud clanking. I sat up and looked out the window. Under a clear blue sky, vendors set up tent kiosks all up and down Novi Varoš.

It was the festival day of Our Lady of Seven Sorrows. All summer, the people of Mrkopalj bragged to us about their *festa;* it was the most important day on the village calendar. In all Gorski Kotar, they said, this church festival was the most popular, with a carnival and street food and more vendors than any shopping mall. We'd seen the festivals in Sunger and other villages. We didn't really believe them. But now the day had come, and before 7:00 A.M., the village was transformed into a tent city. Hundreds of cars streamed up the road.

Željko had told us that whoever made a pilgrimage to Our Lady of Seven Sorrows on festival day would be forgiven all their sins. Jim and I figured that since we were here for a fresh start, we might as well get a few stains off the soul, too. We dressed and waded through the stream of humanity, making our way toward the church.

Just as our friends had told us, you really could get just about anything in those kiosks. Clothes, shoes, candy by the kilo, potato mashers, butter churns, horseshoes. Of course there were fake guns for the kids. We found a ski cap bearing the insignia of Slipknot, the hard-core metal band from Des Moines. Everything, all of a sudden, seemed connected to Mrkopalj.

We walked the streets toward Stari Baća, where pockmarked toothless dudes ran a carnival in a vacant lot across the street. The kids headed directly for the one-gun shooting gallery run by a black-haired woman in similarly colored clothes with a fat stack of kuna bills in her hand. We added to it, and the kids shot the first fake gun of their lives. Zadie won a pair of puppy-dog earmuffs and Sam earned a Spiderman the size of an old-school G.I. Joe. Though Croatia may be a poorer country than the United States, their carnival prizes were way better.

The main ride was the giant twirling swings. The balding carnie in a tracksuit running the thing played throbbing dance music, and when he shifted the motor into gear, blue smoke rose from it and he entirely spaced off in the haze as the children of Mrkopalj spun through the air around him. The kids took advantage of the lack of supervision and swung their legs back and forth, gaining momentum to push off the swings in front of them, then crashing into the chairs behind.

Jim stood with his mouth agape, struck with the horror of a man who knows OSHA codes, while parents stood around laughing at the merriment. As Jim was about to lunge at the carnie and beg him to stop the ride and save the lives of Mrkopalj's children, I pulled him away and we crossed the street to Stari Baća, where Robert and Goranka had set up a food stand. Robert stood wrapped in a blue apron, stirring a vat of *kotlava*—meat cutlets in tomato sauce—with a giant spoon. He seemed mellow, and as far as I knew, sober. I'd decided after meeting Baka Ana that I wasn't going to mention the 262 mix-up to him. I'd probably hounded Robert enough.

Jim, still mildly panicked about the swings, told Robert about it.

"Of this ride, I know," Robert said, nodding gravely.

"You do?" Jim asked.

"Last year, I drink very much. And me and my friends think is good idea to take this ride," Robert said, stirring. "But is not good idea."

"What happened?" Jim asked.

"I cannot say," Robert answered, looking back to his vat of meat.

"Oh, come on," Jim goaded him. "You can tell us. We won't tell anybody."

Robert fished in his apron for a pack of smokes. He tapped one out and lit up, inadvertently ashing into the *kotlova*.

"Me and my friends, we get on this ride. We think we will show kids: This is how you ride! First, we ride good. We push our friends with feet. We fly very fast."

Robert paused, remembering.

"Then, I don't feel good. There is no way I can stop this ride," he said. "I throw up. And throw up goes behind me. On my friends. On other people. So I say: Is not so good, this ride."

We walked on, toward the Church of Our Lady of Seven Sorrows, completing our pilgrimage. People spilled out onto the steps, heads down and hands clasped; the sanctuary was too full to hold everyone. The collection of voices of the Mrkopalj choir wafted over our heads like a blessing.

"Mommy." Zadie tugged on my sleeve. I picked her up and planted her on my hip. "I want sausage."

I leaned over to Jim. "The little carnivore requires meat," I whispered.

"Let's go back to Stari Baća and have lunch," he whispered back. "I want to make Robert tell me the swing story again."

The four of us pushed back through the crowd to the cool, dim sanctuary of Stari Baća. Jim ordered plates of *ćevapčići* and *kotlava*. Stefanija and Pasha were working behind the bar with a smattering of Goranka and Robert's relatives. Cuculić and Nikola Tesla beckoned us over to a table, the same table I sat at when I ate in Stari Baća for the first time, almost exactly a year before.

"Hello, Mizz Veelson!" Cuculić welcomed me. Nikola Tesla wiggled his eyebrows and danced in his chair for me. I had mentioned to the summer girls that I dug Nikola Tesla's Sean Connery vibe, and now I suspected someone had told him.

"Mom? Can we have some pop?" Sam asked.

"No," I told him. "Eat your lunch first."

"Oh, mah!" Cuculić said. Nikola Tesla hustled to the bar, still dancing, biting his lower lip, and fetched the kids two Fantas.

Jim returned with our lunch. The kids wolfed down their food and headed to the pool table just a few steps away.

Stefanija walked over and released the pool balls. "My *baka* says you must come over soon to make *sarma*," she said. "But you must bring the children this time."

"I will," I promised.

"When we are in high school, we sit for hours with Stefanija's *baka*," Pasha called over. "She's the best."

"That is because she loves you," Stefanija murmured, brushing past him.

Pasha said something low and quiet to her, and I wondered why they were no longer a couple. Like magnets, they were pulled together almost as if they couldn't help themselves. But Stefanija dreamed of leaving Mrkopalj. It was taking her a while to finish school—the Croatian education system was complicated, of course, there seemed to be a pay scale based on previous classroom performance—and she had to take classes in small increments in order to afford it. She was sharp and perceptive and possessed an ambition we didn't see in Mrkopalj. But studying didn't come easy to her. She had to focus if she'd ever graduate and run a hotel, which was her dream. And to accomplish all this, I guessed, she would have to focus outside of Mrkopalj.

Jim, Cuculić, and Nikola Tesla were talking like old chums.

"Your children, they are very good," Cuculić said.

Nikola Tesla nodded. He never spoke English. Ever. But he understood it.

"Thanks," Jim said, watching Sam and Zadie. "They've become more valuable to us since they started earning money playing pool."

"Oh ho ho! This is a very American thing to say!" Cuculić said, laughing.

Nikola Tesla nodded and headed to the bar. He returned with beers for all of us and another round of Fanta for the kids.

"*Hvala*," the kids intoned.

Nikola Tesla grabbed his heart and danced over to me. He grabbed my notebook. "Zoran," he wrote. He pointed to himself.

"He is telling you that his name is Zoran," Cuculić said in his same old habit of translating to me things that had already been translated.

"Sarajevo, forty-eight," Nikola Tesla continued.

"He tells you that he is forty-eight years old," Cuculić began.

"Honey, I know." I patted Cuculić's hand.

Nikola Tesla wrote the names of his children. Grown and gone away. He grabbed his heart again.

"Where is his wife?" I asked Cuculić.

"His wife left. She has joined the occult. It is a very sad thing. We are good friends and so he visits Mrkopalj on the weekends."

I looked at Nikola Tesla. He shrugged, closed his eyes, and danced in his chair.

Jim pulled me closer, and I put my head on his shoulder. We watched our kids doing a respectable job moving around the cue ball.

"It takes very good parents to have very good kids. We say *simpatico*," Cuculić said to Jim. "You and your wife do a very good job."

Cuculić rose and corrected Zadie's pool shot, and she sank the ball then. Zadie, miraculously, did not squirm under his guidance.

My husband and I were having fun together the way we had when we were younger and meeting our friends for drinks after work. Even though our kids were a foot or two away from us, I felt as if Jim and I were on a date.

And, God help me, I enjoyed the company of Cuculić. I might say that it was because he was being especially nice that day, but in truth, we were both being nice for once. It struck me that I hadn't been, ever since the first day when I burst through his door wanting to be babied through my job.

Jim and I gathered the kids eventually and walked back to 12 Novi Varoš. The crowd was dwindling. We saw one of the carnies hunched over in the flatbed of a truck, sleeping, but jerking awake just at the point when he was about to fall over. Napkins and beer cups littered the streets. The hawkers were spectacularly aggressive, trying to move merchandise so somebody else would have to carry it home.

"Well, do you think our sins have been forgiven?" I asked. "We made our pilgrimage to the *festa*."

"We just drank in a bar all afternoon while our kids played pool and a video game called Tank Wars," Jim said. "We've got a whole 'nother set of sins to account for."

I held Zadie's hand. Jim held Sam's. He slipped an arm around my waist and we walked home, connected.

That evening was peaceful in the dorm. We'd gotten into our jammies early to lounge around. I was writing down a few thoughts in my notebook. Jim and the kids curled up on the futon watching TV, waiting for the random moment when Conan O'Brien would be on. We never knew when to expect it, but we waited. He'd gotten the *Tonight Show* gig just as we left the States, and he lost the show at about the same time we left Croatia. We considered ourselves fellow travelers. "I like that guy," Sam said. "His forehead is so big that he could fit another face on it."

While they waited for Conan, they watched another dorm favorite: a German show that featured a piece of rotten stinking cheese that talked.

Though it was quiet inside, the streets of Mrkopalj remained in a state of ruckus. The local *festa* parties started. Faint at first, then getting stronger, the sounds of karaoke drifted through the dorm windows, coming from the direction of the convent.

I leaned out, straining to catch a glimpse of the singers.

"Why don't you go out there and have a look around?" Jim asked lazily.

A truly terrible voice hit the karaoke microphone, wherever it was. A real crooner whose singing sounded like a tribal war cry. He sang loud and proud until, in mid-song, I heard an "Oof!," then feedback. Then the music played on, without a singer.

I put down my notebook and pulled on a jacket over my jammies. "Be right back," I said.

I'd only intended to walk the length of Novi Varoš in search of the fallen karaoke performer. But it was pitch dark, and though I heard partying going on, I couldn't see anybody. When I made my way down to the convent, I did discover a stage out front, but it was eerily abandoned, as if I'd been hearing ghost singers. There wasn't a soul in sight.

The streets were cleared of the vendors' wares, and most of the cars were gone. In their wake lay great heaps of garbage. Where was everybody? I still heard partying, and I wanted to see what kind of damage had been done to the rest of the village, so I walked on.

Trash was piled everywhere in knee-high mounds. Here and there, I noticed movement in the shadows, usually a drunken person veering along. People had set up temporary beer stands in backyards, and that's where the remaining partiers were clustered, standing around keg taps and picnic tables, singing local songs, arms thrown around necks, calling for more drinks! More drinks!

I turned the corner from Novi Varoš to Stari Kraj, careful to stay in the shadows myself so no one would see me in my pajamas. Then I heard someone warbling my name. "Jeeee-nnifer! Is that Jeeee-nnifer?" someone called in English.

"Hey Jennifer! Will you have a drink?"

It was Stefanija, walking with Marija, Pasha, and Stjepan. I approached them reluctantly. Stefanija took me by the arm. "Of course you will join us!" Stefanija said.

They hustled me over to a makeshift bar set up outside Cuculić's office. I spotted some Konzum ladies, and they raised their glasses to me as they sang along with an accordion player. We moved through the group over to Goranka, who was nursing a Jägermeister shot. She'd colored her hair Debbie Harry blonde, and it really brought out her brown eyes.

I was never entirely sure how to act around Goranka. We had no common language. Sometimes when I would ask Robert to help me with something, he'd put me off. But if Goranka was around, she'd speak a few soft words and he'd change his tune immediately. I suspected she was his conscience.

Goranka called something over to the bar, and soon I had a Jägermeister shot, too. "*Živjeli*," she said quietly.

I hadn't drunk Jägermeister since a bad experience at a Hole concert years before. But I drank in the spirit of bridging the cultural divide. Plus, it tasted like candy.

Pasha bought a round of beers.

"What happens to the trash in the streets?" I asked. "It's like the sky rained garbage."

"It will be gone by morning," Pasha said.

"Workers will clean it in the night," Stefanija confirmed.

Just then a man whom Jim and I had seen before at Stari Baća lurched into our group. His name was Igor, and he was a tall, rail-thin sailor with a jet-black mop of hair and a sparse mustache. Igor and Jim and I had chatted over coffee one afternoon in Stari Baća about all the places he'd been and found we shared a mutual fondness for Mexico. But it wasn't amiable international Igor who lurched toward us the night of the *festa*. This was way-drunk Igor, who appeared to have lost control of his extremities, his gangly body thrashing dangerously, whacking first into Pasha and then into Goranka.

"Where's your fucking husband?" he slurred to me. His voice sounded as if it had been stretched like taffy.

"Fucking home," I joked. I felt Pasha inch closer to me.

I turned away from the drunken sailor, and he whirled off to harass someone else. When I glanced around the crowd a few minutes later, I saw him crash into another cluster of people. Igor was bothering everyone, but people avoided him carefully, as if they were used to this. He pinballed around until Stefanija's brother, Valentin, the guy with the sideways elbow, stepped in front of him and took a swipe.

The fight didn't work out very well. Valentin's punch missed, and Igor put up his dukes just like in the movies, except that he put them up about forty-five degrees away from the actual location of Valentin. Eventually Valentin's friends pulled him away to administer a "Don't do it, man" talk.

It was Goranka who finally calmed Igor down with a combination of sweetness and stern mothering. This was the smooth work of a woman who ran a bar. She maneuvered Igor to a picnic table and sat him down, and he stayed there, looking bewildered, searching the crowd as if he had lost something.

I turned away from the dispute, ready to make an excuse to walk home myself. But standing in front of me was a short guy so drunk he couldn't swallow his own saliva, which streamed down his chin in a thin trickle.

"Radošević!" he cheered.

"Yay!" I replied.

Then he reached out and grabbed my boob. He lost his balance, and nearly fell over with the effort. Goranka pushed this guy away, too.

I stood there, so incredulous I couldn't speak, hand over my jammied chest. I made my way to a picnic table and sat down hard.

Stefanija joined me. "Are you having fun?" she asked.

"I guess." I laughed. I had gone from feeling the love in Mrkopalj just that afternoon to being baffled and daunted all over again.

Robert wobbled into the fray, shitfaced, and took his place beside Goranka. She'd been smiling and joking, but now she fell silent. Robert glared at her, then at the crowd. I couldn't do all the drama anymore. Drinking made people so unpredictable, and I couldn't bear the thought of Robert and Goranka, two people I liked very much, rolling toward a booze-induced fight.

And so I crept home. Maybe a better traveler would have gone swiftly into the anarchy, but those days, if I'd ever had them, were long past. I scooted up Novi Varoš, the wind piercing through the thin material of my nightclothes.

Jasminka and Jim stood at the end of Robert's driveway.

"It's crazy out there!" I called.

"I'm sorry!" answered Jasminka.

"No," I said, coming up to them. "It's okay. Robert and Goranka are fighting. I figured out what to do with a drunken sailor. And some guy grabbed my left boob. He was so drunk that he'd lost his swallowing mechanism."

"Maybe he'd swallowed enough for one day," Jim said.

"*Joj meni*," Jasminka said, putting her hand to her forehead.

"Pasha and Stefanija are down there by Cuculić's office," I said to Jim. "You should see how Mrkopalj got weird when the sun went down."

We said our good nights to Jasminka, and Jim walked down the street. I went upstairs, where the kids were sleeping.

As I was brushing my teeth, I heard a loud crash downstairs. I spat in the sink, wiped my mouth, and walked over to the rolling door. I stopped and listened. I could hear Robert stumbling around on the second floor. There was another crash. He was falling-down drunk. All three of his daughters were home. It was a school night.

Then I heard the voices of other men. One I recognized as belonging to a guy I saw at Stari Baća sometimes. He was from out of town, big and quiet and wearing thick chains around his neck. People told me he was somehow associated with the Russian mafia.

I couldn't quite identify the other voice.

The three men argued loudly. I heard Ivana yelling something and then a radio blared. The men yelled louder. There were more crashes. I heard numbers. I heard the word *kuna*. Then I am pretty sure I heard the word "američki" a few times. The two male voices seemed to get louder, as if they were moving closer.

I was afraid for Robert's girls. I was scared for my kids. We didn't even have a lock on our door. I stood with my back up against it so it couldn't roll easily aside. Even if they didn't come upstairs, I knew Karla and Ivana and Roberta were down there, alone, their dad no protection whatsoever. I debated going to get them.

I called Jim and got no answer.

I called Stefanija.

She picked up right away. I told her what was going on.

"Tell Jim to get home. Now. Tell Goranka, too."

I flipped the phone shut and stood waiting.

A few minutes later, I heard Jim's footfalls in the driveway. As he walked up the concrete steps, the three guys hailed him in. They were out of *graševina* for *gemišt*. Could they have ours?

Jim came up the steps and grabbed our box of wine.

"They don't need more to drink!" I hissed. "The girls are down there!"

Jim shrugged. "Do you want to wait for them to come up and ask for it?"

He said he knew the guys and they were fine. He'd talked to them and told them our family was upstairs trying to sleep, and if he gave them the wine they had to keep it down and leave when it was all gone.

The whole situation was wrong. Plus, it smelled as if they were smoking about four cigarettes at a time down there.

Jim went back downstairs to deliver the wine. Stefanija called to see if everything was okay. I told her it would still be a good idea if Goranka came home now. I stood alone in the dorm for about a half hour, listening through more arguing and more falling-over crashes.

I heard Goranka's voice eventually.

Jim came back upstairs. I was furious.

"This is what happens when we join the drinking crowd," I said. "What if something really bad had happened tonight?"

"But it didn't, Jen," Jim said. "Those guys are just drunk and stupid."

"Exactly," I said.

What was the worst that could have happened? I don't know. But there would be unhappiness in the house for days now until Robert made it up to everyone for getting so hammered. Before we went to sleep, Jim slid a chair and a box of books in front of the rolling door.

In the morning, Mrkopalj was quiet. Stefanija and Pasha hadn't been joking: The streets were totally clear of debris. Mrkopalj had returned to its usual self. We could hear Robert's sisters downstairs on the second floor, probably giving him an earful that he wouldn't acknowledge anyway. Jim made coffee and we parsed the night's troublesome events as the kids slept.

Mrkopalj had been a protective cove in which to start fresh. It was probably time to finish up my work and go. We were fledglings when we arrived. Now it felt as if we were being pushed from the nest. "Don't worry," Jim said. "We don't have much longer here."

But neither of us was the kind of person who just closed their eyes and waited for life to pass anymore. I would not leave Mrkopalj daunted and skittering away, just like the first time.

I added a spoonful of sugar to my coffee. "It is time for us to go soon, yes," I said. "But I still have a few things I need to do."

chapter thirty-three

Josip stood holding something small and furry in his hand. Upon closer inspection, it appeared to be a rodent. It was also dead.

A *puh* is a vole. Or maybe a dormouse. It looks like a big rat but feels much softer. The one in Josip's hand had been squashed by some kind of blunt trauma, and its intestines hung out of its little *puh* tummy. Blood had dried around its mouth.

We saw it and we petted it. Even Sam had a turn. I held the thing as mites skittered across my hand. Pavice rubbed her belly and said: "Nom nom nom!"

After a while, the novelty of the *puh* wore off. Josip and Pavice headed back to their house, and we thought that was that. Zadie went to biathlon practice with the girls. Sometimes, I wondered if her long-term plan was to abandon our family altogether.

Twenty minutes later, Pavice and Josip returned, carrying a plate. They presented it to Sam, Jim, and me and upon it was very clearly a *puh*—but skinned, fried, and plated.

We really liked Josip and Pavice. We didn't want to be rude. So we ate it. It tasted like chicken.

We enjoyed the novelty of this rodent snack as Zadie returned with the girls and the sky turned dark. The fall night was cold, and we snuggled in to the third-floor dorm. Jim headed out to Stari Baća to meet Stefanija and Pasha after we'd spent the evening talking about what we might do when we left Mrkopalj, trying to pump ourselves up for the inevitable moment when we drove away from 12 Novi Varoš for the last time. We'd soon see all the places that we'd daydreamed of back home. The south of France. Basque country in northern Spain. Barcelona. My grandpa Gino's ancestral home in northern Italy.

It felt as if Mrkopalj was ready for us to go, too. Living in the third-floor dorm had lost its charm. The smell in the bathroom had never been resolved, and now it was joined by an epic flooding in the shower. The futon was threatening long-term nerve damage.

The kids and I curled up like hamsters on the futon. I asked them what they'd miss most about Mrkopalj when we left, which Jim and I had decided would be the following week, at the start of October.

Sam jolted from the crook of my arm.

"We're leaving next week?" he asked. "For good?"

I figured the guy who spent the first month in Mrkopalj weeping openly would be happy to hit the road. I was wrong. "We'll probably come back to visit during the winter when we live in Rovinj," I said. "But we won't be living here anymore."

"Can't we just stay for a few more months?" he cried.

I reminded him that not long ago, he'd hated Mrkopalj.

"Now I want to stay," he wept into his pillow. Within minutes, he fell asleep.

Zadie had been silent the whole time. She sat up and dragged a few strands of hair out of her face. "I'll miss the guwls," she said.

"Karla and Ivana and Roberta?" I asked.

She nodded. "And their ice cream."

"They have ice cream in every country, pretty much," I offered.

"Are you coming with us when we leave?" Zadie asked.

"Of course," I said. "You and I will travel the world like two fancy girls."

Zadie snuggled closer to me. "I'll go then," she said, as if she had a choice. I truly did think she believed she was a de facto Starčević.

If nothing else came of this trip, if I never made one lick of sense out of any of it, I had slowed down long enough to actually get to know my complicated little daughter.

Who, turned out, wasn't all that complicated. She just wanted her ice cream cold, and her parents close by.

Really, that wasn't a lot for a four year old to ask.

I went about finishing up bits of business in Mrkopalj. Most important, getting the recipe for *rakija* that continued to elude me. In the morning, Jim and Stefanija and I headed over for coffee in Anđelka and Željko's backyard. They were huddled with Viktor around the picnic table.

"So," I began, trying a little small talk to loosen up my favorite tough guys, "are there many wolves around here?"

"Before forty years, there was a reward for killing the wolf," Željko said. "The wolf killed the farm animals. When I was a child, if someone kills a wolf, you go see it. Now, there aren't so many wolves, so they have protection from the government."

"What would you do if you saw one now?" I asked.

"Stand back," Viktor offered. "Only he who doesn't know the woods is scared." Eighty-four pounds of twisted steel, that one.

"Viktor, you've *never* been afraid in the woods? Come *on*," I said, egging him on.

"*Nisam*," he said slowly, his Croatian stare boring holes into my skull.

"Hey," I said. I had a thought. "Do you think we could get a wolf to eat Cesar?"

"Wolves like to kill dogs," Viktor said helpfully.

"Oh, Jennifer!" Anđelka laughed, clasping her hands together. "You just have to come back and visit us again."

"Anđelka, of course I'll come back. I have unfinished business here," I said, taking advantage of the convivial spirit. "Everybody knows I want to learn to make *rakija*."

"Yes, everybody knows!" said Stefanija. "And so nobody tells you!"

I ignored her. "Anđelka, I was wondering what you and Viktor were doing the other day, with those jugs on the picnic table," I began.

Anđelka busied herself with coffee cups. Party over.

"I thought maybe you were making *rakija* out here," I said.

"Vinegar of apple," she answered.

"Applesauce!" Željko hollered over his shoulder, heading inside.

I turned to Stefanija. She shrugged and slipped her purse over her arm. "Perhaps they are making cider."

Viktor stood. "Or juice."

"Oftentimes in Mrkopalj we store water in jugs," Stefanija suggested as she headed toward the road.

Jim and I walked back to Robert's yard.

"Wow. I think you're really breaking them down," Jim said, draping an arm around my shoulder. "Nice work, Angela Lansbury."

chapter thirty-four

Jim and Robert had argued about our going-away party in Mrkopalj. They'd decided on a date—October 3—and that we'd slaughter a sheep. But they differed on the vibe. Jim wanted something simple and communal. Robert wanted a formal, sit-down affair in Stari Baća. Against our better judgment, we'd let Robert have his way again, so I wasn't looking forward to the party. Robert even told us we had to dress up.

"It is what it is, Jen. Just roll with it," Jim said as we drove to Tomo's for breakfast the day of the party. Tomo was the architect for the sheep, and therefore had offered to have a pre-party at his house.

At Tomo's we ate grilled pork chops, calamari, onions, and zucchini that he'd roasted on the open fire below the spit in a giant stone fireplace he built himself. There was a bowl of olive oil with diced garlic and fresh parsley sprinkled in for dipping bread. Ashes floated through the air, and people lounged on a goldenrod-colored upholstered sectional sofa.

Sam stood before the spit, fixated on the stomach of the sheep, which had been gutted, then knit together with its own fibia bones. He turned and retreated to Tomo's weight room beyond the breezeway to punch a bag. He remained vegetarian for many months after.

An unshaven and gaunt Cuculić stopped in to pick up the sheep's head and guts so he could take them home and eat them.

Robert lounged on the couch with his guitar. I'd been icy toward him since the night of the Mrkopalj *festa*. He could have put both our families in danger that night. But Robert always tried to repair the damage he did when he was drunk. That may have been why he was making such a big deal about the party.

"Jenny," he called to me. "You ask for to hear 'Bijele Stijene.' Favorite song that I write."

"I did," I said.

"Now is song," he said.

I was dreaming that
I'm standing at the top of Bijele Stijene
And looking somewhere in the distance
Into the storm and sea.

While the moon shone
And gave nobody peace
Like he's torturing me
And crushing my dreams.

Am I running from the truth?
Am I still too young?
I don't want to be a skeptic
But where should I go now?
Let them lie
Go fuck them
I am a man and I know that
I just want some perspective
But I don't wanna change a thing.

I like when they spit at me
Because then I am myself
Never mind because I am just
Spinning in the circle
Of an illusion.

I will fight with myself
With my own blood and sweat
Even if I go somewhere
Far more just, and better.

Robert propped himself up on the couch and laid his guitar against his chest. Standing next to me, Zadie and Sam clapped their applause. Jim and I clapped for Robert, too. He was a train wreck. But he was *our* train wreck. As he smiled and lit a cigarette, ashes from the cookfire rained down on him.

"Thanks, Robert," I said. "I'm glad I finally got to hear it."

"Where you go today?" Robert asked as Jim and I gathered our things.

"Jen's got some things to do," Jim said. "I'd like to walk Bobi one last time."

I had told Baka Ana I'd stop by before the party. She wanted to see the kids, and to show me her great barrel of fermenting sauerkraut. I did as she asked me—you really don't argue with the Baka; once, I'd turned down a shot of *rakija* on my way home from the morning walk to Tuk, and she'd bodychecked me—and we surveyed her garden as the kids played in her field. She picked up a single cabbage, twice the size of her head, and held it up to me. Its giant leaves were entirely sturdy, perfect for the *sarma* that we had spent a few hours in the kitchen making the night before.

"The best cabbage is from Mrkopalj!" she said. "It hardly needs any pepper or salt!"

"What's the secret of happiness?" I asked, fishing for something meaningful, half joking.

Baka Ana cackled loud.

"Use cow shit on your garden!"

I laughed and sent the kids home to take a walk to the mountain with Jim and Bobi and the girls. Stefanija and I walked to Zora and Dražen's place, pausing at the former Radošević family land, now occupied by the Horaček family garage. I promised I'd visit before we left the village so they could tell me the full story.

Dražen came outside. He'd built his white and dark green stucco house with his own hands, he said. The latest addition was a smokehouse, where he would hang for forty days the hams he'd cut on pig slaughter Saturday in November. Mario built the smokehouse doors, Dražen pointed out, because Mario was better with doors, and everyone in Mrkopalj knew that.

The Horaček kitchen was warm and cozy when Stefanija and I entered. Dražen's kids gathered as we settled around the table. Dražen poured wine. Zora emerged from her bedroom in a housedress.

"*Moja ljepa!*" she said, kissing my cheeks. "Are you ready to hear a story?"

"I am," I said, sitting down.

Zora told me the long history between our families. Petar and Katarina Radošević had lived on the sliver of land between the Horaček garage and House No. 262. When their family left Mrkopalj, the property they left behind deteriorated. One house collapsed completely. Zora said that Katarina 2 and her sister had come to the Horaček home to warn them that they intended to sell the land, because they were very poor.

"If we didn't buy it, they were going to offer it to someone else," Zora explained. That was in 1979. "I remember the day. I gave each of them eggs and one sausage. They were crying so. The money from us was the first thing they ever got out of that land."

To the Horaček family, purchasing the land meant they didn't have to farm at the *polje* anymore, that they had more space at home to expand.

"Our families are connected," I said, smiling.

"Yes," Zora nodded, her thick glasses magnifying her blue eyes.

I thought about House No. 262, how it had been abandoned, as if someone had left it in haste. Now it sat, unused and unloved, like a creepy relic. But next door, the *real* land of my ancestors was being used by one of the hardest-working families in Mrkopalj. It made me happy to know this.

Dražen beckoned me outside to his tidy workshop. He smiled as he pointed to the old stone base of a new wall, the foundation of the Radošević family home he'd left intact, as a reminder. I reached out and touched the stone, connecting.

"This land has more value than the house on it had," said Dražen.

When we went back inside to eat and drink at the kitchen table, Zora handed me a pair of red and purple socks. "I made these for you," she said.

"They're perfect!" I said.

"Benetton colors." She winked. "If you visit again, I will show you how to knit. If I am alive."

I would never learn the full story of what happened to Valentin Radošević and Jelena Iskra in Mrkopalj. Somehow, I knew with absolute certainty that this wasn't the point. The point was getting here. To Mrkopalj. To the old women. I had come to the village missing a grandmother who loved me, and now I had many. Valentin and Jelena, through Mrkopalj, had given me back my family. And it was a beautiful, all-encompassing thing.

"Are you satisfied now?" Zora asked me, patting my back.

"Yes," I said. "I am satisfied."

chapter thirty-five

While I was blow-drying Zadie's long hair in the dorm before the going-away party, there was a tap at the rolling door. It was Ana Fak. I motioned her inside.

Her eyes were teary as she pressed a gift bag into my hand. I wanted to talk to her, but we didn't have an interpreter, so I led her to my computer. I opened a translation program and showed her that I could type things, and they would be instantly translated.

"*Dobro!*" she said gently, smiling at me.

I opened her gift. Inside was a medal depicting Our Lady of Seven Sorrows, her heart pierced with swords. I put it on.

I looked up. "Are you coming to the party?" I typed my words into the computer. She read them and shook her head.

She picked up a piece of paper and pen from my desk. She wrote: "You are my own dear family. The day that you leave I will be very sad. Please visit again."

"I will miss you, too," I typed. "I wish we could talk. You remind me so much of my grandma Kate, whom I miss very, very much."

"The grandma who smoked?" she asked. The one who wore medals, like the one she had just given me?

"Yes," I nodded.

"Happy travels, and much, much happiness," she said, putting her warm hand on my arm one last time.

It was the first of many good-byes. Jim was helping with last-minute preparations at Stari Baća. When we joined him, we were all taken aback.

"What happened in here, Mom?" Sam asked.

Zadie, disoriented, lifted her arms up for me to hold her.

The room had been transformed. The tables were joined into one long harvest table set formally with white cloth, wineglasses, and flowers. Robert hurried from behind the bar to greet us. He was wearing a dinner jacket.

"I want to go outside and play," said Zadie. "I don't want Robert to wear a suit."

Sam was slowly backing out the door with a look of horror on his face at the sight of formalwear Robert. I pushed Zadie toward him. "Keep an eye on your sister," I said. "Stay close by."

Mile came in first. I fetched him a drink at the bar and we stood uncomfortably, not really sure what to say without the common goal of the Book of Names. Helena came in next, all dressed up and bearing a bottle of Chivas Regal and DVDs for the kids. Mile excused himself and returned later with a box of wrapped chocolates. I wasn't the only one who had been surprised by the formality of the occasion.

Others trickled in slowly. The summer girls delivered a steady stream of food to the table—wild boar goulash, potatoes, big lumps of Goranka's *gnocci*, made with bread and green onions and chunks of ham. Giant plates of onions and tomatoes. A cold salad of vinegar, beans, and more onions. The roasted sheep.

People sat, visiting politely. I fetched drinks at lightning speed, desperate to loosen up the place. Goranka set up the kids to eat in the back room. Ivana had been charged to babysit, and she carried Zadie around on her hip until they all had eaten and she herded them to the Starčević house, where Jim had arranged a full spread of junk food and movies, American style.

Soon, the party was rolling. Pavice, Josip, Viktor, Manda, Anđelka, and Željko arrived together, looking reluctant and subdued in dinner jackets and sweaters. How I wished we were all wearing the same old coats and hats we wore in the backyards every day! Nikola Tesla and Cuculić came in. Cuculić's wife, Dragica, had made the trip. She kissed me on both cheeks.

"I make apple cake!" She held up a bag of groceries.

Scruffy Tomo had even shaved. Baka Ana and Zora were escorted on the arm of Dražen. I seated them at the head of the table. Stefanija swooped down beside us.

"This is probably the last party we'll be invited to," Zora said matter-of-factly, and to me, this felt like a great honor.

"It's a very nice party to be our last one," Baka Ana assured me, reaching over to pat my hand. "Now open my present."

Inside her gift bag was a bottle of *rakija* so enormous that it could not be poured from. It had its own silver spigot.

"She said this is only for you," Stefanija said. "Not to share with Jim!"

"I promise not to share," I said, winking.

Mario and Jasminka arrived. I positioned them at the other end of the table. They presented me with a frame of hand-pressed flowers from the *polje*.

Pavice, not to be outdone, handed me a marigold-colored table scarf she had embroidered with brown snowflakes. Robert's sister-in-law Snow Girl gave me a hand-carved polenta spoon made by another villager. Željko and Anđelka set upon the table a miniature of the sculpture by the Croatian artist Ivan Meštrović called *The History of the Croats*, one of the most important icons of Croatia, depicting a seated woman with the Glagolitic stone tablets upon her lap.

"When you see that, you can only think about Croatia," Željko said.

Cuculić presented me with a wood sculpture of the Mrkopalj crest, also burned into wood, with the original Mrkopalj coat of arms on it. "From Queen Marija Terezija times, four hundred years ago," he said, shoving his hands into his pockets. I kissed him on the cheek, which seemed to blow both of our minds.

At Robert's signal, we ate. At last, the party grew loud and happy, and I sat back in my chair next to Zora and Baka Ana and watched as these people who had been strangers to me just a few months ago broke bread like family.

Robert demanded a toast. I began to sweat under my right armpit as I stood up. Helena rose to translate.

"Thank you for allowing us to share this time with you," I said. "Thank you for being patient with our photos. Thank you for being patient with our questions. And thank you mostly for sharing with us your history, which now, after a hundred years, is my own family's history once again."

I thought it was a pretty good speech. I cried, and people clapped. But Stefanija leaned in to tell me that none of the translation made any sense. People were just clapping out of politeness. I sat down.

Then Robert took the stage and kept it for the rest of the night. He toasted my Mrkopalj roots, toasted my family, which had livened up the village for the summer. As if on cue, a giant and burly man with a tiny jet-black mustache stepped forward. Robert said Zvonko ran the grocery store next to the Konzum, and his family had once lived in House No. 262. Zvonko then handed something to Robert before turning to give me a mighty hug that nearly crushed my sternum. With a flourish—I am certain he would have gotten a drumroll if drums had been available—Robert presented me with a rusted metal plate bearing the old house number: 262. Zvonko and Robert had sneaked down Novi Varoš in the middle of the night to remove it from the house I had thought was Valentin's, but was not Valentin's.

I turned it over in my hands. The plate was gouged with fresh scrapes across the old paint where Zvonko and Robert had labored to unscrew it under cover of darkness. My heart swelled in my chest and the tears welled up all over again. I gave Robert a hug. Maybe No. 262 was not my family's house, but that didn't diminish the magnitude of the gift. In Robert's mind, it was my true home, and now *that* house was part of my family history, too. Robert tried to kiss my cheek, but I still got the European kiss backwards, and he ended up kissing my eyeball in front of all those people.

Glasses were raised. The din of the room rose to a pleasant chaos. Jasminka and Snow Girl admired the house number as we huddled together at the end of the table, speaking Croglish and trying not to cry.

Then the room quieted. I looked behind me, and Robert was signaling for silence again. I sat down, I think on Jasminka's lap. Helena translated as Robert spoke.

"And then there is Jeem," Robert began. "Jeem, who come to this place to help his wife find her Croatian roots. Everyone in this room is Croatian but Jeem."

Jim shrunk back in his chair in mock temerity. Robert let silence hang in the air. People nodded. A few toasted this fact.

"But it turns out, Jeem is the most Croatian of us all," Robert said, his face turning pink and his eyes growing wet. "He has been a good friend to this village. A good friend to me. To Jeem, the lost son of Mrkopalj!"

Stari Baća erupted in cheers, as it often did regarding all matters Jeem, its best new customer, astute town gossip, expatriate who quietly steered away from all talk of Croatian politics in favor of the Ožujsko-Karlovačko beer debate. My husband was presented with glasses and glasses of *gemišt*, the halp-halp he had embraced immediately and wholeheartedly—none of that fancy red wine for Jeem!

If Jim were to stay, I thought as I propped my elbow on the table and dropped my cheek into my hand as my husband basked in this murky sun, he would likely be elected the next mayor of Mrkopalj.

In Stari Baća, the light was dim but golden, the air hot and moist. Robert had picked up his guitar, and people got up from their chairs to gather around as he played the ballads of Croatia and John Denver's "Take Me Home, Country Roads," just for us.

People clapped as they sang. They beat the tables with their fists. They got up and danced, linking arms and jigging in circles. They bounced along in their chairs. They roared in song, whether they sounded any good or not. The singing of Mrkopalj dwarfed everything, as it always had.

I hardly drank a drop. I didn't want to miss a thing. A few of the guitar-playing Anthony Hopkinses we'd seen so long ago in the Sunger church parking lot even showed up. Robert sang so long and so loud that he sounded like Joe Cocker as the night wore on. He was truly at his best commanding center stage. It was a delight to be part of his audience, and I glimpsed the wild beauty of the boy inside him. He worked the room until everyone was a flush-faced fan. Sometimes he stood. Sometimes he dramatically wiped sweat from his forehead and flicked it to the ground. Sometimes he whacked the guitar like winter wood. Sometimes he held it as if it were a woman and plucked tenderly, his ear pressed against the side of it, as if he was listening for something very faint and far away.

Stari Baća was filled with music and laughter and cheering. It would be filled with the same energetic pride four months later, when my family returned for one last time on a bone-cold February, Valentine's Day night, just to watch with the rest of Mrkopalj as Jakov competed in the Winter Olympics. We crowded around a tiny television at 3:00 A.M. to see our hometown boy ski and shoot and ski and shoot, jumping up and down and hugging around the hearth of Stari Baća when he did it—Jakov Fak won the bronze medal!

The frenzied magic of our going-away party was the stuff Jim and I would dream about for the rest of our lives. But my posse of eighty-somethings had long ago pooped out, and I was close behind them. I took one last look through the window of Stari Baća and smiled at the crowd: flushed, sweaty, singing. Stefanija looked up and saw me. She raised her hand in a small wave that I returned with a smile. I stepped away and walked alone to 12 Novi Varoš, loving my new family with all my heart, even though the next day, Robert presented us with the bill for the party, about double the price he and Jim had ultimately agreed upon, calculating our farewell down to the last lipa, and then some.

Still, Robert had been a good guide. He was our passport into the Old World, and we emerged from it squinting and blinking into a strange new light. In his Blue Period, the Brown Bear had more questions about his life and his surroundings than ever before. My husband and I felt exactly the same way. But if Robert was at his best when he didn't know a damned thing for sure, I had to consider that perhaps we were, too. Sureness, as we'd seen in Mrkopalj, hadn't done anybody much good.

In the end, it was easier to tell Robert good-bye like this. If Mrkopalj was family, then Robert was my troubled brother.

I loved him as much as I loathed him. Halp-halp.

chapter thirty-six

When I finally found my ancestors' graves, it was All Saints' Day, November 1, the only holiday that all religions and all ethnicities celebrate together in Croatia. We'd been traveling around Europe in the Peugeot before settling into Rovinj for winter. We returned to Mrkopalj to pick up the last of our stuff from Robert's place, then drove to the cemetery to locate those overgrown graves once and for all. This time, I knew where I was going.

Hundreds of people gathered in the cemetery dressed in wool coats against the forty-five-degree cold. The new priest spoke into a boxy PA system, but the microphone was broken, so no one could hear his blessings. Instead, the choir sang. The sound carried loud and pure and strong on the brisk air.

The kids and I made our way to the graves of Jelena Iskra's parents. Jim grabbed his camera to photograph the choir's silhouette against the blue sky. Sam and Zadie held my hands, theirs little pulses of warmth better than gloves.

Finding the graves of Jelena's parents really had been as easy as asking Pavice. Her relative just gave us directions to the family plot over the phone. Josip and Marija Iskra were buried with their children on the far south side of the cemetery in a grave marked, oddly enough, Radošević. The family from Germany still visited often, from the looks of the tidy white cinder gravel. Silk roses and daisies in urns decorated the grave, alongside three red candles that once danced with flame.

The simple black metal cross with a gold plate read *Počivaju u miru Božjem*, roughly meaning "Here they rest in peace with God."

It's difficult to manufacture the emotions of loss and sorrow in a culture where the dead felt just as present as the living. Anyway, I wasn't here to mourn. I was here to acknowledge a feeling that grew clearer every day: I was grateful.

The village had taught my family a deep gratitude for what we had. We'd been spared the senseless murders, persecution, sorrows. We'd been spared hunger. The old ones in Mrkopalj knew hunger like they knew their backyards, because they were one and the same. Our trip hadn't been about finding these graves. It was about losing what didn't matter, and gathering to us all the things that did. It was about discovering the sacrifices of my ancestors that had spared me and mine, so we could find a better way. And for that, we would live with gratitude.

Gratitude didn't mean groveling to the boss or buying everything we could get our hands on or indulging our children so much that they expected everything yet appreciated nothing. It meant respecting our place in the world, actively embracing it as citizens of the best and brightest among them, starting by teaching our kids more about it.

Because when we lost that knowledge, we lost what it meant to be American in the first place.

I had been a fool to think that this trip was only about my family. It had been about the whole family—those who left, those who stayed, and all those connective tissues on either side of the journey my great-grandparents made. The journey that began with *their* parents. Mrko-palj had needed to tell its far-flung family its difficult story.

Josip and Marija Iskra, whose house stood on gypsy ground, had ushered their tall and by all accounts unattractive daughter out the door of House No. 40 to embark on a journey into the unknown. Jo-sip and Marija had lost five children either at birth or during their childhood. Then they gave up their daughter to America. For this, I got down on my knees to thank them and asked my children to do the same. I straightened a red candle that had fallen over and smoothed the cinder with the flat of my hand.

The altar boys for the Church of Our Lady of Seven Sorrows swung censers full of incense, the little pots on brass chains scenting the air just enough that we caught whiffs as we moved on.

We used the grave with the porcelain face of Ana Crnić on it as a guide, and followed the row toward the cemetery fence. Petar and Ka-tarina were buried with their daughter-in-law, Matilda Kružić, who had married their son, Matej. The grave was inscribed with Matilda's name only, and the words *"Podižu, kćerke,"* or "Arise, daughter." But Petar and Katarina were in there too, added to the plot in lean times, keeping their daughter-in-law company as their son had not. Perennial bushes sprouted from the ground alongside a yellow spray of button flowers and a white vase of pale-pink roses. Candles flanked the marble headstone, atop white posts marked with a cross and an olive branch.

The kids and I knelt, then just sat down and listened to the choir. I was content near Petar and Katarina. Their son Valentin had pioneered my American family, though he'd abandoned his own to do it. He'd become "Wally" in America, a funny little guy shaped like a gourd, a man who'd loan money to anybody who asked for it. Because of that,

his family rode a constant roller coaster between prosperity and poverty, as Wally Radošević handed out cash in America rather than
send it to the Old Country. He had left Mrkopalj without a trace,
never looking back. There was a good chance that Petar and Katarina
Radošević had told him to do so. And because he did not, there I
stood, alive and unscarred and a citizen of the only country in the
world that didn't believe in carrying its baggage. And everyone knows
that when you travel without baggage, you're free.

I had spent a whole summer looking for these people, hunting
down their physical remains in the vast graveyard of a village that
once seemed small to me. All were nothing now. They didn't even
have a stone that bore their names. But through their children, they
had placed their own cog in the machinery that powered a Nation of
Immigrants, a brand-new country that restored the idea of possibility
in a world that had been ravaged again and again by the same old
mistakes, a world in which each village had, in Cuculić's words,
burned to the ground at least five times in the last two centuries.

The stories of each of us mattered, every step of the way, from the
dust below us to me and the kids sitting above. The connection was
bigger than I was. It was bigger than Petar and Katarina Radošević
and Josip and Marija Iskra. Bigger than the families they'd raised,
and their families, and their families, and my own. I had come to witness because this had been forgotten. What happened to these people
happened to me and mine. The reverberations were like rings in a
pond. This was the lesson that I would pull back home and make part
of the essential DNA of my own family. The newspaper story about
Serbian and Croatian leaders exchanging apologies for wartime crimes
gave me hope, because I understood it, not dwelling on the past but
witnessing it, so I could know better than to stand idly by if it threatened to repeat itself. To build on its foundations instead of coasting
into the sort of laziness that's easy to fall into when you've got it pretty
damned good.

The bell atop the yellow church tolled. Jim joined us, crouching
on the cinder of the old grave. I thought of the parable told by Jesus in

the Book of Luke about prudent and grateful servants who stood in greeting when the master returned from the wedding party: "From everyone to whom much has been given, much will be required; and from one to whom much has been entrusted, even more will be demanded."

It all came down to dust beneath the feet, and the simple question from an old man: *What kind of Radošević are you?*

To which my family and I had heard the resounding response, channeled through the warm hands of old women: You were the very best of us. Do not forget.

glossary of croatian people, places, and words

baka (BOCK-ah). Grandmother.

čaj (CHAI). Tea.

Čelimbaša (CHELL-eem-bash-ah). The ski hill in Mrkopalj.

Željko and Anđelka Crnić (JHEL-ko and ON-jell-kuh TSER-nitch). Our next-door neighbors to the north in Mrkopalj. Owners of the best backyard in town.

Željko Cuculić (TZU-tzu-litch). The tourism director for Mrkopalj; my former nemesis.

Delnice (DELL-neets-uh). The biggest town in Mrkopalj county.

džezva (JEZ-vah). A small pot with a long handle designed for making Turkish coffee.

gemišt (gem-EESHT). A popular Mrkopalj drink—half white wine, half fizzy water.

Gorski Kotar. A forested region of Croatia that roughly translates to "mountain district." Its main cities are Rijeka and Karlovac. It is separated from Slovenia by the Kupa River.

groblje (GROBE-lee-yay). Cemetery.

Joj meni (YOY MAN-ny). Oh my!

Karlovačko (KAR-loe-vatch-koe). A brand of Croatian beer.

Mrkopalj (MER-koe-pie). The village of my great-grandparents in the Gorski Kotar region of Croatia where my family and I lived in 2009 for a period of about four months.

Novi Varoš (NO-vee VAR-osh). Our street in Mrkopalj. It means "new way."

Ožujsko (OH-zhu-skoe). A brand of Croatian beer.

Pavice and Josip Paškvan (PAH-veets-uh and YO-seep POSH-kvan). Our farm-family neighbors and owners of the evil dog Cesar.

Valentin and Jelena Radošević (VAL-en-teen and YELL-eh-nuh rad-OH-sheh-vitch). My great-grandparents on my mother's side. They left Mrkopalj in the early 1900s.

rakija (ROCK-ee-uh). A clear liquor made by the people of most Slavic countries, but distilled particularly well in Mrkopalj. Good luck trying to get their secret recipe, though.

Rijeka (ree-YAY-kuh). A major port city thirty minutes from Mrkopalj.

Viktor and Manda Šepić (SHEP-itch). Our elderly next-door neighbors to the south in Mrkopalj.

The Family Starčević (STAR-cheh-vitch). The family we lived with in Mrkopalj. Parents Robert and Goranka and daughters Ivana, Karla, and Roberta.

Stari Baća (STAR-ee BOTCH-uh). Robert's café-bar.

šuma (SHOE-muh). Forest.

Šume Pjevaju (SHOE-meh PYEH-vah-you). The oldest bar in Mrkopalj.

Ustaše (OO-stash-ee). An ultranationalist Croatian movement that became the pro-Nazi, eastern European arm of Fascism responsible for the World War II Yugoslavian genocide.

Zagmajna (zag-MINE-uh). The biathlon training field on the outskirts of Mrkopalj.

živjeli (ZHEE-vell-ee). Cheers! Locally, it is said that one must maintain eye contact when making this toast, or suffer seven years of sexual bad luck.